I0803196

IMAGES
of America

DeSoto Parish

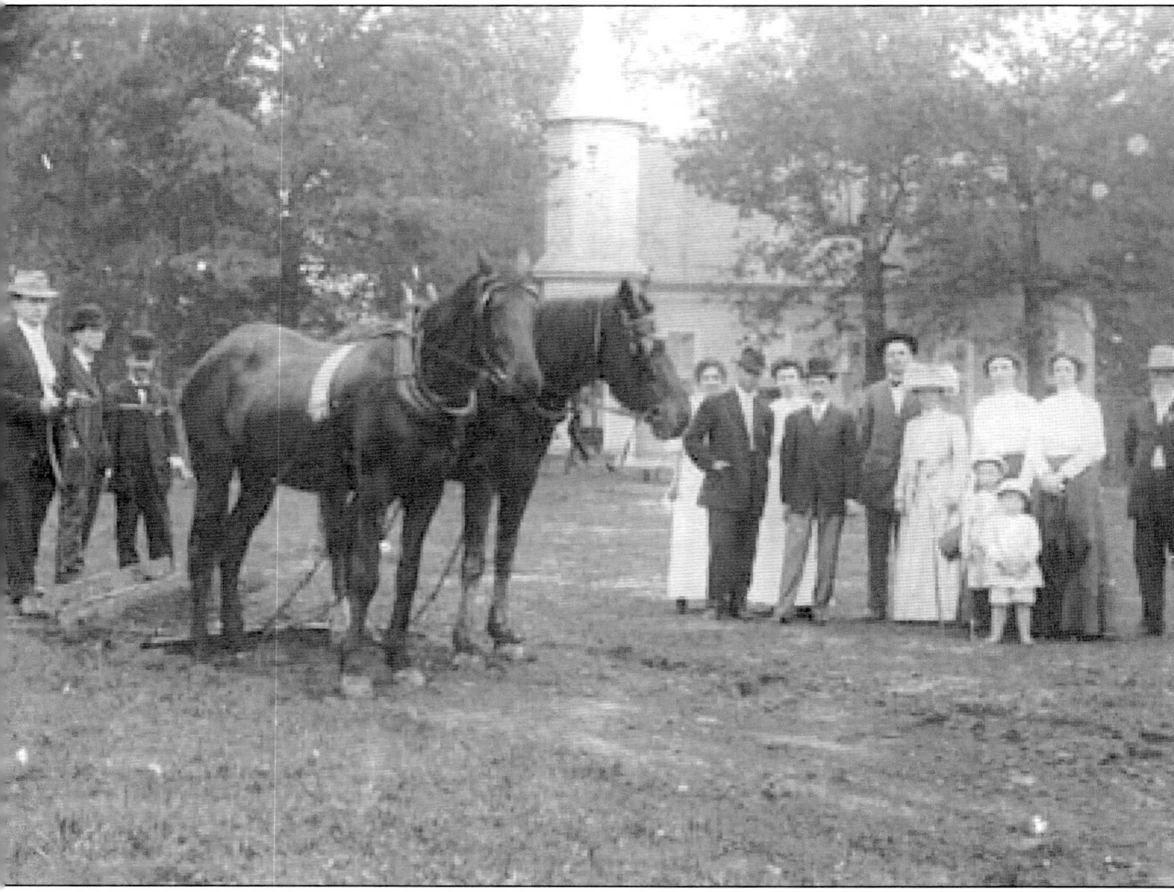

CAPTION NEEDED.

ON THE COVER: Pictured in 1908 is Stonewall Methodist Episcopal Church South Drag Road Rally. People in the community would bring their horse teams and drag equipment to smooth the roads. Possibly this one was to improve the road in and around the church. The church was the center of the community in small rural towns. Additionally, the churches were able to influence the residents; therefore they were responsible for many community improvements. Pictured are Dr. Floyd O. Brinkley of Gloster, Dr. W.R. Dodson (later dean of agriculture at Louisiana State University), Roselyn Liverman (piano teacher), S.R. Cummings (DeSoto superintendent of schools), W.I. Roy (president of Louisiana Normal College), John Rogers (president of DeSoto Parish Schools), a Mrs. Kimball, Mrs. W.L. Gilmer and son W.L. Gilmer Jr., Mrs. Floyd O. Brinkley and son Floyd O. Brinkley Jr., and W.L. Gilmer of Stonewall. (Courtesy of Libby Dady Alcorn.)

IMAGES
of America

DeSoto Parish

Emilia Gay Griffith Means
and Liz Chrysler

ARCADIA
PUBLISHING

ISBN 978-0-7385-8723-3

Published by Arcadia Publishing
Charleston, South Carolina

Printed in the United States of America

Library of Congress Control Number: 2010935200

For all general information, please contact Arcadia Publishing:
Telephone 843-853-2070
Fax 843-853-0044
E-mail sales@arcadiapublishing.com
For customer service and orders:
Toll-Free 1-888-313-2665

Visit us on the Internet at www.arcadiapublishing.com

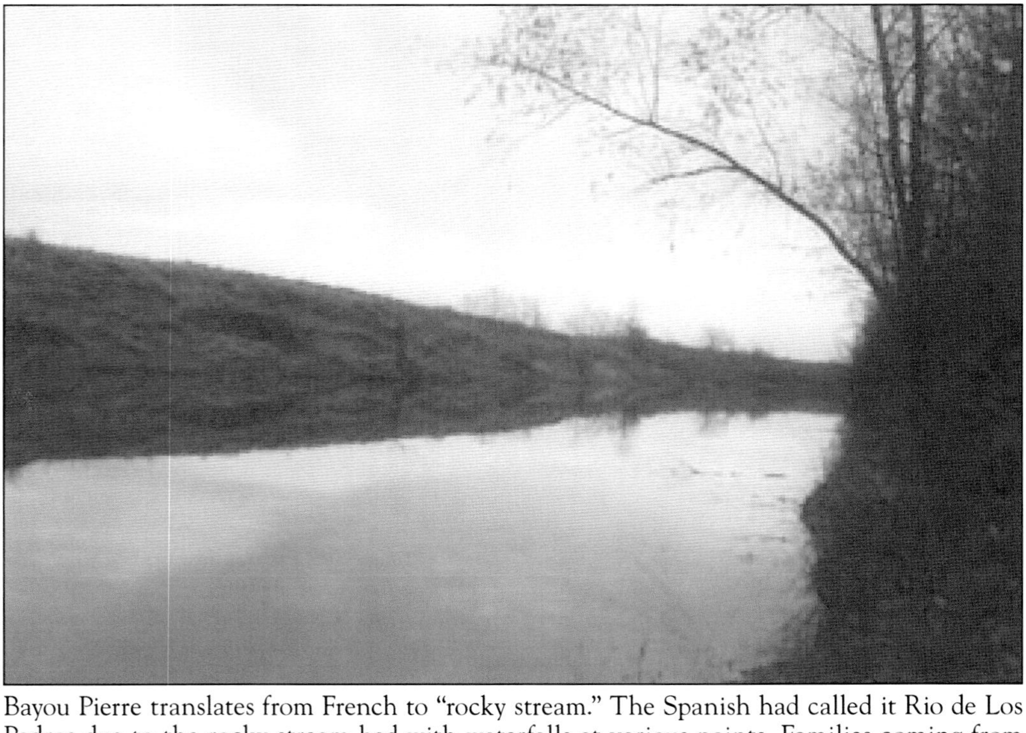

Bayou Pierre translates from French to "rocky stream." The Spanish had called it Rio de Los Pedros due to the rocky stream bed with waterfalls at various points. Families coming from Natchitoches traveled on Bayou Pierre further north into what is now DeSoto Parish. (Courtesy of Liz Chrysler.)

Contents

Acknowledgments

The authors wish to thank their editor at Arcadia Publishing, Amy Perryman, for her guidance. Deepest appreciation goes to Raymond Powell of Mansfield for his help in providing numerous images of that town as well as other images from around the parish and to George Meriwether Gilmer Jr. of Stonewall, who lent numerous images from his own collection and went out of his way to obtain other images from around the parish. Thanks to Mayor Curtis McCune of Stonewall, who lent images of several important places in Stonewall. Additionally, Edith Burgess Herring obtained important photographs of Grand Cane. Thanks go to Kathleen Myers and Margaret Joyner of Pelican, Louisiana, for lending their important photographs of that town. Furthermore, Glenn Crockett Price of Logansport provided his photographs of riverboats and paved the way for other information. Mary T. McGuire of Houston, Texas, went to her invaluable collection and chose important images of the town of Keachi. Libby Dady Alcorn of Houston went out of her way by taking her rare photographs to a professional photographer in Houston to have them scanned to the proper specifications for the book as well as providing a properly sized scan for the cover and valuable suggestions for the publication.

Others who deserve appreciation are Nancy Beard Wilson, Franklin Rembert, M.D., Ina Larkin, Janet Boyett, Delores Caldwell,Cheena Robbins, Edna Thornton at the Mansfield Chamber of Commerce office, Patricia C. Hesser, Vicki Gourley, Glenda Sharbono, the DeSoto Parish Library, and the Mansfield Enterprise Offices. Scott Solice, Monica Pels, and W. Conway Link assisted in providing images. Richie Self went out of his way to scan in images from his collection of rare manuscripts. Willy Bearden of Rolling Fork, Mississippi, and Rick Sherrod of Stephenville, Texas, provided suggestions.

Lastly, the entire staff of the Louisiana State University in Shreveport, Noel Memorial Library, Archives and Special Collections were extremely helpful. Special thanks go to Shawn Bohannan, who scanned in numerous images both from their collection and those lent to the authors. Furthermore, he made suggestions since Publishing. Dave Bland, always helpful on any project, provided some of his own photographs. Domenica Carriere, Furman Garlington, and Laura McLemore of the archives provided assistance also.

Nathaniel Means, Ph.D., helped in scanning, editing the cover text, and made invaluable suggestions. Gary L. Fox deserves thanks for help and encouragement to finish the publication.

INTRODUCTION

DeSoto Parish rests in northwest Louisiana as a stopping point along the wagon roads of American westward expansion. Following the prescriptive of Horace Greeley's "Go West, young man," immigrants poured into the region from such eastern states as Georgia and South Carolina. Often spurred by letters from family and friends extolling the fertile soil and salubrious climate of northern Louisiana, South Carolina slaveholders transplanted their way of life to northern DeSoto Parish. Such settlers might have thought of themselves as pioneers pouring into new and unchartered territory, but the land on which they would build farms, towns, and communities already had a long and rich history.

The geographical confines of what would become DeSoto Parish encompassed a small part of the Caddo Nation, a tribal confederacy with roots and branches that extended across north Louisiana and eastern Texas. The Natchitoches and Yatassee, part of that broader nation, inhabited lands along small bayous and depended on trails for trade. They cultivated maize in rich river bottomlands, hunted the deep forests, and built a rich civilization.

At the dawn of the 18th century, Caddo Indians and French and Spanish settlers opened a new era of contact and contest in the land that would become DeSoto Parish. Led by Louis Juchereau de St. Denis, in 1714 French newcomers founded the community of Natchitoches, France's first permanent settlement in their Louisiana territory. St. Denis sought to make Natchitoches economically viable by opening trade with the Spanish, who claimed a vast territory of New Spain. As he trekked across the land that would later be known as Texas, Spanish soldiers arrested him on the Rio Grande River. While captive in the home of Don Diego Roman, Louis Juchereau de St. Denis fell in love with Roman's granddaughter Manuela. The marriage of St. Denis and Manuela brought a temporary respite in the French and Spanish conflict on the contested borderland of Louisiana and New Spain. Their grandson Joseph Marcel DeSoto married Marie Baillio, began a family, and accepted a Spanish land grant of three leagues for bringing 30 permanent settlers into what the Spanish claimed as their Nacogdoches territory.

The syndic of Bayou Pierre, Marcel DeSoto, established his settlement along what translates in French to "rocky stream." Bayou Pierre had become a relatively large stream in the level lowland due to the great raft, or blockade of Red River by falling trees. DeSoto's contingency became known as the Bayou Pierre Settlement. The settlement extended from just north of Natchitoches along Bayou Pierre all the way through the hills of Pierre Dolet's land grant and upward to an area later called Wallace. Until recent times in Louisiana, waterways were the preferred mode of long distance transportation, due to seasonally impassible or nonexistent roads.

Economically, the early American period between 1803 and the 1840s offered limited opportunities. Hunting, subsistence agriculture, and cattle occupied the attention of settlers, who depended upon crude cattle trails and rivers and bayous for transportation. DeSoto built his first bousillage home on one of the hills that rose up from the Bayou Pierre Lake, where he ran a trading post to earn additional income.

After Louisiana was recognized as part of the United States, Marcel DeSoto was named justice of the peace by Thomas Jefferson and was authorized to perform marriages and notarize deeds. Early settlers had to refile their land under American claims. The Spanish and the Americans continued to dispute the borders of the Louisiana Territory until the signing of the 1819 Adams Onis treaty, which not only set the borders between modern-day Louisiana and Texas at the Sabine River, but also set the border of the future parish of DeSoto. By 1819, the early history of DeSoto Parish as contested ground between international powers had come to an end.

In the summer of 1808, Marcel DeSoto recognized the need for a priest who could serve his community, which had no church closer than Natchitoches. He and other settlers formed a delegation and rode on horseback to the capital of New Spain, near present-day San Antonio, to request a priest for the Bayou Pierre Settlement. The governor was impressed and wrote the Very Reverend Father Bernardiono Vellejo, president of the Franciscan Mission, to initiate arrangements for a priest. The Franciscan missionaries stationed at Nacogdoches began making mission tours to the coast of Bayou Pierre, baptizing, instructing, performing marriages, and celebrating Mass at private homes or in open arbors. This persisted until the mid-1800s, when Father Pierre traveled up from Natchitoches to establish the first church in the region. In the late 1800s, Carmelite monks came from south Texas to establish a monastery and convent and built the Rock chapel, now on the National Register of Historic Places. At the convent, nuns taught girls, and a monastery was erected for the separate instruction of boys.

Recognizing the rapid growth of the region between Natchitoches and the Sabine River, the State of Louisiana carved out DeSoto Parish from portions of the parishes of Natchitoches and Caddo in 1843. It was created by Act 88 of the 16th Legislature of Louisiana and named in honor of Marcel DeSoto, who brought the first settlers to that area. Anglo American settlers from crowded eastern states moved west into northern Louisiana as the cotton regime became to unfold

A contingency of settlers moved to an area just west of Bayou Grandes Cannes and established the village of Screamerville. A dispute emerged between the residents of Screamerville and another settlement at Augusta over which location would become the seat of the new parish. In 1843, a police jury decided to locate the parish seat by sending a horse-drawn wagon from each of the suggested sites. Where the wagons met at sundown would be the parish seat. They met at the foot of Hungerbeiler Hill, where the town of Mansfield was established slightly south of that point due to the inadequate water supply on the hill. A respected parish resident named Thomas Abington presented an eloquent story of the English lord Chief Justice Mansfield, after which a new name for the parish seat had been found.

The opening of the Great Cotton Kingdom of the 1840s lasted to the early 20th century and defined life in DeSoto Parish for this era of development. Anglo American settlers eager for land on which to earn a better way of life came westward to establish their own farms. They left home from places like Society Hill, South Carolina, and came to DeSoto Parish, where they built houses virtually identical in architectural style to those they had left behind. Large two-story houses arose amongst the most successful, and small frontier dog trots, dotted the landscape. Farmers continued to raise cattle. Hunting remained a mainstay of social life, but cotton was king. As the parish developed, new communities arose, and settlers built such institutions as churches and schools.

Soon after the founding of the parish seat, residents came together to found a college that would advance the education of women in Louisiana. In 1855, the Mansfield Female College opened to offer its students a classical education. Located on the highest point of the parish, the college completed its new building in 1857, which became a fixture over Mansfield's skyline. In 1860, a crop failure hit DeSoto Parish, and consequently the school's source of generous donations evaporated. The school property fell into the hands of the parish sheriff, but an original incorporator managed to buy the campus. After the Civil War, the Methodist Conference was able to buy the property and reopen it to students.

As in other areas across the South, the Civil War was a pivotal event for DeSoto Parish. The war affected every individual in the parish. Enslaved men and women whose forced labor made possible the explosive growth of the cotton regime found liberation in the war's aftermath. Thousands of young men from the parish enlisted, fought, and perished in the war. On April 8,1864, DeSoto Parish men prepared to defend their homes, fields, and families from the impending invasion by Union soldiers in the Red River Campaign. Louisiana and Texas farmers fighting for the Confederacy defeated the attempted conquest of Shreveport, the capital of Confederate Louisiana, at a battlefield just south of the town of Mansfield. Approximately 1,000 Confederate soldiers were killed and wounded, and the Union side suffered approximately 2,400 casualties in the Battle of Mansfield. The campus of Mansfield Female College was turned into a private hospital, and private homes cared for the wounded and dying on both sides. Confederate soldiers pursued retreating Union soldiers and met at a small town south of Mansfield. Both sides suffered another 2,200 casualties at the Battle of Pleasant Hill on the April 9, 1864. Union dead were buried in mass trenches behind Pearce-Payne College. A store and a Methodist church founded in the 1850s were both used as hospitals.

Following his engagement at Pleasant Hill, Gen. Nathaniel Banks of the Union army halted his offensive. It was the only such retreat by the Union army in a year that witnessed both the determination of Ulysses S. Grant, who smashed into the heart of Virginia, and William Tecusmseh Sherman's capture and destruction of Atlanta. The United Daughters of the Confederacy organized a chapter named for the Prince de Polignac, a French aristocrat who served as an officer at the Battle of Mansfield and played a pivotal role in the establishment of a state park at the site of the engagement. DeSoto Parish Episcopalians renamed their parish church Christ Memorial in memory of both Union and Confederate dead.

Rural outreaches of the southern frontier like DeSoto Parish depended on crude wagon trails, small streams, and bayous to transport commodities like corn and cotton to markets abroad. Northern Louisiana farmers and planters, desperate for a more reliable means of transportation, clamored for railroads, which might solve their problems. The Texas and Pacific Railway Company acquired the New Orleans Pacific Railway Company on June 20, 1881. The New Orleans Pacific Railway Company had been chartered in June 1875 to build a line of track from the upper Red River country to New Orleans. The Texas and Pacific completed the rail line between Shreveport and Provencal on October 1, 1881.

The town of Mansfield did not grant a right to the railroad through its limits; therefore, Mansfield was left off the main track of the Texas and Pacific. The result was the chartering of the Mansfield Railway and Transportation Company in 1881 for the purpose of connecting the town with the Texas and Pacific. Subsequently, the town of South Mansfield developed at the junction of the Mansfield Railway and Transportation Company line with the Texas and Pacific.

Other new towns developed. The New Orleans and Pacific sold lots and laid out towns to finance and develop the line. Such settlements and towns as Stonewall, Gloster, Grand Cane, Oxford, Benson, and Pelican soon arose and obtained their names from the railroad workmen. The settlement of Old Pleasant Hill became new Pleasant Hill (Sodus) as the railroad rolled along in its track building. With the Texas and Pacific came cotton fields, the development of sawmills, and the quick rise of the lumber industry in DeSoto Parish. Among the list of lumber mills that operated in north Louisiana were McGill's Mill at Pelican, Boling Williams near Mansfield, and Oxford Lumber Company at Oxford. The railroad line changed the settlement patterns and, at its peak, the New Orleans and Pacific can be considered the river of DeSoto Parish. It was now possible for "Mr. Ogilvie from Shreveport to send Mrs. Joyner of Pelican in little or no time fresh fruit such as bananas."

In 1885, the Houston East and West Texas railroad line had been completed from Shreveport to Logansport. The rail line went on to the west and was completed from Houston to the Sabine River at Logansport. About two years later, the bridge over the Sabine River was completed, linking Shreveport and Houston by rail and ending the era of the steamboats operating on the upper Sabine.

In the late 1890s, another railroad arrived in DeSoto Parish this time receiving encouragement from Mansfield as well as those who had a definite interest in the promotion of the lumber industry in the area. This was the Kansas City Southern Railway Company, earlier known as the Kansas City, Shreveport, and Gulf Railway Company. Mansfield now realized the opportunities the railroad would bring to the entire parish of DeSoto, boosting the local economy.

Over the late 19th century, cotton, horses, a thriving dairy industry, and beef cattle remained an important part of the parish's economy, but by the turn of the century, the parish's economy had diversified with large-scale timber harvesting. Developed concurrently were lumber mills that provided finished building materials to towns and cities and cross ties to a burgeoning railway network that eased transportation across the parish and the American South. In the early 20th century, an oil boom came to the paris,h leading to a more diverse economy.

DeSoto Parish continued to offer a rich social and cultural life in the 20th century. Until it closed its doors in 1929, Mansfield Female College was a premier educational institution the South for the training for young women as teachers and musicians. In addition, Mansfield's schools educated prominent men in letters, business, the armed forces, and sports.

The environs of the land that became DeSoto Parish fulfilled the vision of many families moving west. These settlers established homes and fought to defend their livelihood. Railroads brought new life and prosperity to DeSoto Parish for coming generations.

One

The Early Years

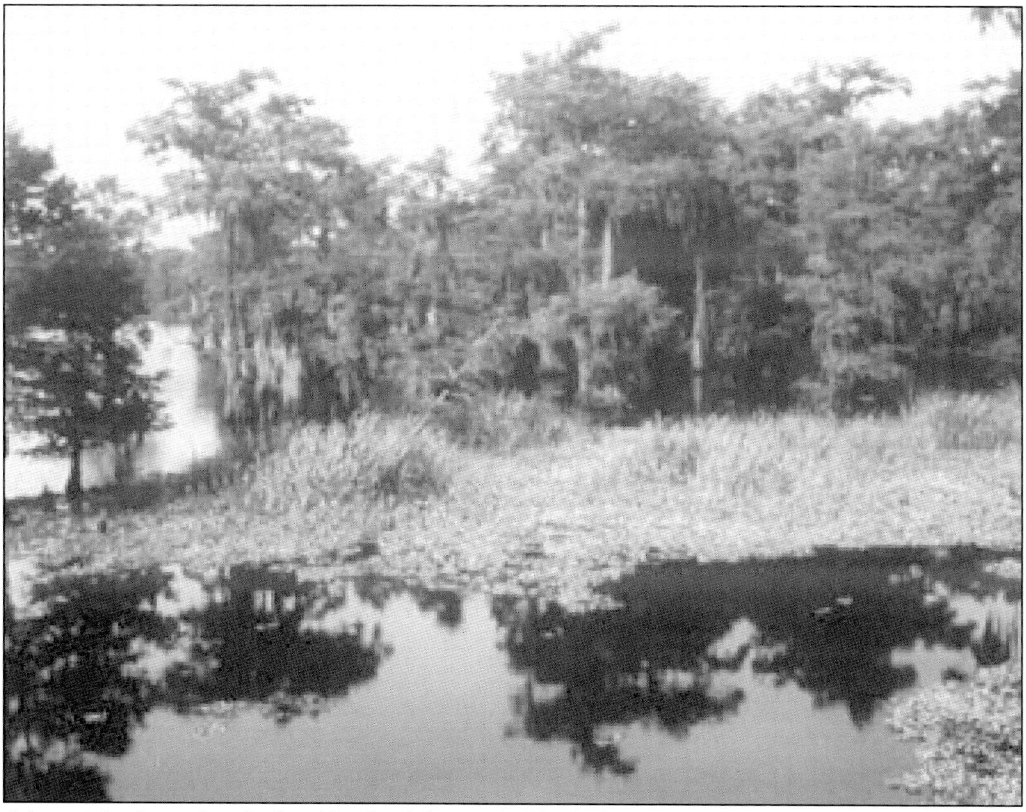

A huge lake formed in the level lowland due to the blockade of Red River by falling trees and Bayou Pierre becoming a larger stream. That lake was called Bayou Pierre, and finally the new settlement became Bayou Pierre Settlement. The settlement extended from just north of Natchitoches along Bayou Pierre all the way through the hills (later named for Pierre Dolet, whose grant was there) and upward to an area later called Wallace. (Courtesy of Liz Chrysler.)

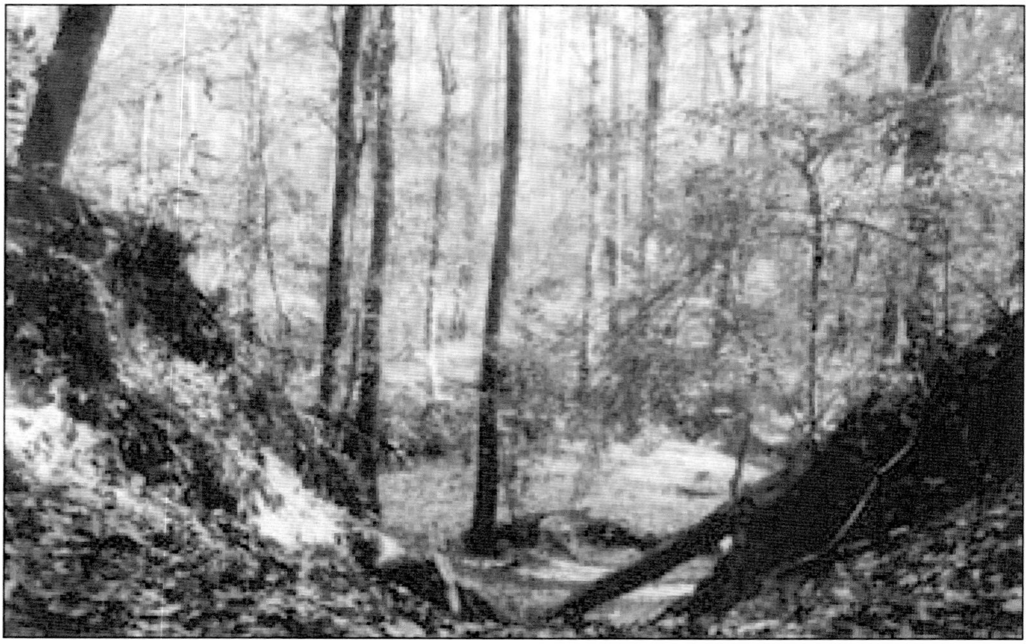

One of the first means of making a living Marcel DeSoto and St. Denis' son, Louis, would capture wild horses from the area northwest of Bayou Pierre, then keep them in the caves and break and train them for the Spanish Army, who paid for well-trained horses. The caves in Dolet Hills from the inside looking out where Marcel and St. Denis son captured the wild horse and kept them. (Courtesy of Liz Chrysler.)

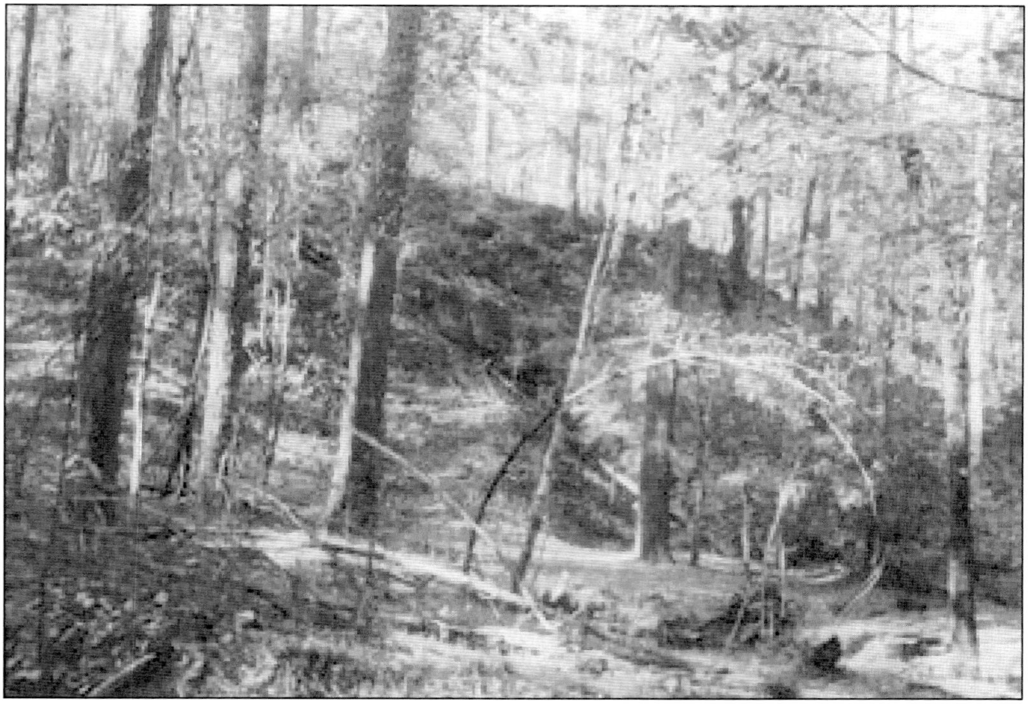

This is the outside of the caves where wild horses were kept. It is said that many newly arrived Anglo settlers lived in these caves until they could build a house. (Courtesy of Liz Chrysler.)

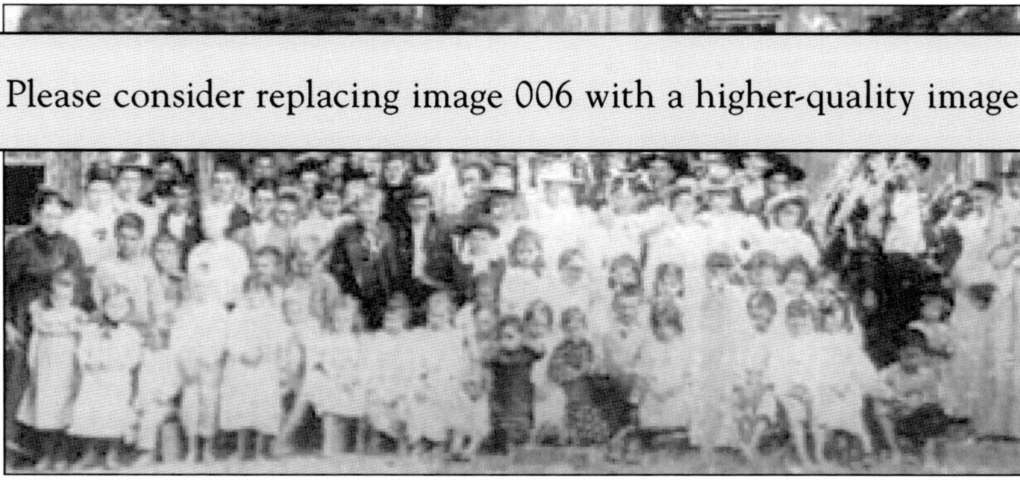

The settlement kept the name Bayou Pierre until 1890, when the Carmelite monks came to establish a convent and monastery. The community was renamed Carmel, which translates into "Garden of God." Father Pierre traveled up from Natchitoches to establish the first church in the region. The monks constructed the Rock Chapel, now on the National Register of Historic Places. Shown here is a photograph of a group picture at the Carmel Monastery around 1898. At the convent, nuns taught girls, and a monastery was erected for the separate instruction of boys. (Courtesy of Liz Chrysler.)

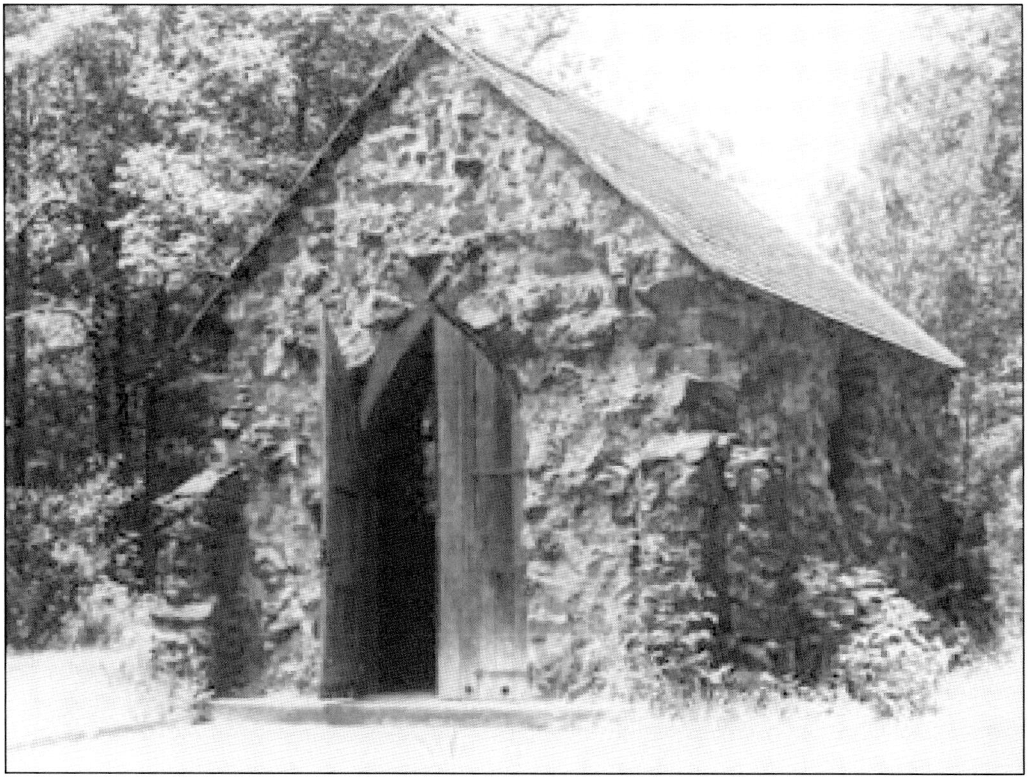

Rock Chapel has been restored or repaired several times. Shown in this illustration is the latest restoration of the "Little Rock Chapel," as it was known. In this restoration, the front doors are hung and the ceilings have been restored with beautiful artwork. (Courtesy of Liz Chrysler.)

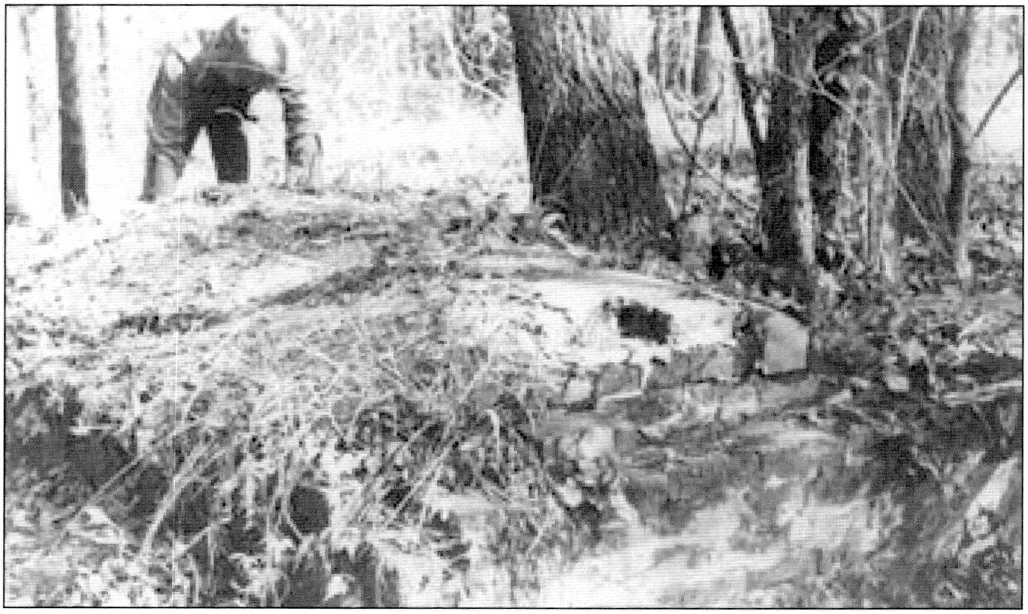

One of Marcel's sons was Simeon DeSoto, who purchased land and built a home and farm atop the highest point in the Dolet Hills. This was a generation after Pierre Dolet lost land and then passed away. Simeon was later buried in the family cemetery bordering his land, alongside his wife, Marie Tessier DeSoto. Simeon served on the first DeSoto Parish police jury and represented the Bayou Pierre Settlement at the meeting to choose a parish seat. Photographed is the DeSoto Cemetery, Simeon DeSoto's grave marker of handmade brick, on the hillside of his family home. (Courtesy of Liz Chrysler.)

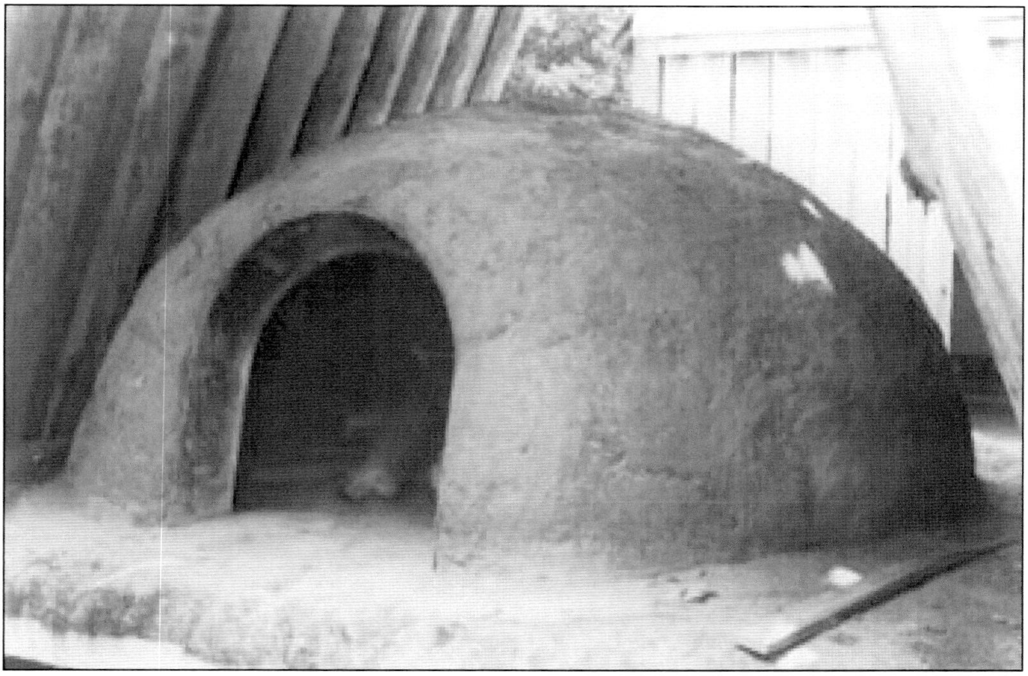

Pictured is an original clay oven used for summer baking in the backyard. It has been preserved. (Photograph by Liz Chrysler.)

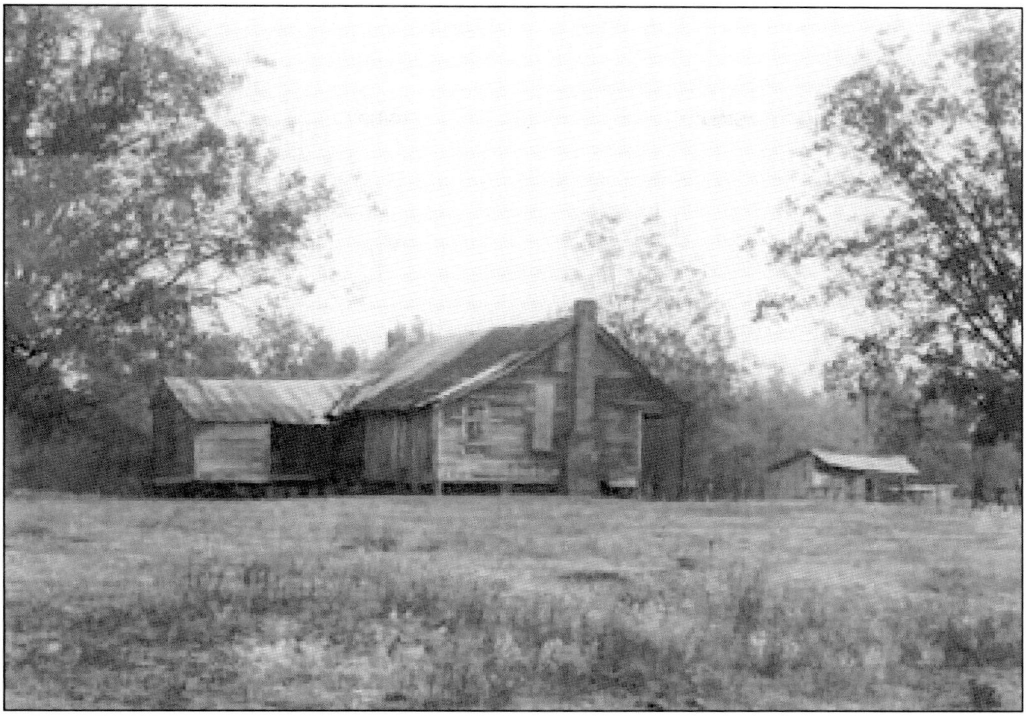

Shown is an early DeSoto Parish home located at Carmel. This home was typical of those near Carmel and of the early settlers. (Courtesy of Liz Chrysler.)

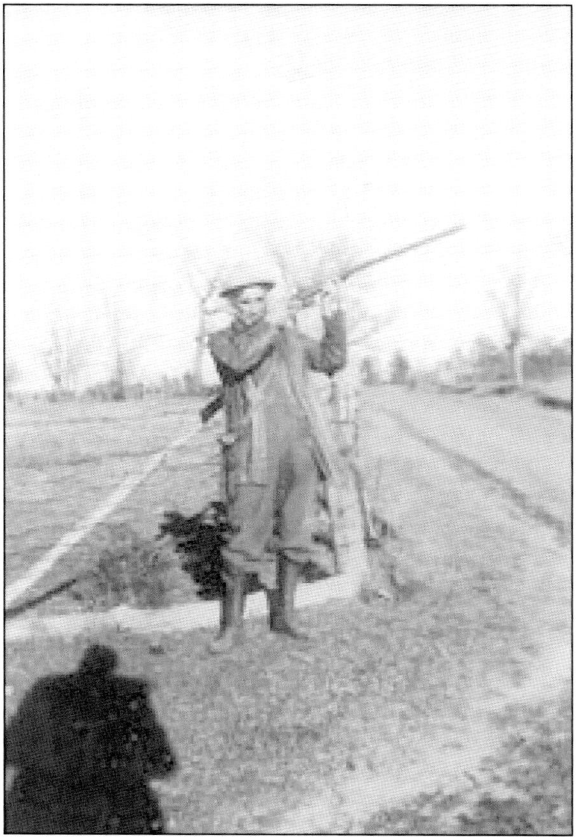

This photograph shows Uncle Edgar Vascoque with his gun. In DeSoto Parish and especially in the Bayou Pierre, area hunting was not considered a sport but was a source of meat for the table. (Courtesy of Liz Chrysler.)

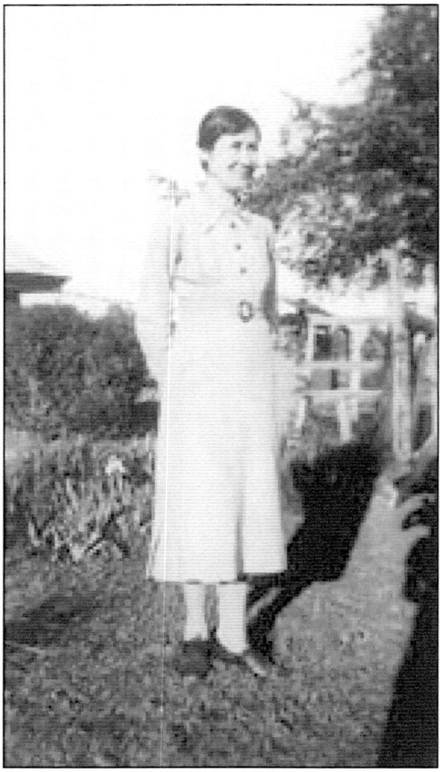

Shown is Elizabeth DeSoto, wife of Edgar Vascoque. Many of the early settlers in the Bayou Pierre region were intermarried. Elizabeth DeSoto was a direct descendant of Marcel DeSoto, for whom the parish was named. (Courtesy of Liz Chrysler.)

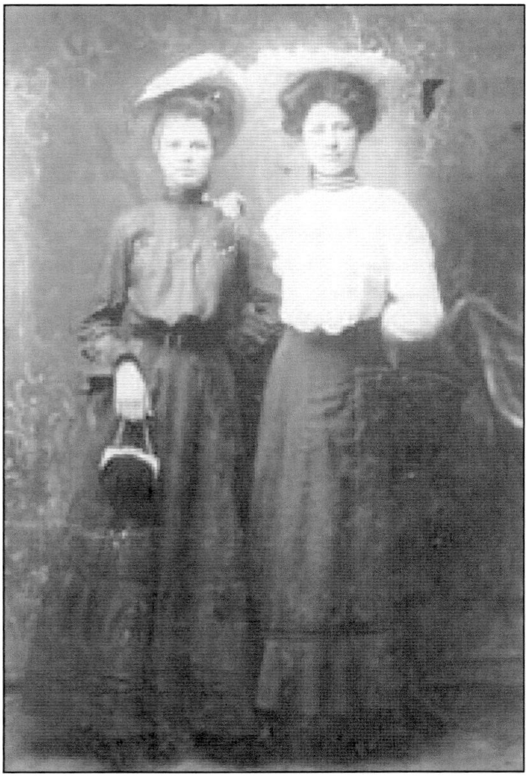

Pictured are Edna Dill and her friend and sister, Emily Vascoque. (Courtesy of Liz Chrysler.)

Carmel schoolchildren are pictured in front of the school at Carmel, one of the early public schools in Louisiana. (Courtesy of Liz Chrysler.)

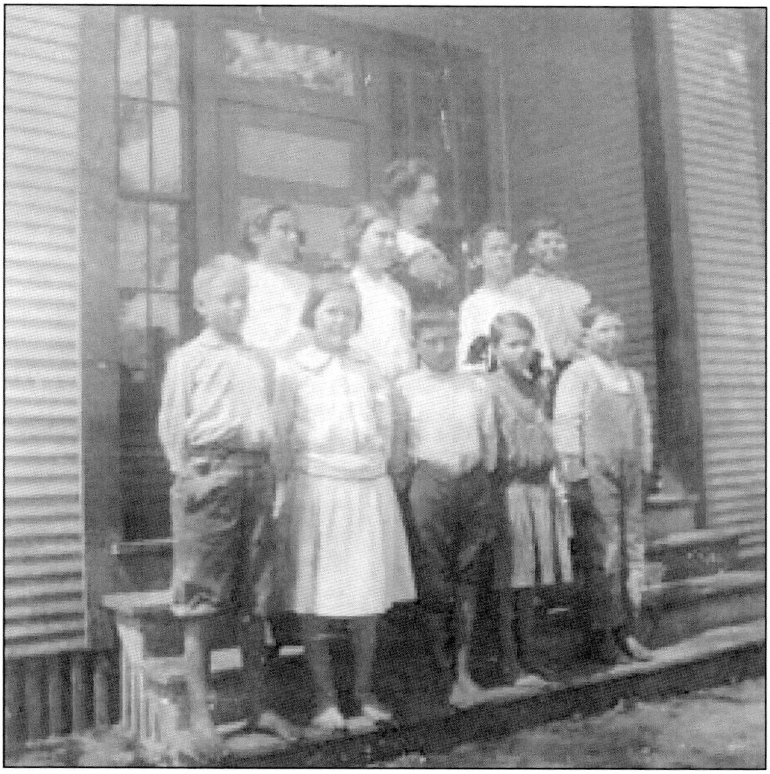

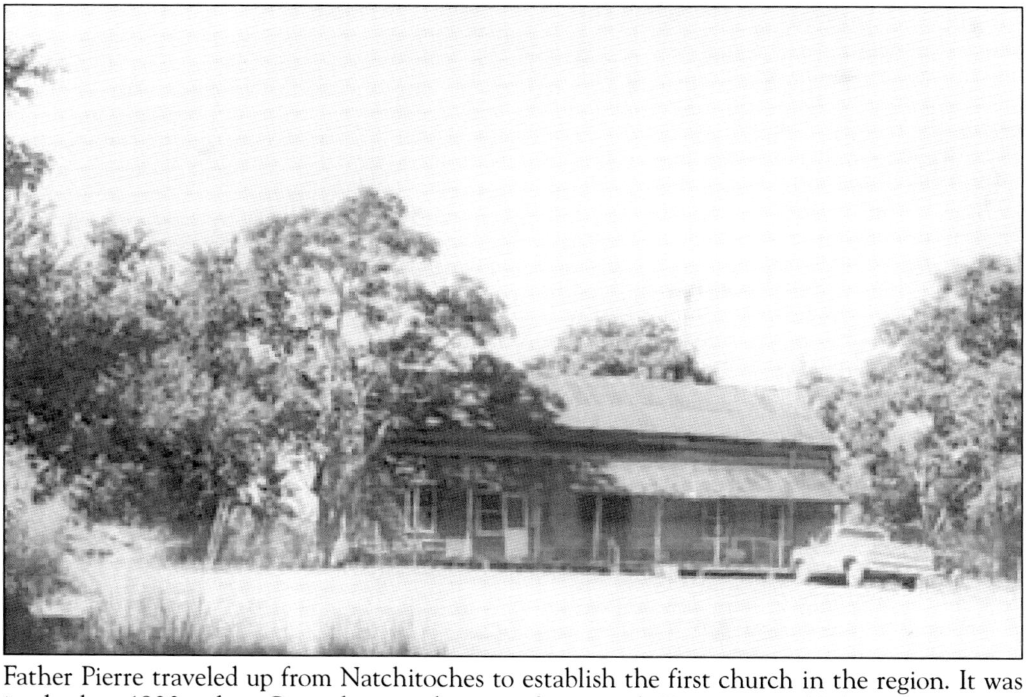

Father Pierre traveled up from Natchitoches to establish the first church in the region. It was in the late 1800s when Carmelite monks came from south Texas to establish a convent and monastery. Shown here is a photograph of the convent, where girls were educated by the nuns. (Courtesy of Liz Chrysler.)

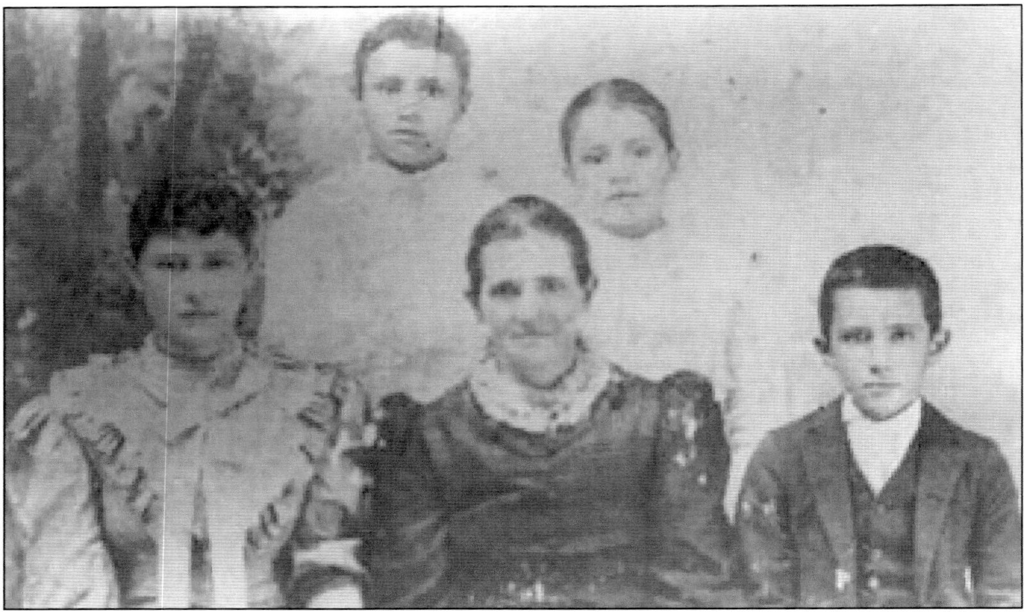

Shown are the descendants of J.P. Laffitte and A. Vascoque. These are (first row) Eliza Vascoque, Matilda Lafitte, and Edgar Vascoque; (second row) Edna and Ora. (Courtesy of Liz Chrysler.)

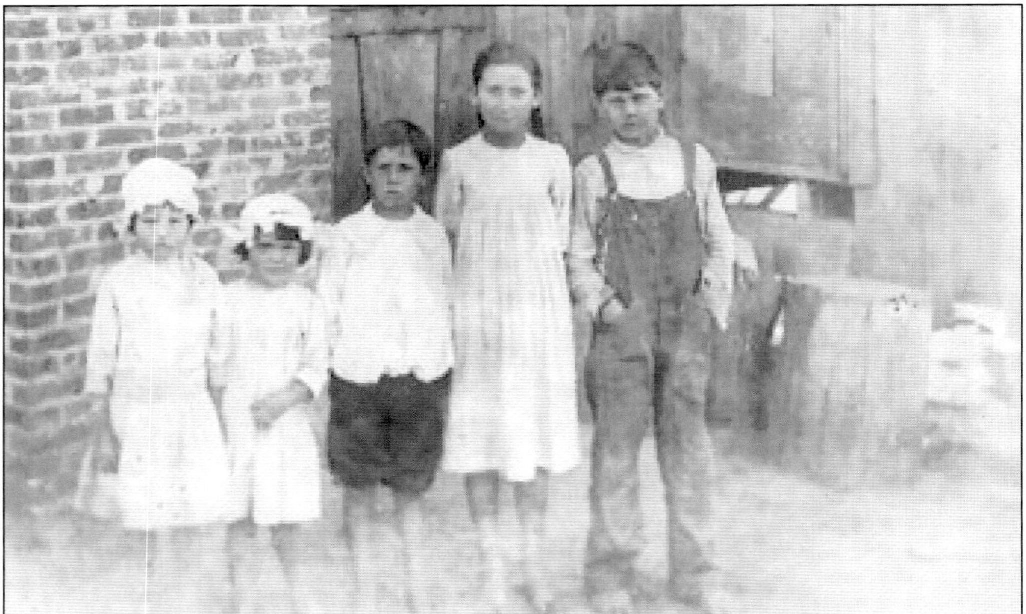

In 1843, Act 88 of the 16th Legislature of Louisiana formed DeSoto Parish from portions of the parishes of Natchitoches and Caddo. It was named in honor of Louis Rambin's grandfather, Marcel DeSoto, who brought the first settlers to the area. The first public school was organized by Mrs. L.B. Rambin, who taught in a spare room of her home. A building was erected in the 1880s, named the Virginia School by Louis M. Rambin to honor his wife A post office was established at Rambin in the early 1880s, located in a general mercantile store owned by Charles Rambin. Pictured are Susie, Flossie, Alto, Eliza, and Julius when they were children at the Rambin school. (Courtesy of Liz Chrysler.)

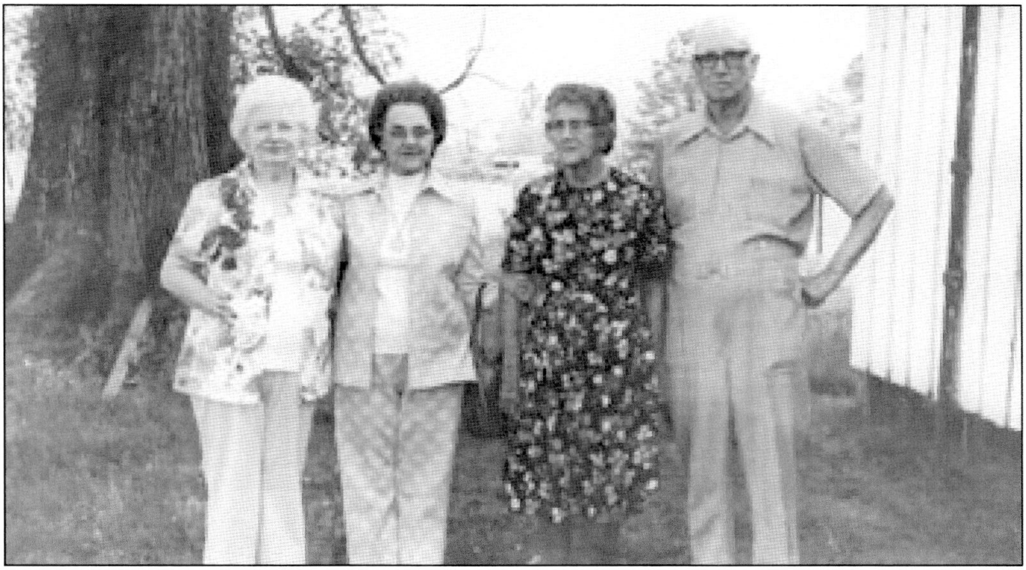

Louis Marcel Rambin became governor of the neutral territory, often called "No Man's Land" because it was disputed between Texas and the Louisiana Territory. This land was all part of the Bayou Pierre Settlement, which ran from the town of Augusta all the way down Bayou Pierre to just north of Natchitoches. Since no one was recognized as governing the area, it became a haven for robbers, rustlers, and murderers. Rambin became a community with a school and Catholic church. The picture shown here is of Susie Chaffin, Flossie DeSoto Williams, Dabney DeSoto Flores, and Reuben Williams in April 1976. (Courtesy of Liz Chrysler.)

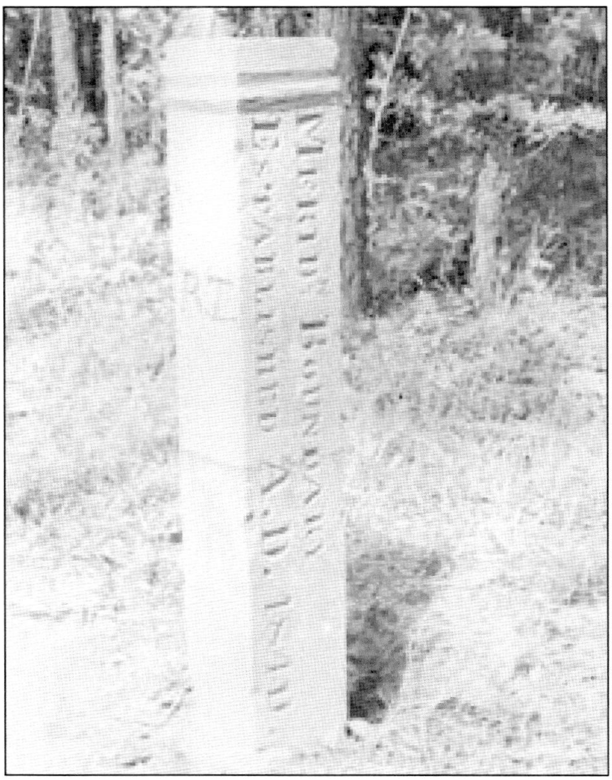

This settlement was by descendants of French and Spanish settlers in No Man's Land. Since the area had no official governance, it became a haven for robbers, rustlers, and murderers. An international boundary marker was set in 1841, placed by engineers as they shot the boundary northward from the Sabine River. The Sabine had been officially the boundary between the United States and Spanish Mexico, set by the Adams-Onis Treaty of 1819. A convention between the two governments was held in Washington, D.C., to establish the official line in the middle of the Sabine River. After the line was marked, the two governments were able to clear out the bands of outlaws in the neutral ground. The international boundary is still the only one within the United States. (Courtesy of Liz Chrysler.)

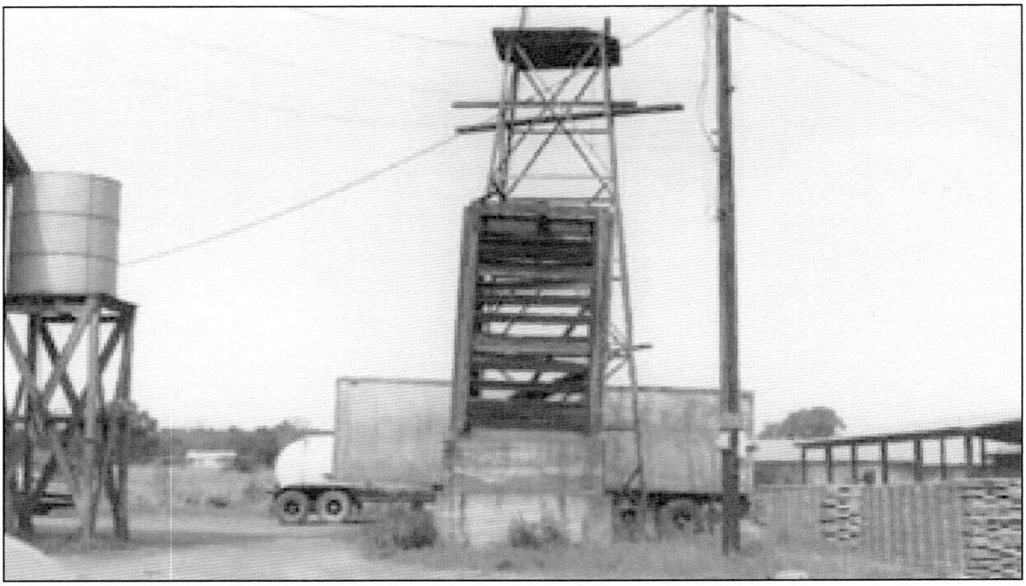

Pictured here is the Lafitte Lumber Company at Carmel. As immigration continued westward, lumber for houses grew in demand, and lumber mills developed. At the Bayou Pierre Settlement in the early 1900s, the Laffitte Company began a commissary store, run by Edward Laffitte on his farm. By 1911, he had been running a small cotton gin for several years. The equipment was moved to the lumberyard property, a five-acre tract. A new building was constructed in 1912 for the gin. The sawmill equipment was purchased in 1912 from A. G Faggard. A shingle mill came with the sawmill, and cypress shingles were cut for a year or more by the Laffitte Company until the new building was erected for the sawmill at its final site. deep well was dug for drinking water at the multiple developing industries, and a pond was developed for boiler water. Beginning at its new location in 1913, The Laffitte Company furnished lumber for most of the homes around the Carmel and Smithport area, constructing many of the new homes. (Courtesy of Liz Chrysler.)

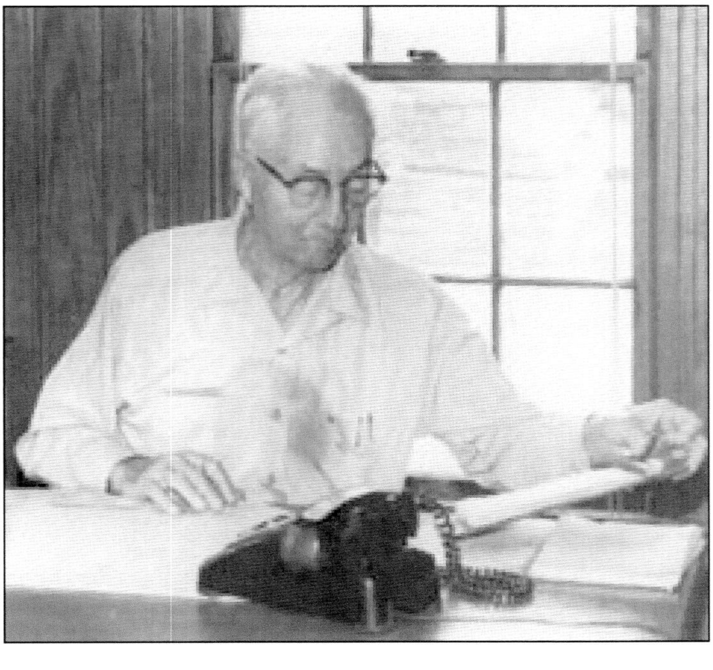

Earnest Lafitte is shown at his desk at his lumber mill. Depression struck in late 1929, and money grew scarce. With 10 children to support, the Laffittes had to cut corners, but the business continued. When America entered World War II, Ernest ran the business alone with the younger men gone to war. After the war ended, postwar production increased. The company began shipping lumber by truck, first into other North Louisiana and East Texas markets, gradually expanding the mill. (Courtesy of Liz Chrysler.)

Two

Arrival of Anglos and New Towns

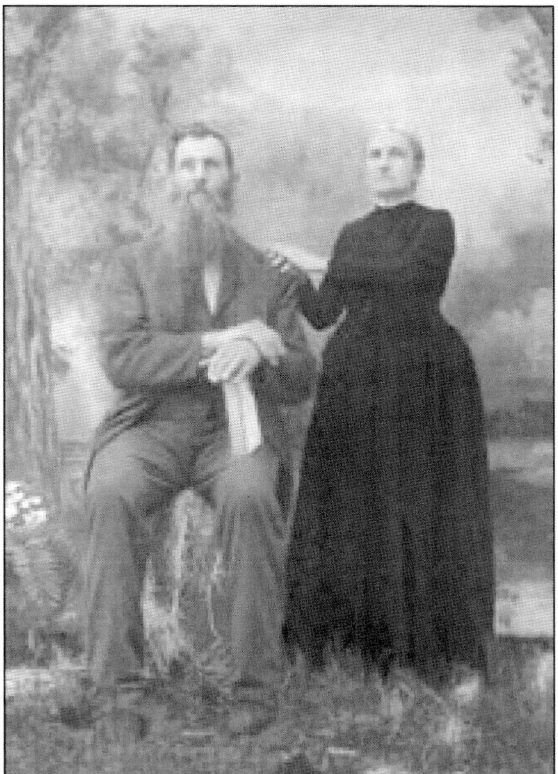

Among the first Anglo settlers were those who came to the Dolette Hills as part of the westward migration from Georgia, Alabama, and South Carolina. Pictured are Margaret Jane Pace who married Edward Joseph Griffith in DeSoto Parish in 1859. She came to DeSoto Parish with her mother Elizabeth Horton Everett Pace and two sisters, Mary Thomas Pace and Harrett Rebecca Ann Pace, from Georgia in the early 1850s. (Courtesy of Emilia Gay Griffith Means.)

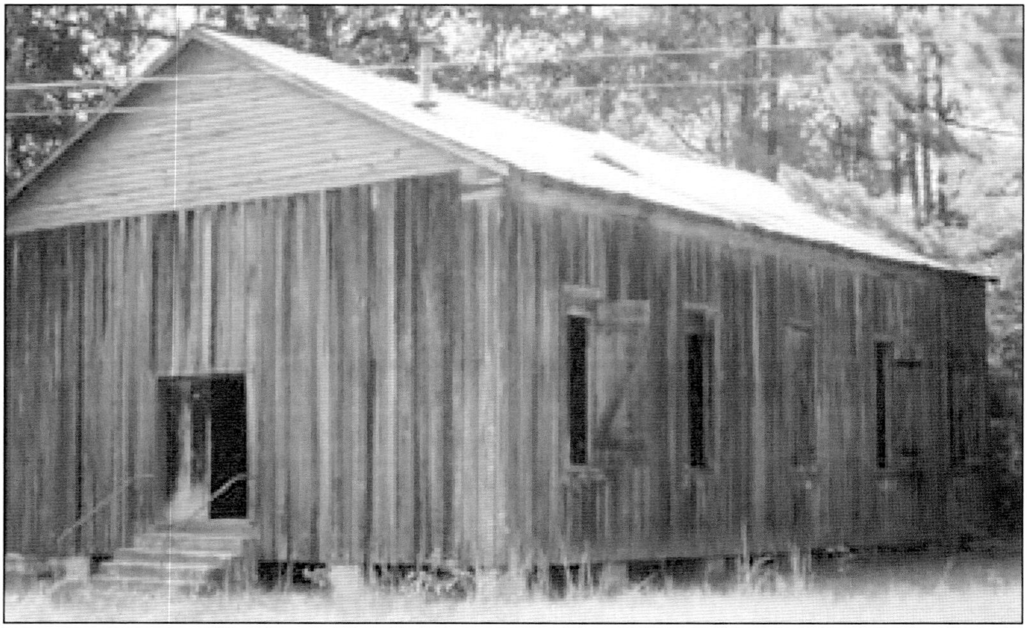

Grove Hill Baptist Church was organized in 1859 and remains the last structure standing in this once viable Dolet Hills community. It was one of two churches, the other being a Methodist church. The community was known as Double Churches and had a doctor and a school as well as the post office. Many families lived once there, but this building and the cemetery are all that remains. A reunion is held every year on the first Saturday in June. Some of the families who once lived there were the Lords, the DeSotos, the Bowdens, among numerous others. The cemetery is in excellent repair. (Photograph by Emilia Gay Griffith Means.)

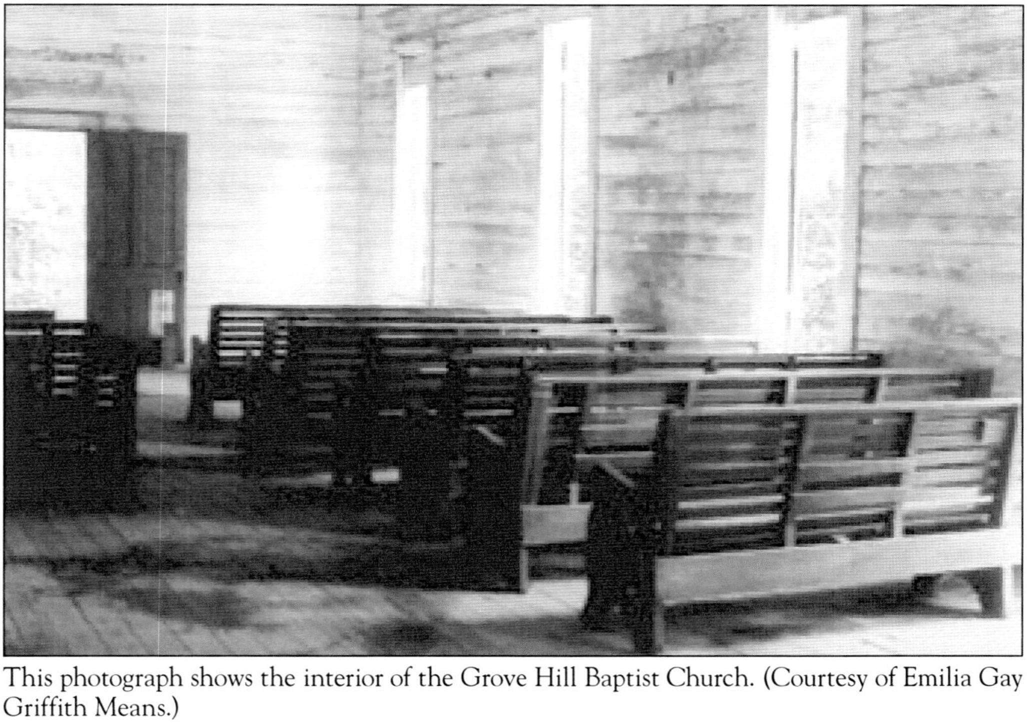

This photograph shows the interior of the Grove Hill Baptist Church. (Courtesy of Emilia Gay Griffith Means.)

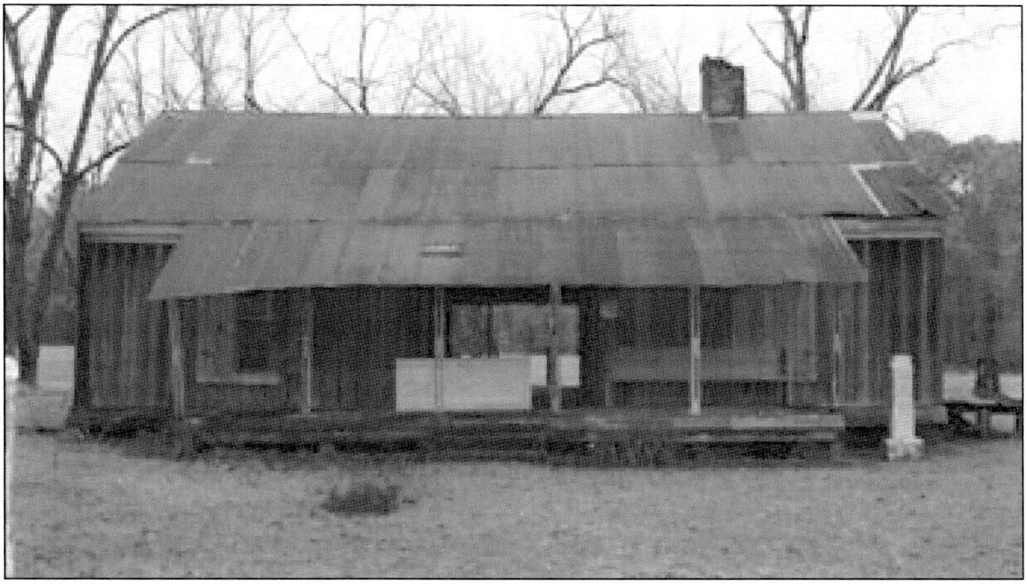

The Elam House was built by John Waddell Elam, sheriff of DeSoto Parish from 1858 to 1862. He fought with the Second Louisiana Volunteers in Virginia with Robert E. Lee and Stonewall Jackson. He was wounded at Antietam, captured, and paroled back to Louisiana. He was a scout at the Battle of Mansfield and Pleasant Hill for Richard Taylor. After the Civil War, he came home and farmed. His brother was J.B. Elam, speaker of the Confederate House of Representatives. The house was used as a hospital during the Battle of Pleasant Hill. It and the cemetery are all that remain of this settlement. (Courtesy of Scot Solice, photographer.)

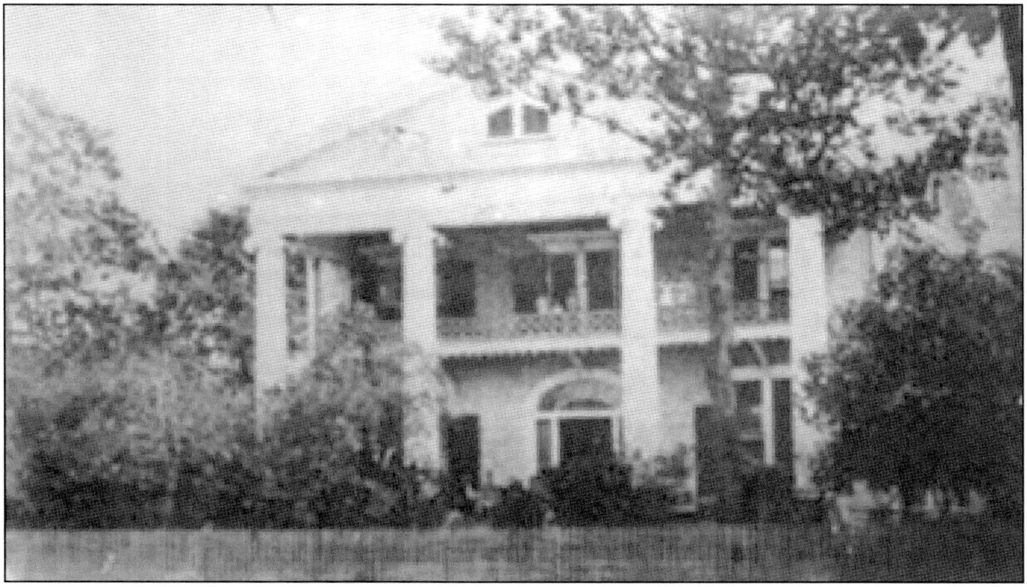

The Childers Home, built in 1859 by John S. Childers, was used by General Banks of the Union army headquarters at the Battle of Pleasant Hill on April 9, 1864. After the battle, the home was used as a hospital for Union and Confederate wounded. Capt. Elizah Parsons, an attorney from Texas, died in the Childer's Mansion and was buried under a tree. He came with Walker's Greyhounds, a Confederate division made up of Texas troops. (Courtesy University of Louisiana in Shreveport, Noel Memorial Library, Archives and Special Collections.)

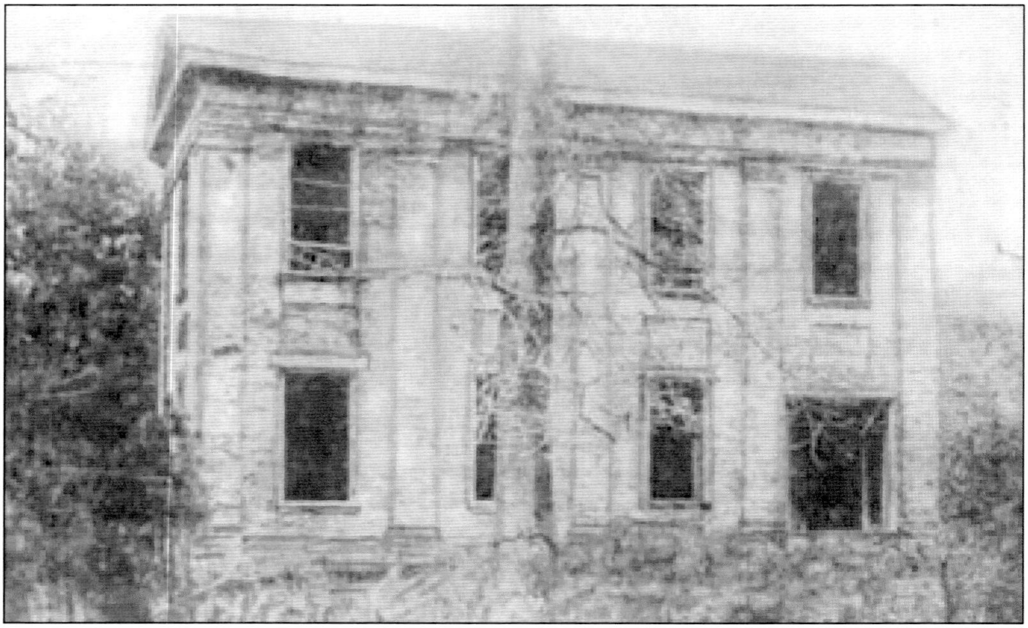

Pearce-Payne College was a school for boys operated by the Methodist Church. The school saw many boys off to the Civil War who were severely wounded or never returned. After the Battle of Pleasant Hill, it was used as a hospital for Union troops. Near the college was a store, and the Pleasant Hill Methodist Church was at the site of the battleground. (Courtesy of Raymond W. Powell.)

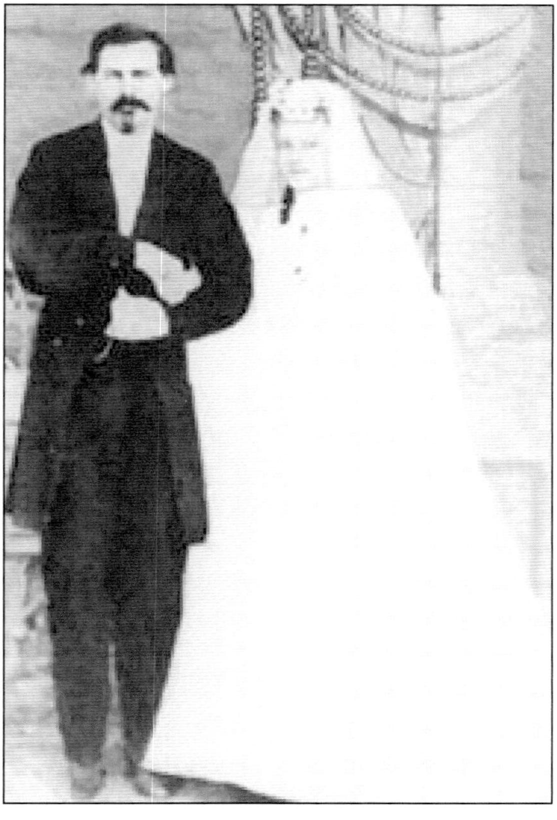

Robert Abijah Rembert, born 1846 in Selma, Alabama, was reared and educated in DeSoto Parish. Robert married Sarah Helen Chapman, daughter of early settlers Stephen Decatur and Caroline Elizabeth Chapman. Sarah Chapman's family owned a much smaller dogtrot house across the road from the mansion. They had a cistern in their backyard where dead soldiers' bodies were dumped after the battle. She was born in near Macon, Georgia, and came to Louisiana in a caravan from Selma, Alabama, as a young girl. She was the last resident survivor of the Battle of Pleasant Hill and was an eyewitness the battle. (Courtesy of Dr. Franklin Rembert.)

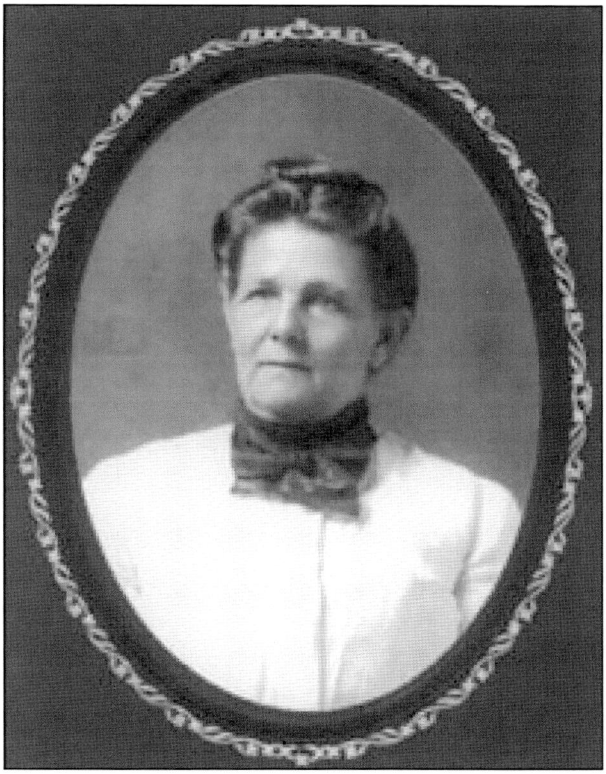

Sarah Chapman Rembert watched the 1864 Battle of Pleasant Hill as it unfolded in the fields behind her home. She died on December 23, 1940, at the age of 93, and was the last surviving witness of that battle. She is buried next to her husband in the new Pleasant Hill Cemetery. (Courtesy of Dr. Franklin Rembert.)

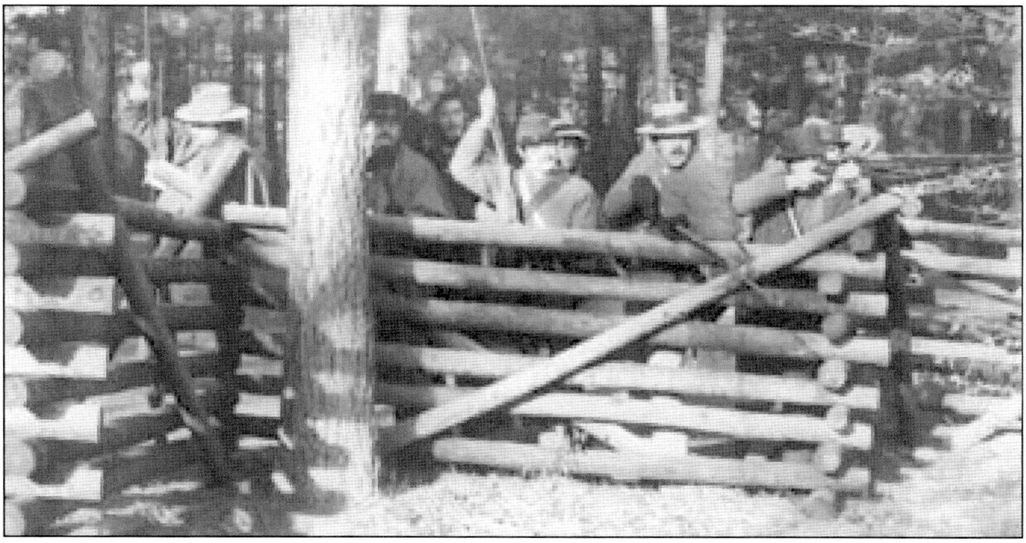

Now all that remains of Old Pleasant Hill are the Elam House, the cemetery, and a popular reenactment of the Battle of Pleasant Hill. The Elam House is still used as headquarters for the officers of the Confederacy and a few widows in mourning and their families. The reenactors set up tents around the area and cook their own food. Entire families come and camp out. Suttlers come with their goods, photographers demonstrate the techniques of 1864, and reenactors roam the cemetery. Once the battle begins, no automobiles are allowed in sight, and all who are dressed in civilian clothes are asked to step out of the campground. On occasion there is an artist dressed in period clothing with his sketchbook. (Courtesy of Liz Chrysler.)

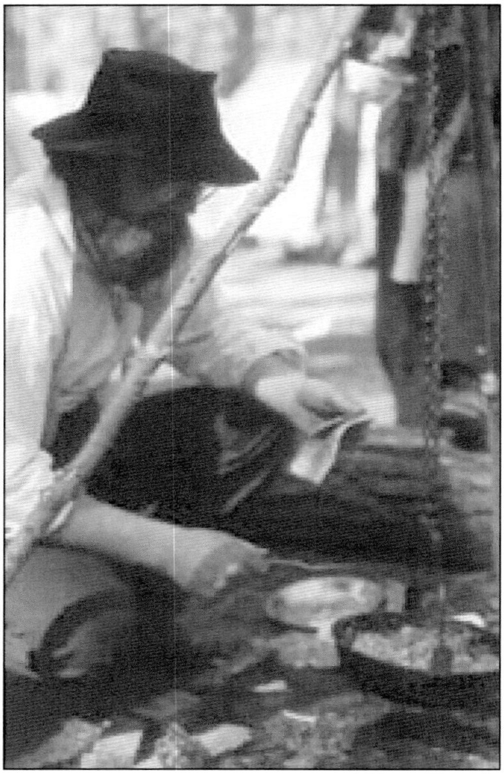

Shown is reenactor dressed in period clothes cooking for his comrades and anyone else interested in the food he has to offer. The reenactors take pride in making certain that their clothing, guns, cooking utensils, silverware, and shoes are as authentic as possible. Some use original rifles. (Courtesy of W.Conway Link, photographer.)

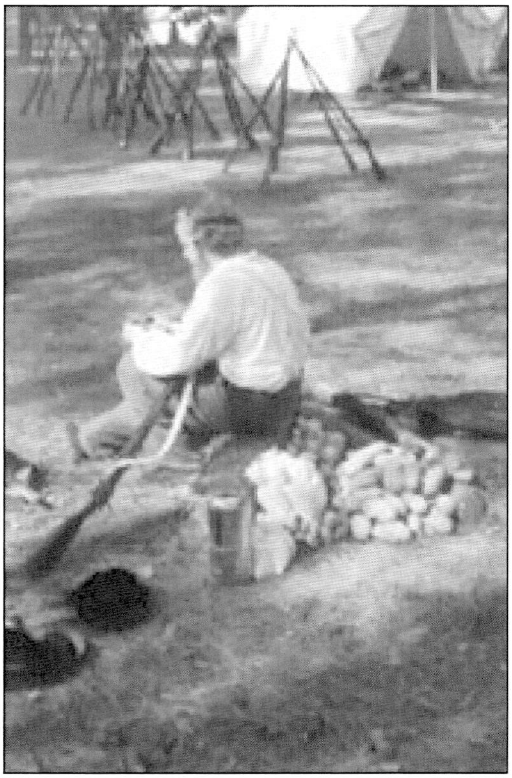

Shown is reenactor in period clothes peeling potatoes—probably to contribute to a stew. The tents and stacked rifles are traditional when the soldiers are in camp. (Courtesy of W.Conway Link, photographer.)

This photograph depicts Old Hazelwood Cemetery 1848-1934 as now forgotten. The cemetery is all that remains of this lost community and at the date of this photograph contained some very impressive vaults stones in dire need of repairs. This small community was located on the middle stagecoach route between Mansfield and Shreveport. (Photograph by Libby Dady Alcorn.)

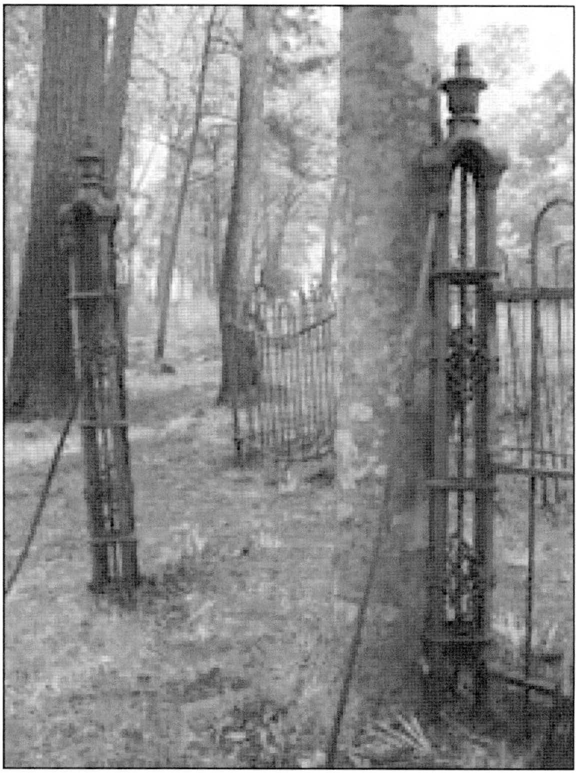

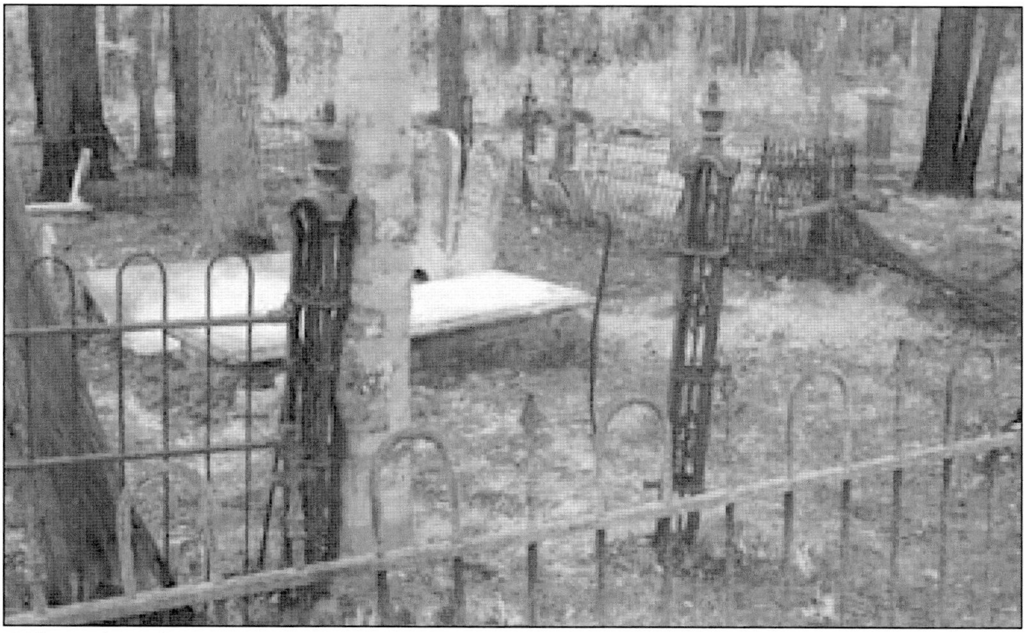

Old Hazelwood Cemetery Fence Post speaks a thousand words. In this cemetery are the gravesites of some of the earlier settlers in DeSoto Parish. The once beautiful grave stones from days gone by, the antique iron fence, pitted with rust, bent in places with sections of the fence lying on the ground is still depicted by the beauty of flowers planted by someone who ones cared. (Photograph by Libby Dady Alcorn.)

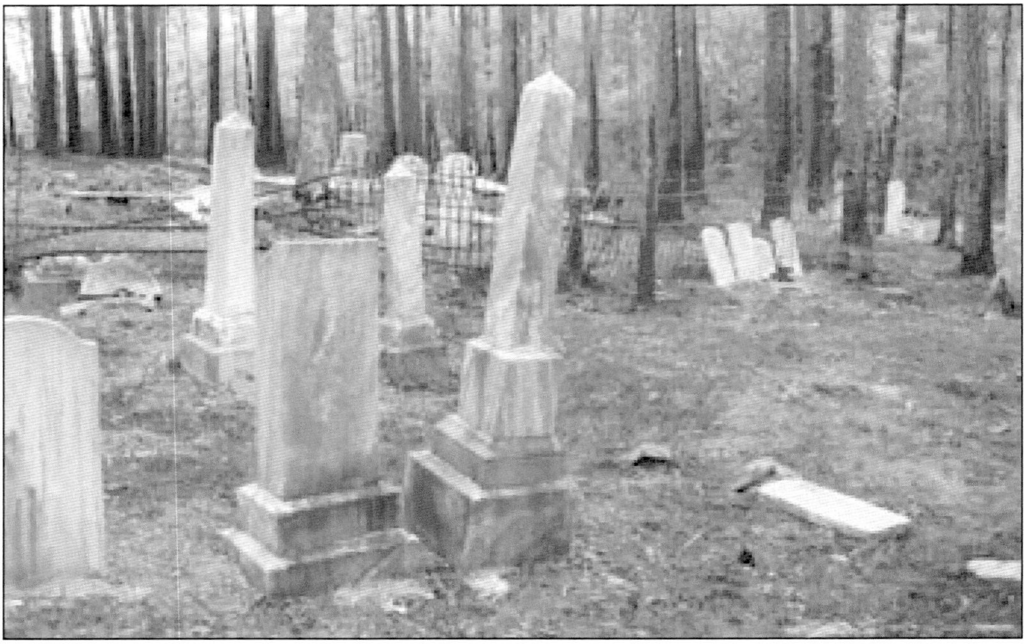

This picture of fallen gravestones in Old Hazelwood Cemetery was taken before Libby Dady Alcorn undertook a restoration project with the help of Jay Burford and some of his young parishioners. The cemetery is 162 years old and had been forgotten in time. In this cemetery are the gravesites of some of the earlier settlers of DeSoto Parish. (Photograph by Libby Dady Alcorn.)

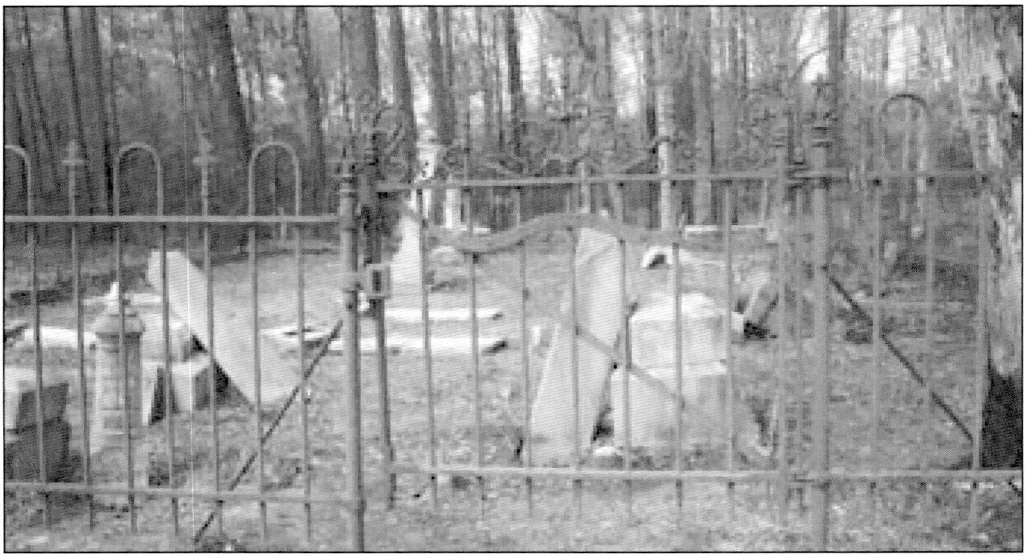

James Cowley was a deacon of the Hazelwood Baptist Church, which was located adjacent to the cemetery. The church is no longer in existence and all that remains is the cemetery. The oldest gravesites in the old Hazelwood cemetery are the ones of the three young daughters of James Cowley, who died within weeks of each other in the spring of 1848. Perhaps influenza or another contagious disease might have been the cause of death for these three young girls because the dates of their deaths are so close. This was not long after the Cowleys arrived in DeSoto Parish from Alabama. Each gravestone has a story to reveal about the joys and sadness that occurred in this lost community. (Photograph by Libby Dady Alcorn.)

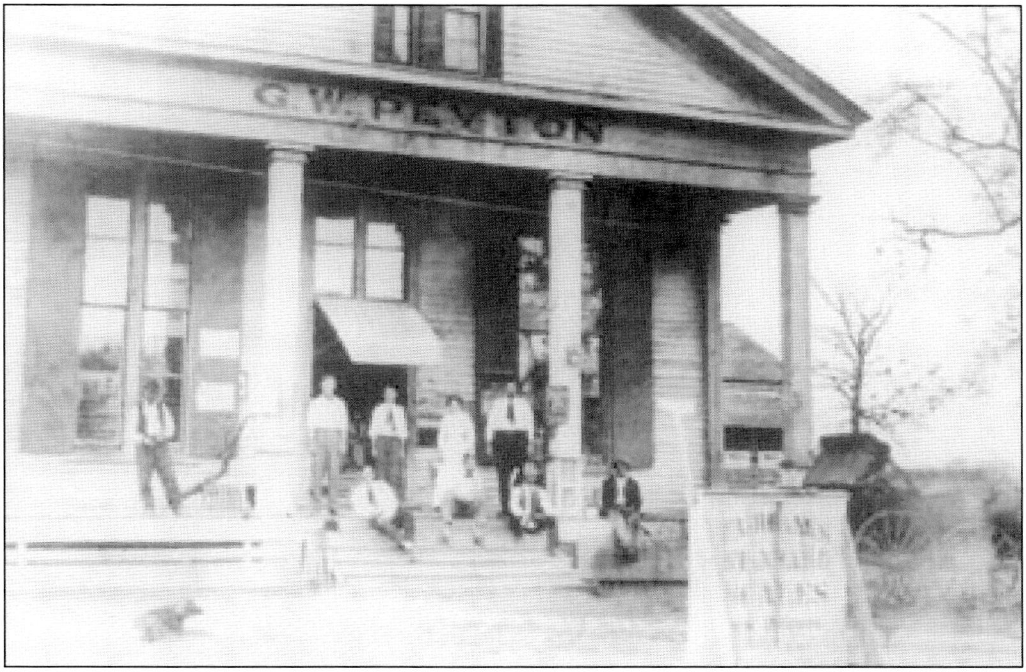

Built in the 1840s, Keachi store is a frame, temple-style, Greek Revival commercial building located in the crossroads community of Keachi. The store features a broad porch in front and a long rectangular shape with office in the rear. Pictured is the store during the ownership and management of G.W. Peyton, around the turn of the 20th century. (Courtesy of Nancy Beard Wilson.)

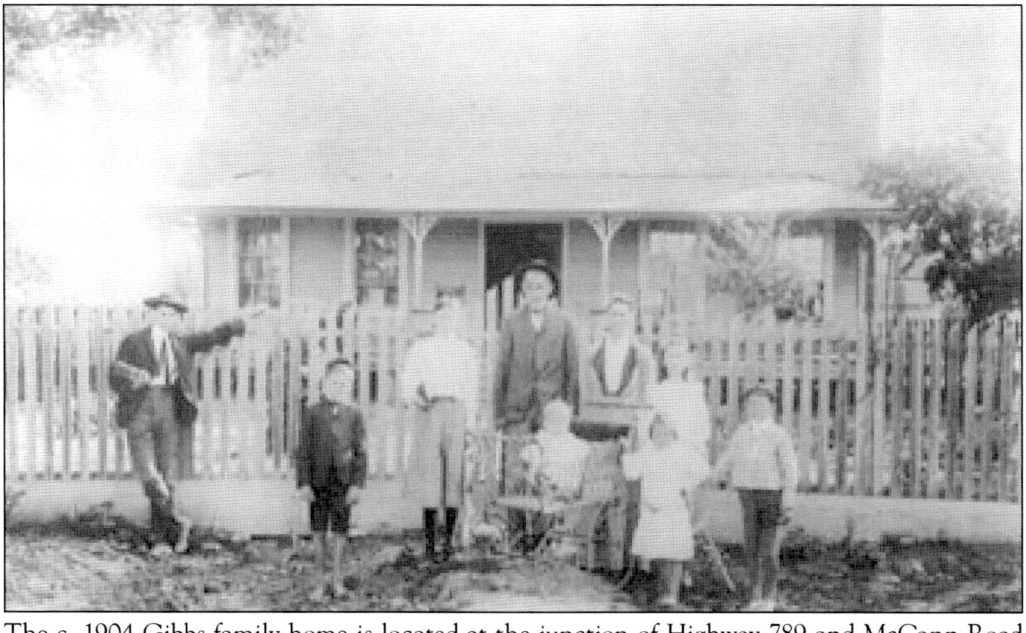

The c. 1904 Gibbs family home is located at the junction of Highway 789 and McCann Road in Keachi, Louisiana. Pictured from left to right are Byron Bennett Gibbs, Edwin Harp Gibbs, Marth Laura Gibbs Lyons, Archibald Palaski Gibbs, Marth Elouise Gibbs, Archer Lita Gibbs, Wesley Waits Gibbs (in carriage), Mena Mae Gibbs Dawson, and John Alvin P. Gibbs. (Courtesy of Lisa Owens.)

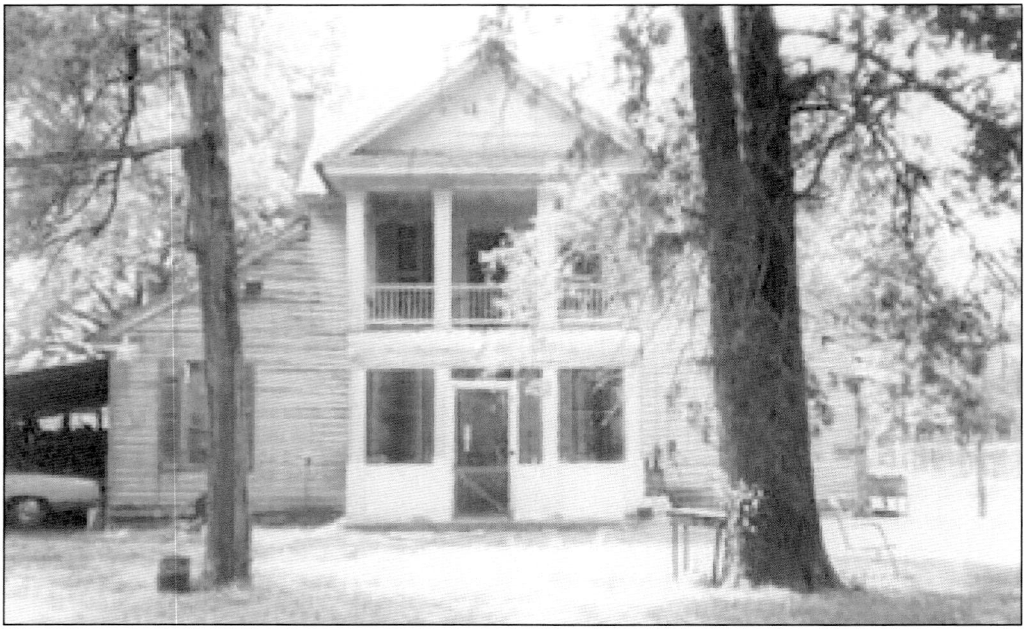

Known most recently as the Jackie Vile home, this house on Smyrna Road is very near the Gamble – Mason – McMichael cemetery. One story told about it is that it was built by John Akin Gamble (1796-1851) from South Carolina. The Gambles had two daughters and a son. Amanda married into the Mason family, and Jane married into the McMichael family. Although John Akin Gamble may have constructed the basic one-story home, it is believed that his son was the builder of the home as it appears in these photographs. This house, probably the one known as Mrs. Gamble's Stagecoach Inn by diarists and travelers during the Civil War, was originally located on 16,000 acres. Presently, the home is in a state of disrepair. (Courtesy of Raymond W. Powell.)

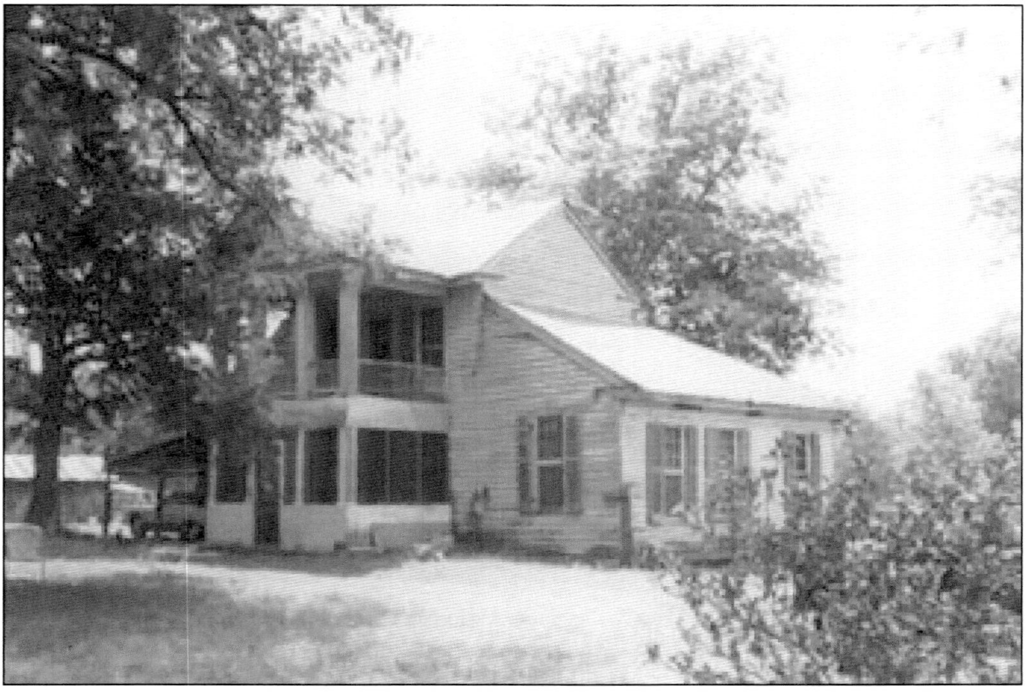

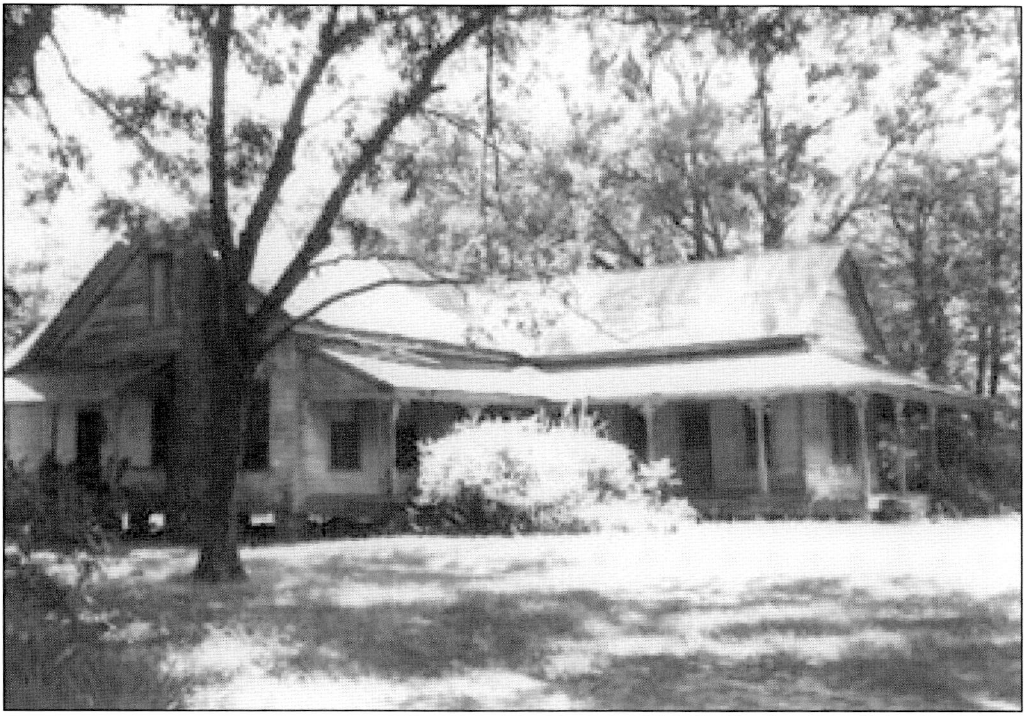

The Patton House was built by William B. Patton in the early 1850s using slave and servant labor. George Washington Patton, who owned a store in Keachie, bought the house and added a Victorian front room where his daughter was courted by suitors. The house is almost directly across the road from the home of Travis Whitfield, which places it behind the Masonic lodge. To this day it is occupied as a residence (Courtesy of Raymond W. Powell.)

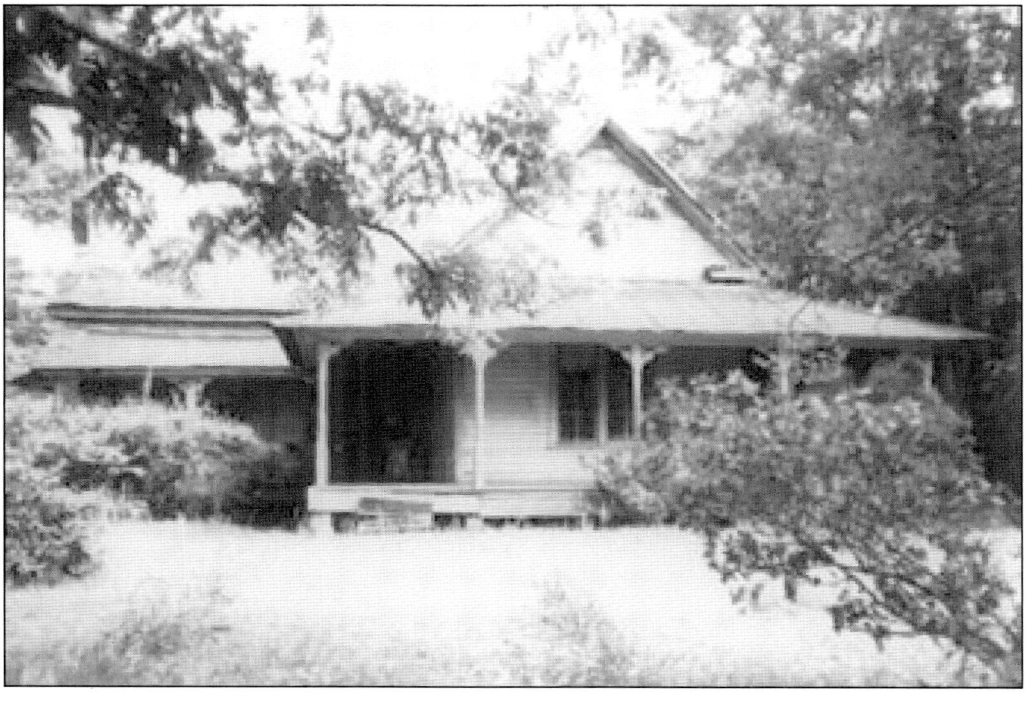

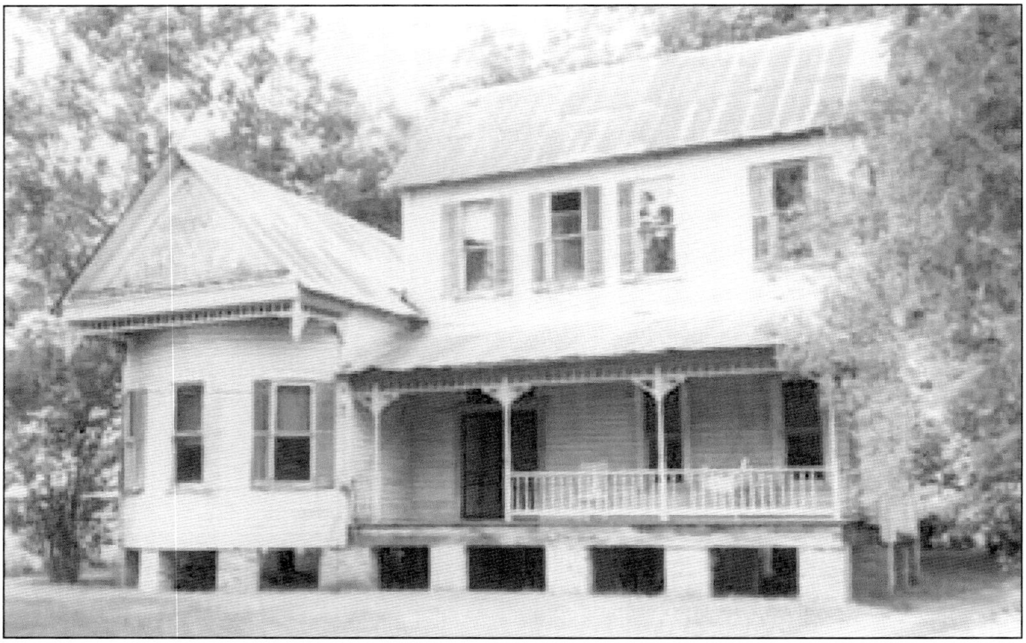

The Travis Whitfield Home, one of the Victorian homes in Keachie, sits high off the ground on brick piers. When Beauregard Talbert built the house in 1898, he used it as a townhouse. In 1917, a Mr. Wyatt bought the house, which has extra trim, banisters, and 14-foot ceilings. Travis Whitfield, the present owner, bought the house in 1976. Whitfield is the mayor of Keachi, a well-known artist, and a preservation specialist. Those who have visited him say that their favorite place in Keachi is to have coffee with him on the back porch of this house and enjoy the view. (Courtesy of Raymond W. Powell.)

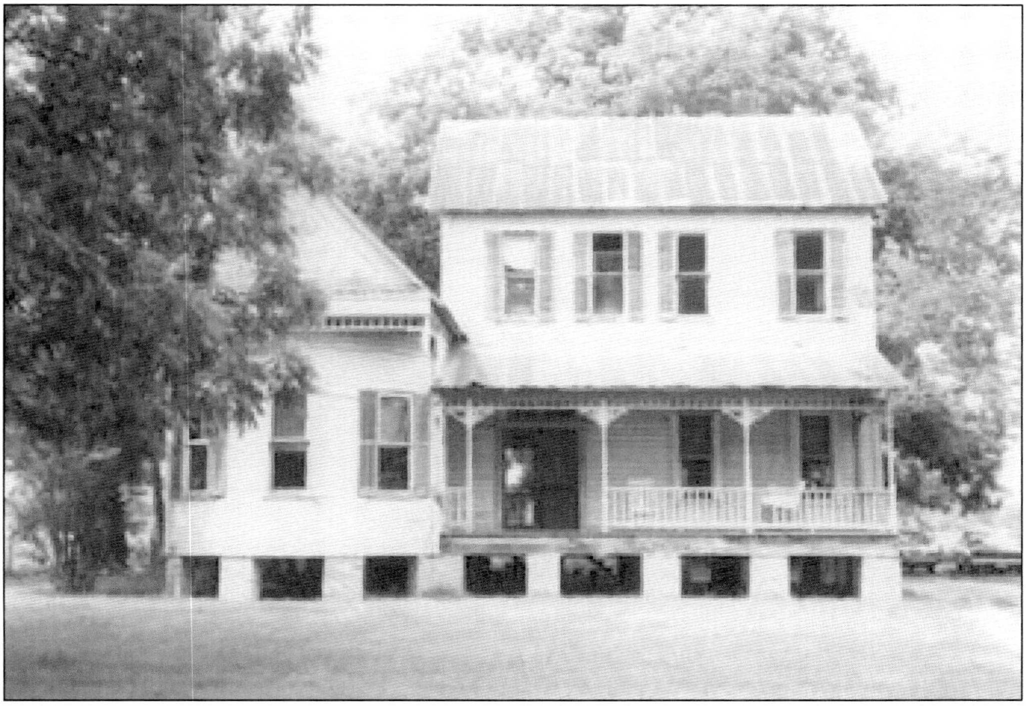

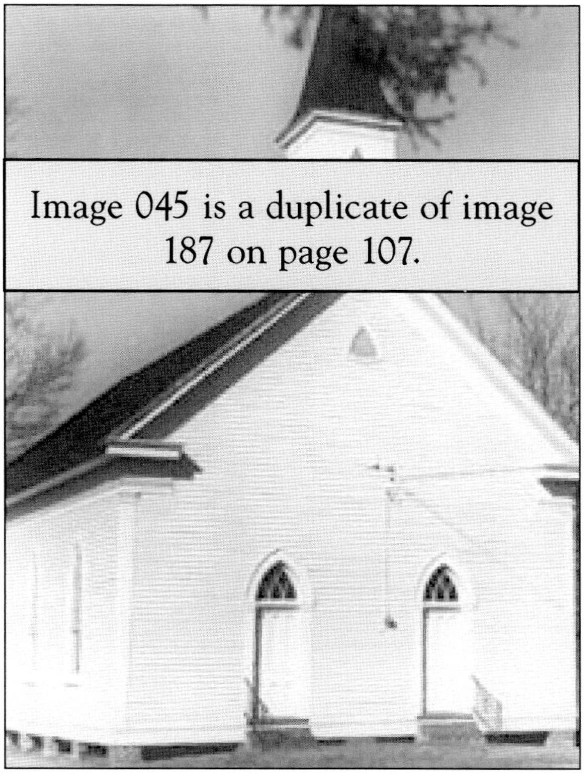

About 1848, the Bethel Presbyterian Church was organized, and it was the first frame house of worship erected west of the Mississippi River. In 1856, the building was sold, and the church moved to its current site, where the present building in 1858. In 1859, the presbytery changed the name to the Keachi Presbyterian Church. Basically the church remains in its original state. The benches are hand-hewn and have on been cleaned and varnished. The chairs on the pulpit are among the first used in the church. On the right is a pump organ, which still plays but is not longer used. The light fixtures are also original and have been only silvered and converted from coal oil to electricity. The wood burning stoves located on either side of the church have been removed and gas burning heaters installed. (Courtesy Noel Memorial Library, Louisiana State University in Shreveport, Archives and Special Collections.)

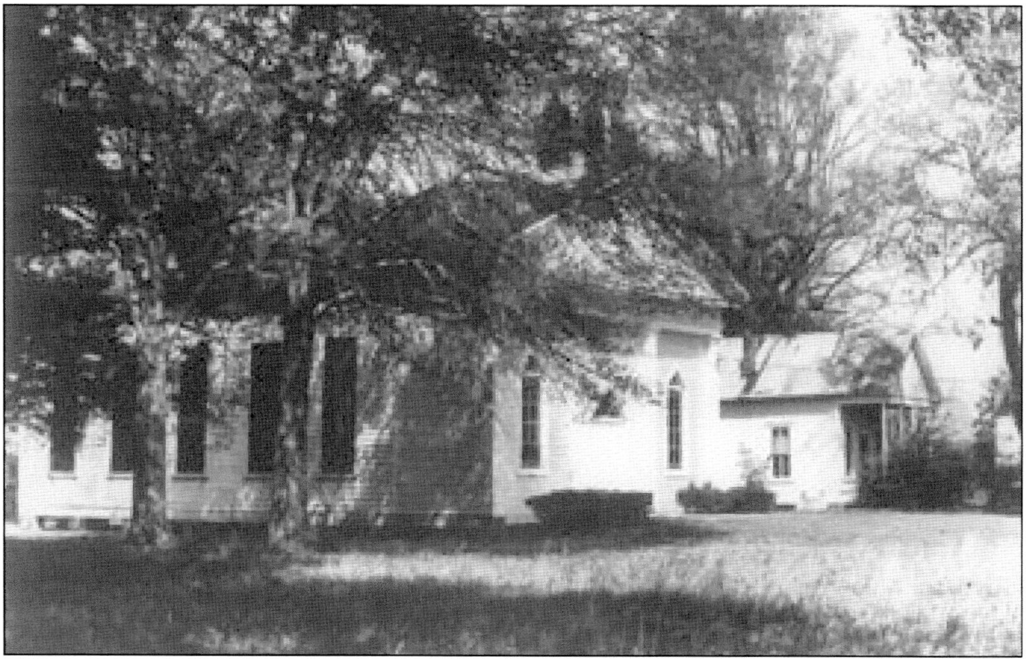

Shown is a side view of the Keachi Methodist Episcopal Church South. Constructed in 1856, the building is listed on the National Register of Historic Places. William A.Thorpe, who donated a three-acre lot next to the church, was one of its early trustees. (Courtesy Noel Memorial Library, Louisiana State University in Shreveport, Archives and Special Collections.)

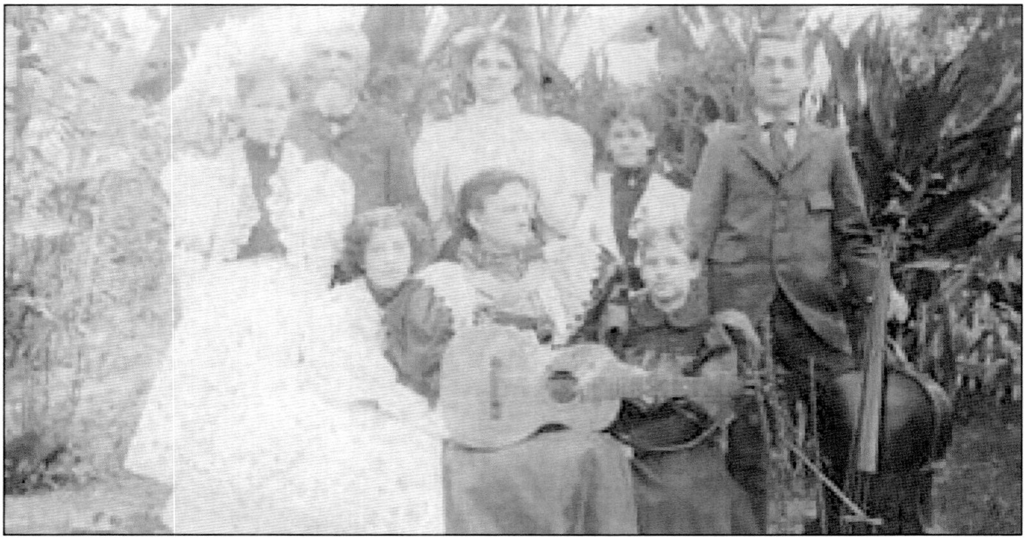

Pictured is the Ernst Schuler family of Keachi. Front left to right are (first row) Nanetta Schuler; Evelyn Fullilove Schuler; and Florence Schuler; (second row) an unidentified Hollingsworth; Ernst Schuler; Eoline Schuler; an unidentified Hollingsworth; and Ernest Schuler. Evelyn Fullilove eloped to marry Ernst Schuler. Their four children were Eoline, Nanetta, Ernest, and Florence. Evelyn bought the Schuler-Cathy home from her mother, Elizabeth Foster Fullilove, and was responsible for most of the additions to the home. (Photograph by David B. McGuire, courtesy of Mary E. and Mary T. McGuire.)

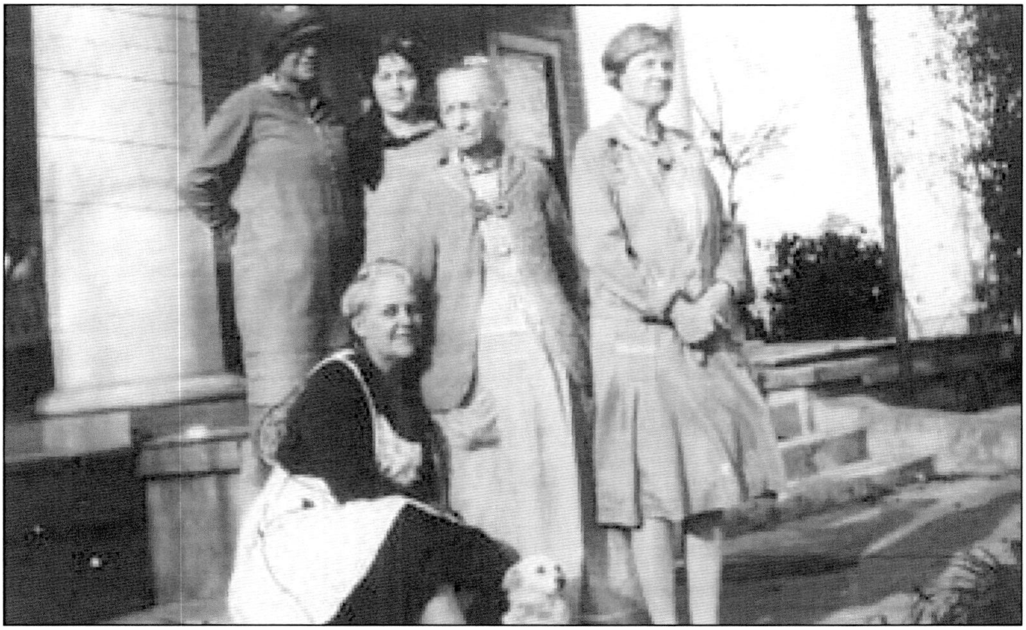

Shown from left to right are (first row) Eoline Schuler (Mrs. Hill) Fullilove and Snowball; (second row) Nanetta Schuler (Mrs. T.F.) Bell, her daughter, Mary Evelyn Bell, Evelyn (Ma or Old Miss) Schuler, Florence (Mrs. O.C.) Cathy. One son-in-law said, "The Schuler women had 'a decided mind set.' " Evelyn Schuler was the second woman to own the Schuler-Cathy home, and Florence (Foncy) was the last resident and part-owner. (Photograph by David B. McGuire, courtesy of Mary E. and Mary T. McGuire.)

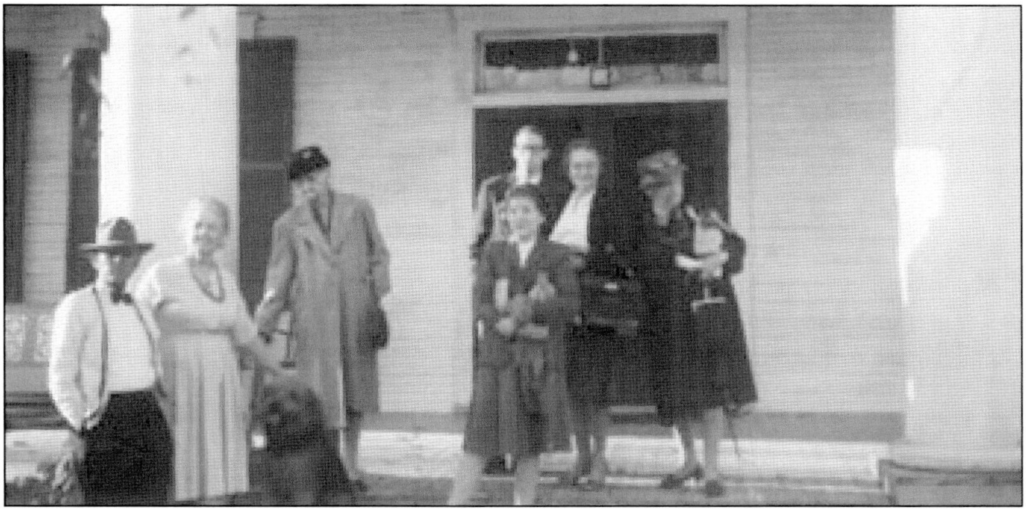

This is after a Sunday lunch in 1963. From left to right are (first row) Mary T. McGuire (granddaughter to Nanetta and great-niece to Foncy and Sallie) (second row) O.C. Cathy, his wife, Foncy (with her hand on their dog Buck), Sallie Ross Bell (sister-in-law to Nanetta Bell), E.L McGuire III (grandson of Nanetta Bell), his mother, Mary Evelyn Bell McGuire, her mother, Nanetta Schuler (Mrs. T.F.) Bell. Later that year, Sallie died, and Nanetta broke her hip. This is their last recorded visit to Keatchie. (Photograph by David B. McGuire, courtesy of Mary E. and Mary T. McGuire.)

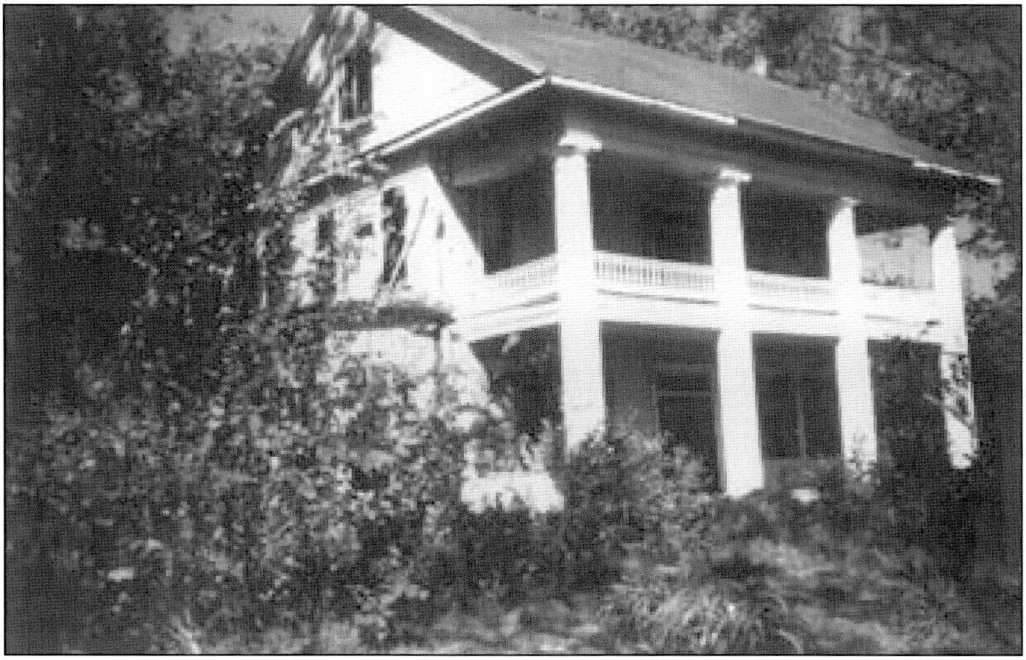

Shown is a 1963 view of the Schuler-Cathy home from the front on the front porch. A more appropriate name should be the Fullilove-Schuler-Cathy home as these are the of the 4 generations of women who have owned this home. The house was first bought in 1859 by Elizabeth Foster Fullilove and probably used as rental home, yet she would stay there when she was in town. She had a concrete edging added to the front path, embedded with sea shells she collected from a 1890 trip to Santa Barbara, California. (Photograph by David B. McGuire, courtesy of Mary E. and Mary T. McGuire.)

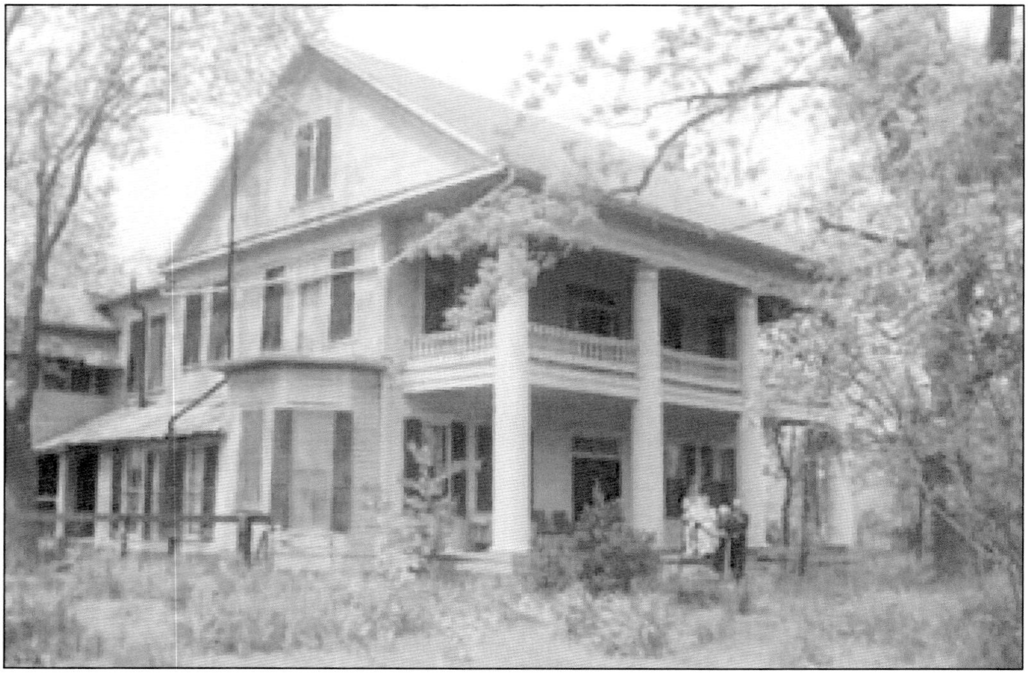

Here is a view of the Schuler home in June 1962, with family members on the side. The bay window, second floor, and columns were all Evelyn's additions to the original structure (Photograph by David B. McGuire, courtesy of Mary E. and Mary T. McGuire.)

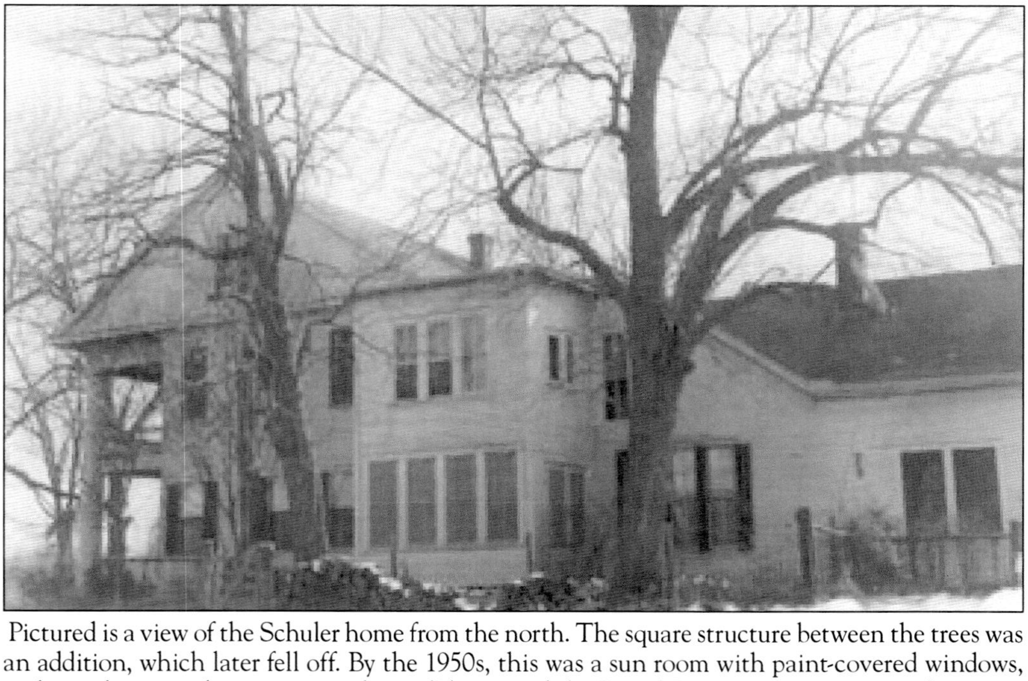

Pictured is a view of the Schuler home from the north. The square structure between the trees was an addition, which later fell off. By the 1950s, this was a sun room with paint-covered windows, rocking chairs, and a sewing machine. (Photograph by David B. McGuire, courtesy of Mary E. and Mary T. McGuire.)

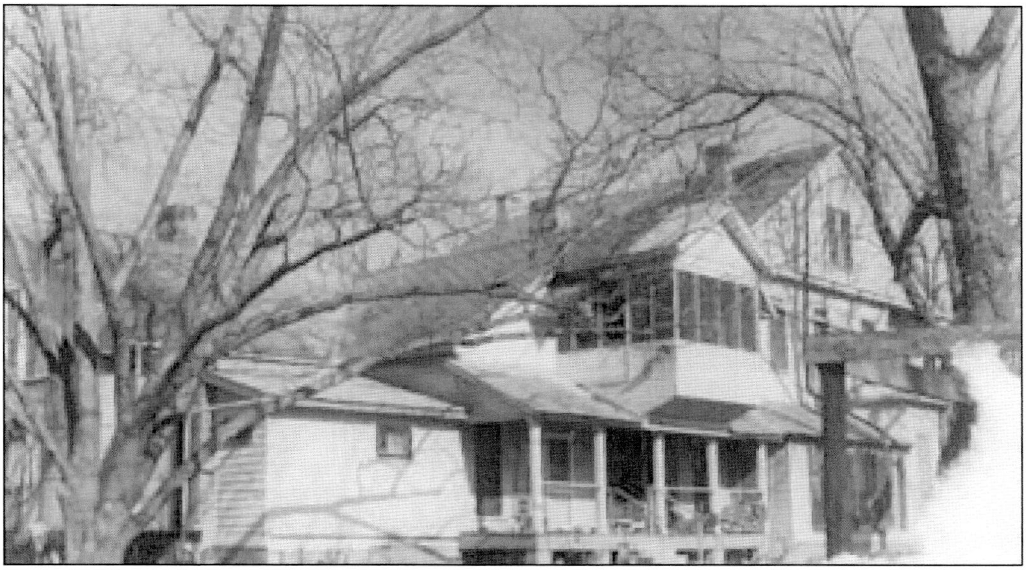

This is a southwest view of the Schuler home. In the 1950s, there was a chicken coop on this side. The back room was added to accommodate Foncy and O.C. Cathy moving back to care for Evelyn Schuler, who died in 1932. Mary Evelyn McGuire remembers her aunts and mother sitting on this porch weaving a blanket of flowers for their mother's casket in 1932. (Photograph by David B. McGuire, courtesy of Mary E. and Mary T. McGuire.)

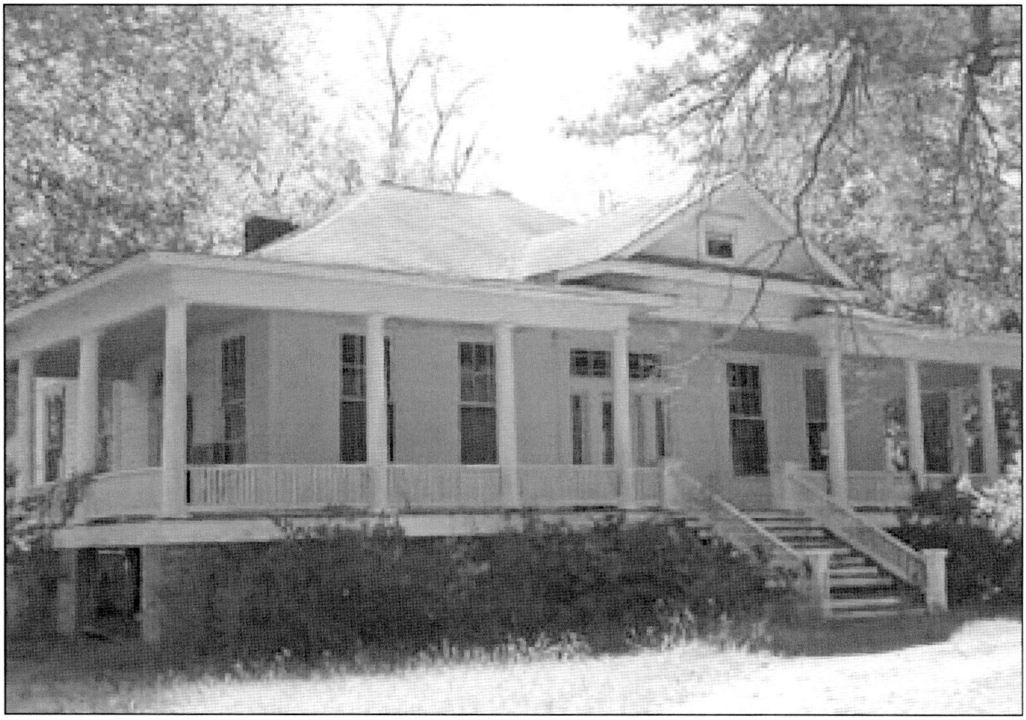

The Crawford Williams Home can be dated to at least 1848. It is one of the oldest homes in Keachi and across the street from the Presbyterian church. Peter M. Crawford became president of Keachi College in 1866. His daughter Martha married Joseph Williams. (Courtesy of George Meriwether Gilmer Jr.)

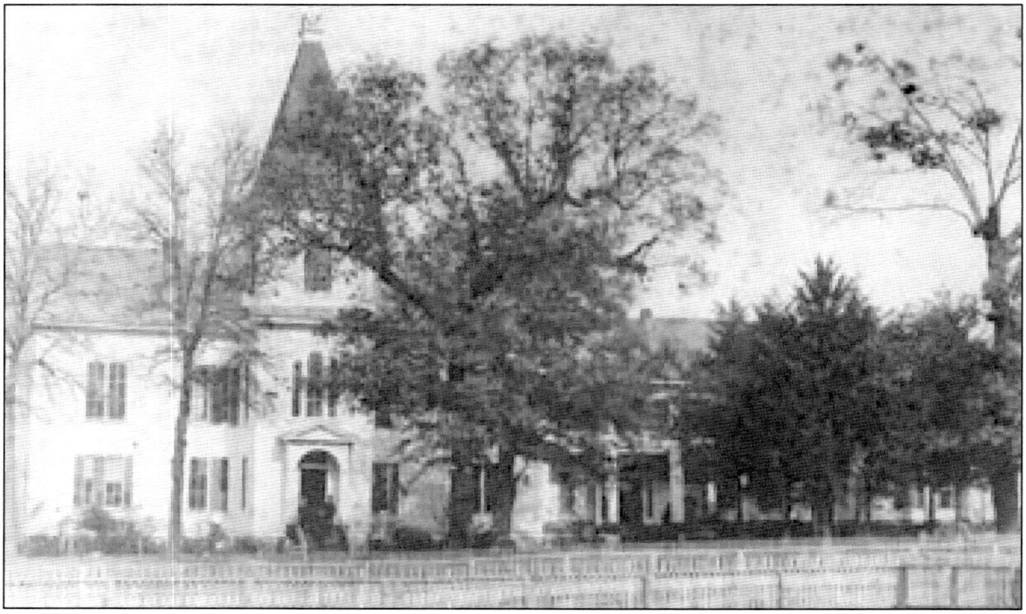

The Louisiana Female College was located in Keachi. The buildings were a donation from Thomas M. Gatlin, and the school opened in 1858. The college prospered, and when the Civil War began there were 125 young ladies attending. During the Civil War, the college was closed and the buildings were used for a Confederate hospital. The college reopened after the Civil War, but a tornado struck the building in 1880, and the college was closed by the end of the century. (Courtesy of George Meriwether Gilmer Jr.)

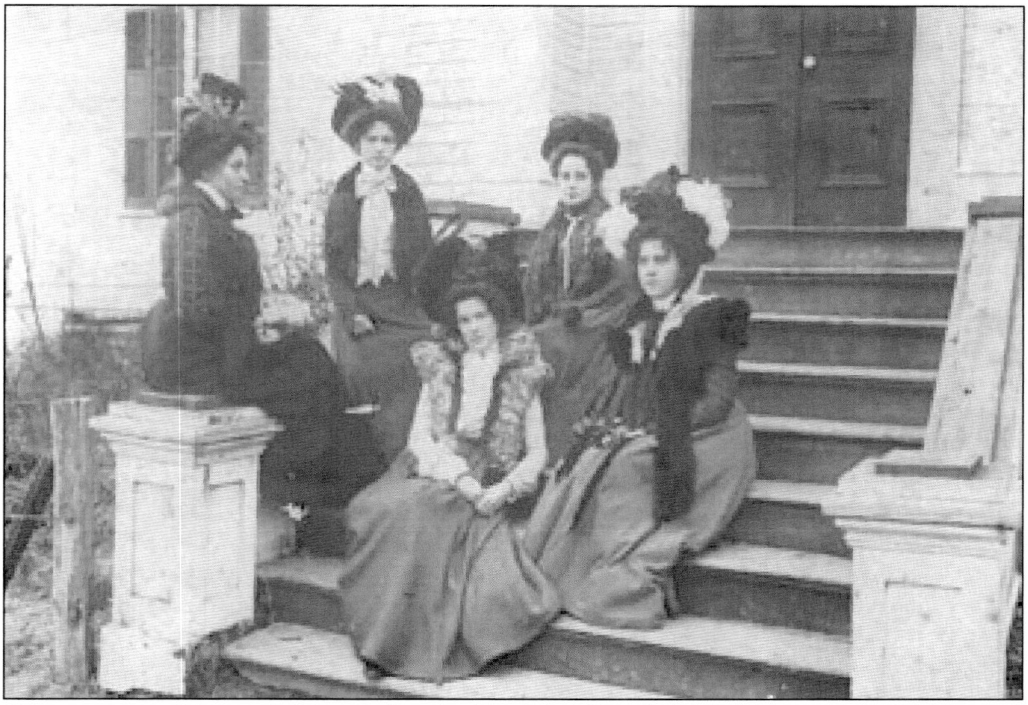

Shown is a group of young ladies seated on the front steps of Keachi College. (Courtesy Noel Memorial Library, Louisiana State University in Shreveport, Archives and Sprecial Collections.)

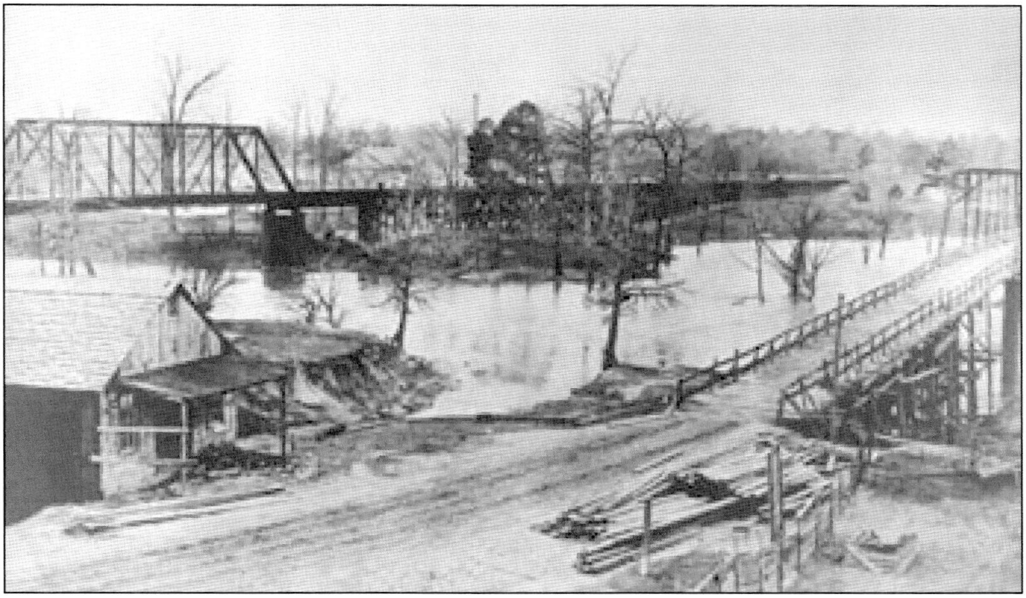

Logansport, a major transportation center in the late 1800s and into the 1900s, provided access to south Louisiana, south Texas, and the rest of the world by way of steamboats. Cotton, lumber, barrel staves, and other products from the region made their way down the Sabine River aboard some of the finest steamboats of their time. Most became victims of the railroad. Pictured is Logansport around 1900. (Courtesy of Glenn Price.)

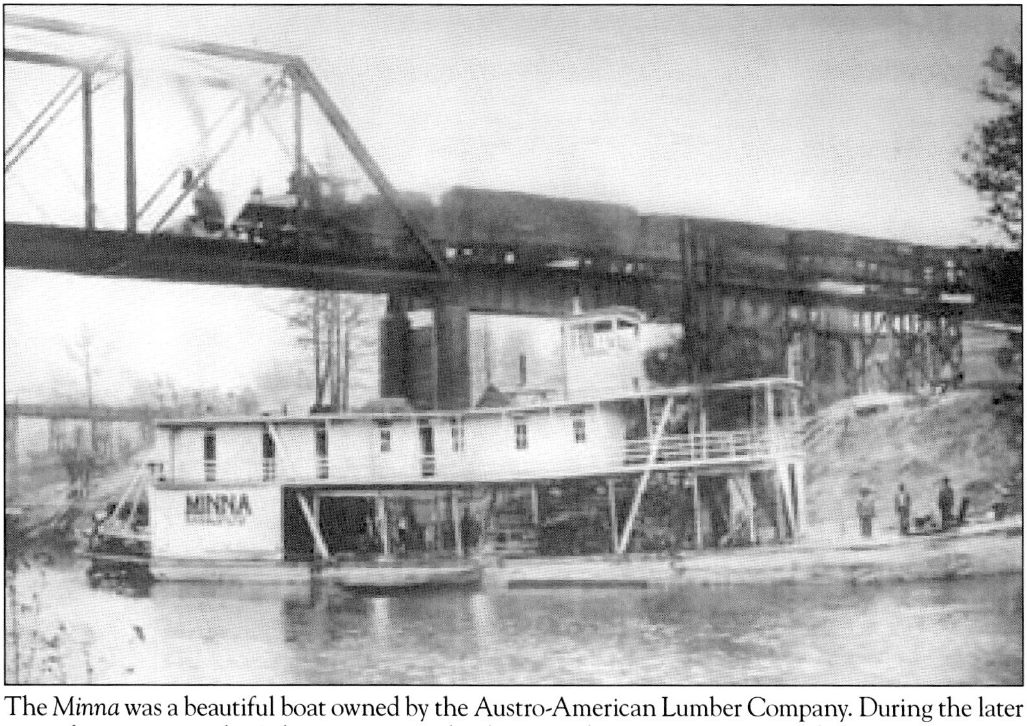

The *Minna* was a beautiful boat owned by the Austro-American Lumber Company. During the later part of its career on the Sabine, it was used to bring timber up to Logansport for the construction of the railway trestle. The captain was E.E. Price. The *Minna* is shown docked near the railroad bridge at Logansport as a train passes overhead. (Courtesy of Glenn C. Price of Logansport.)

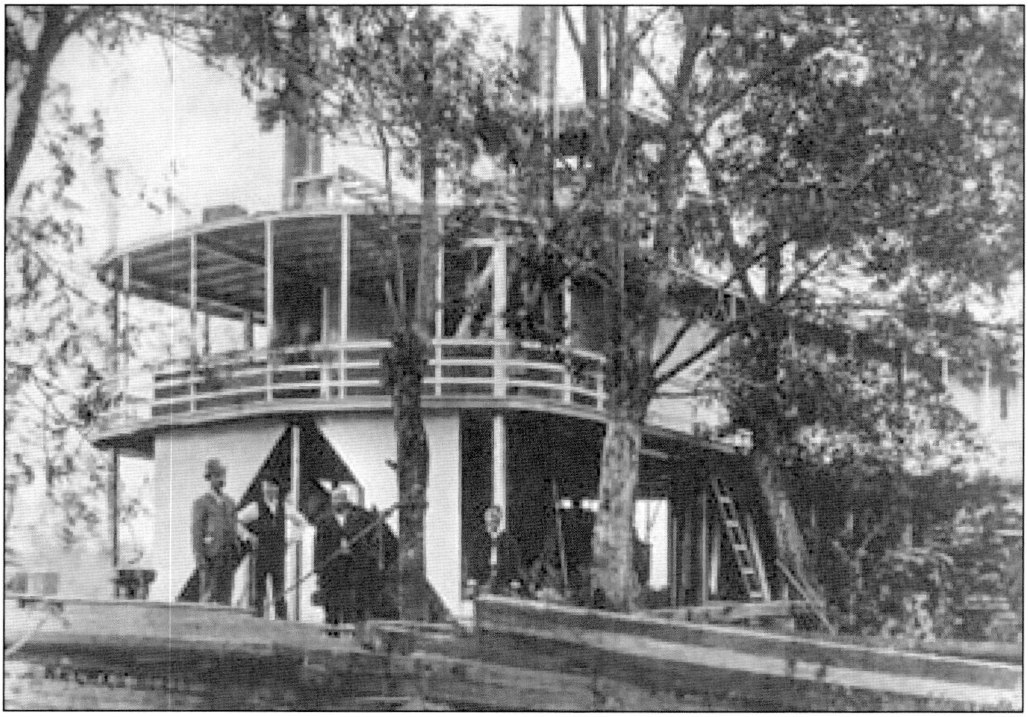

The *Neches Belle* was built in Beaumont, Texas, in 1890 at a cost of $3,000, not including machinery. The machinery came from another boat, the *Vicksburg*. On the main deck, it carried 1,000 bales of cotton. On the second deck, it boasted a saloon and a band for the entertainment of the passengers. (Courtesy of Glenn C. Price.)

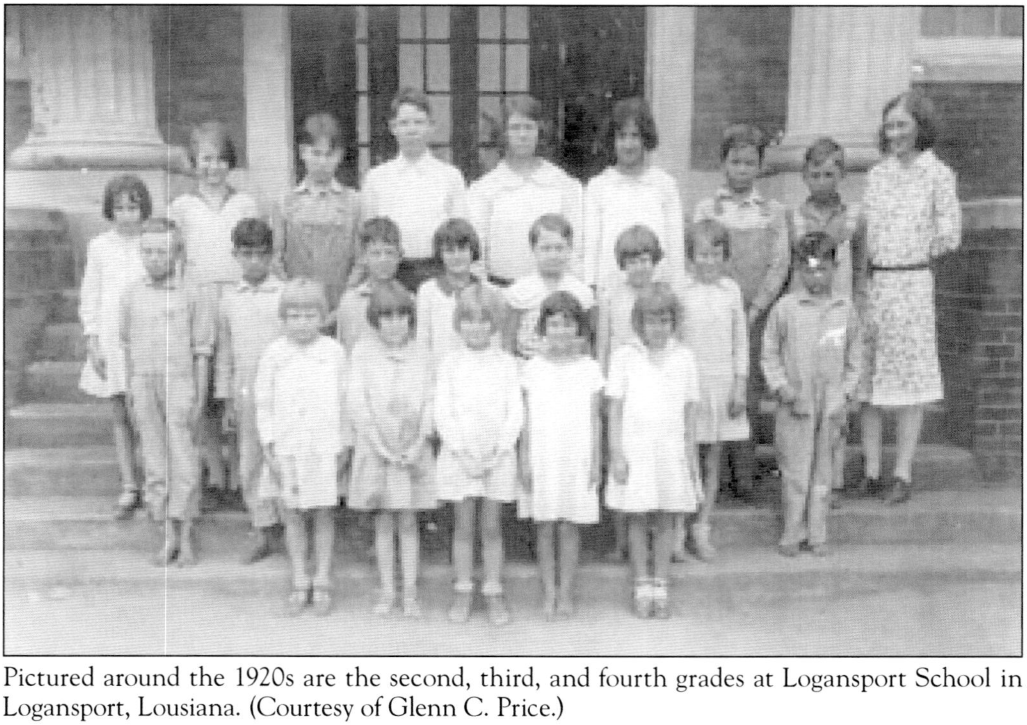

Pictured around the 1920s are the second, third, and fourth grades at Logansport School in Logansport, Lousiana. (Courtesy of Glenn C. Price.)

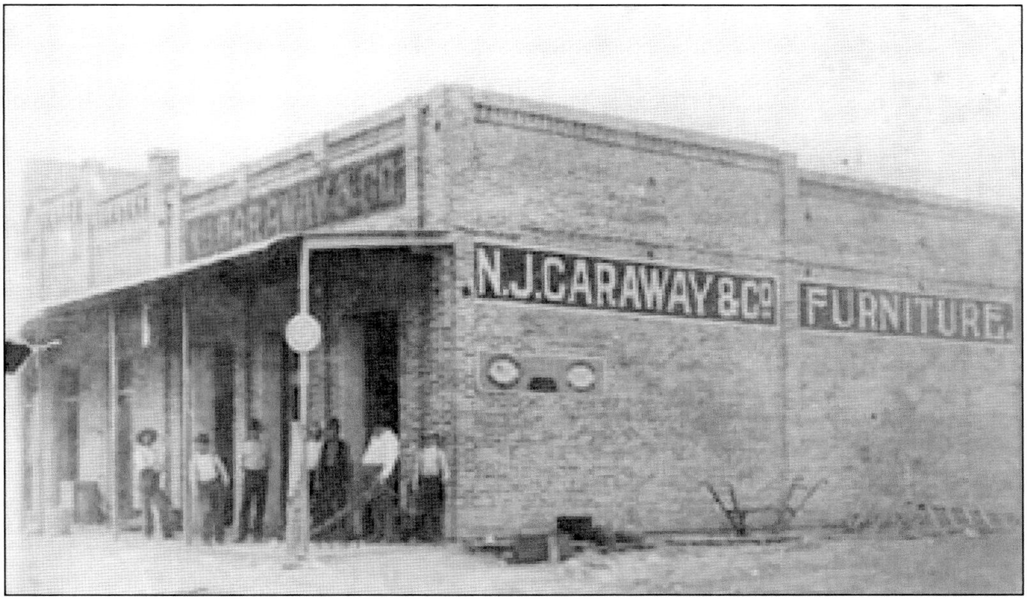

N.J. Carroway Furniture Store on the northeast corner of Main and Second Streets was built in 1902 by N. J. Carroway. The original structure was only one story; however, in later years a second story was added. Now a hardware store that sells everything, it is the second oldest continuously operated store in north Louisiana. The oldest is Kaffee Friedricks Hardware in Natchitoches. (Courtesy of Raymond Powell.)

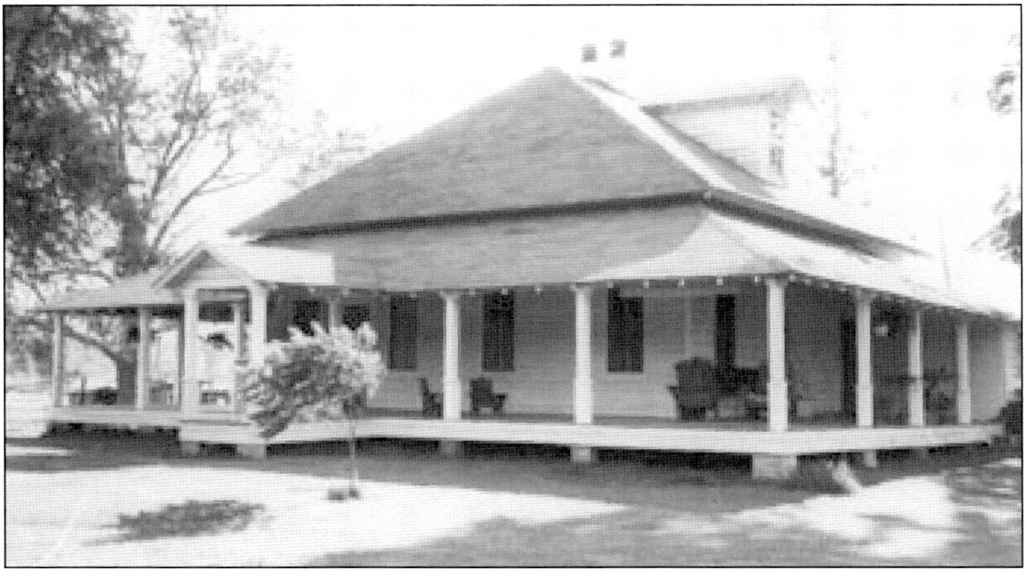

The Blunt house was built in 1890 by Lawrence C. Blunt, who was well known throughout the countryside for performing cures for spider bites, snake bites, and other ailments. Originally there were four fireplaces, all using the same chimney; now there are two working fireplaces and one false. All the boards for the house were kiln dried before construction began. The boards for the house were kiln dried before construction began. The boards, all heartwood pine, were hand planed with tongue and groove. Square nails and pegs were used extensively throughout. What was once a side of the house is now the front due to the change of the road's direction. (Courtesy of Raymond W. Powell.)

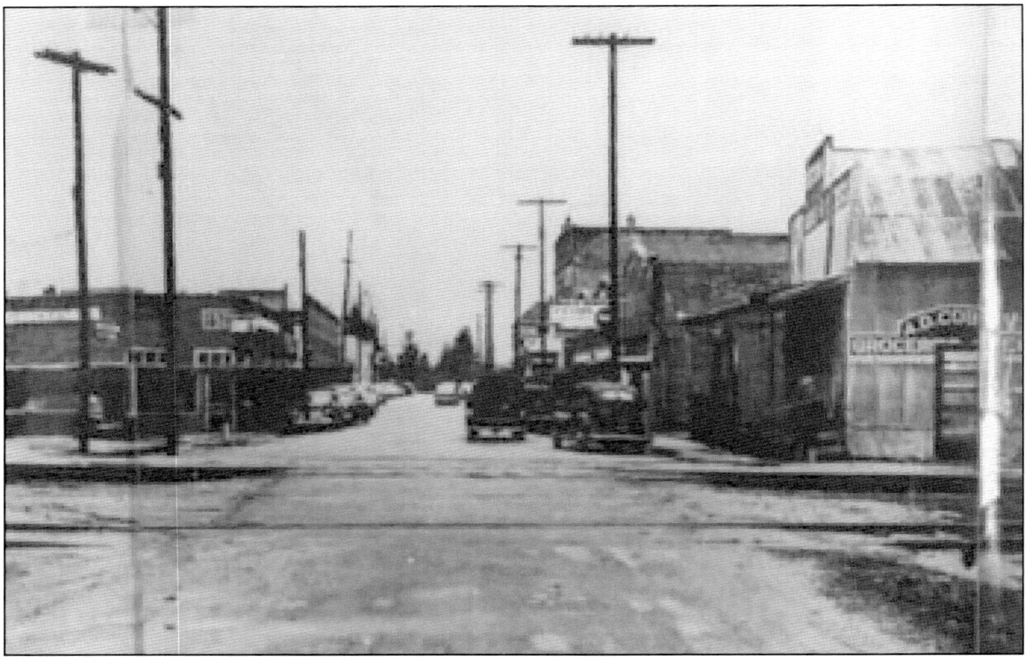

This is a photograph of downtown Logansport around the 1930s. (Courtesy Noel Memorial Library, Louisiana State University in Shreveport, Archives and Special Collections.)

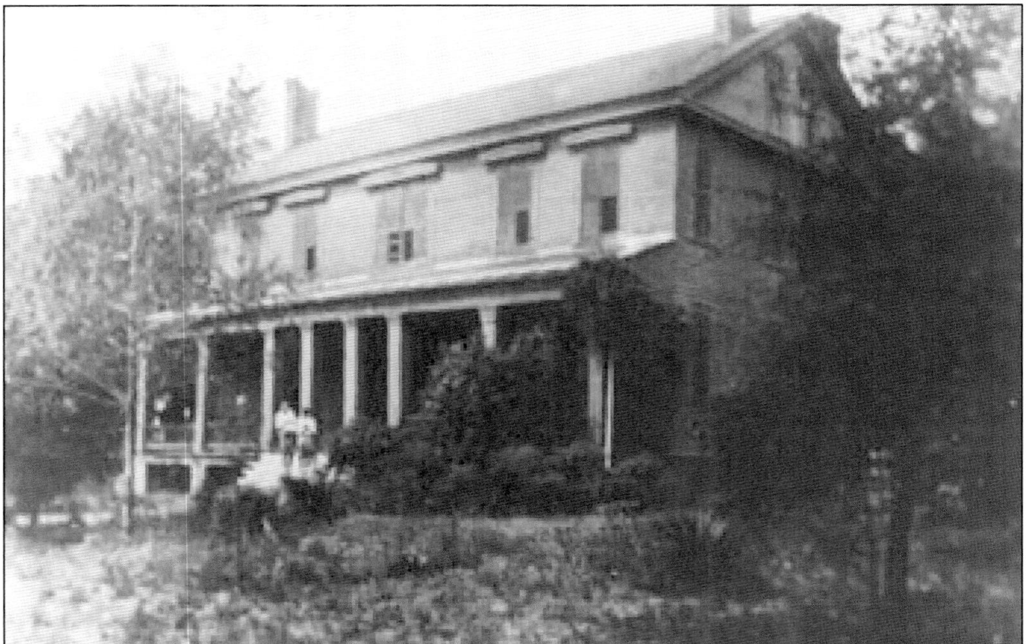

Auburnia Plantation home was located at Kingston, a settlement near Frierson. The home was built originally by John Francis Tomkies. The Tomkies' daughter Kate married James H. Beard, who was fatally wounded at the Battle of Mansfield. After Tomkies died, Kate and her daughter Corinne, later the wife of Robert Hall Scott, lived here. The house was torn down about 1946. (Courtesy Noel Memorial Library, Louisiana State University in Shreveport, Archives and Special Collections.)

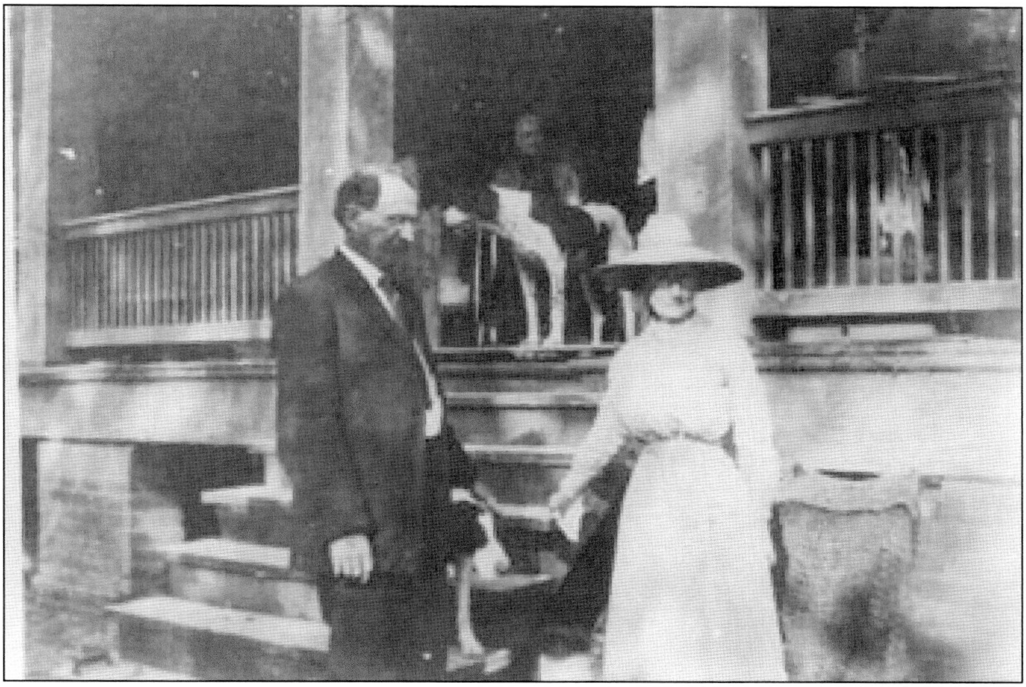

Corinne and Robert Hall Scott are pictured here in front of Auburnia with their dogs. (Courtesy Noel Memorial Library, Louisiana State University in Shreveport, Archives and Special Collections.)

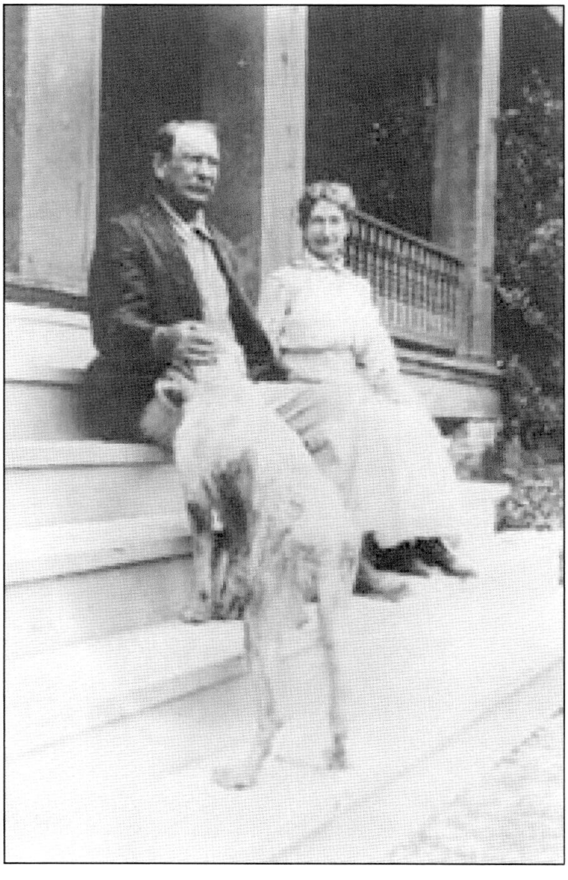

Shown are Corinne Beard Scott and her husband, Robert, with a dog. Corinne appears to be much younger or maybe it is the lack of a hat. (Courtesy Noel Memorial Library, Louisiana State University in Shreveport, Archives and Special Collections.)

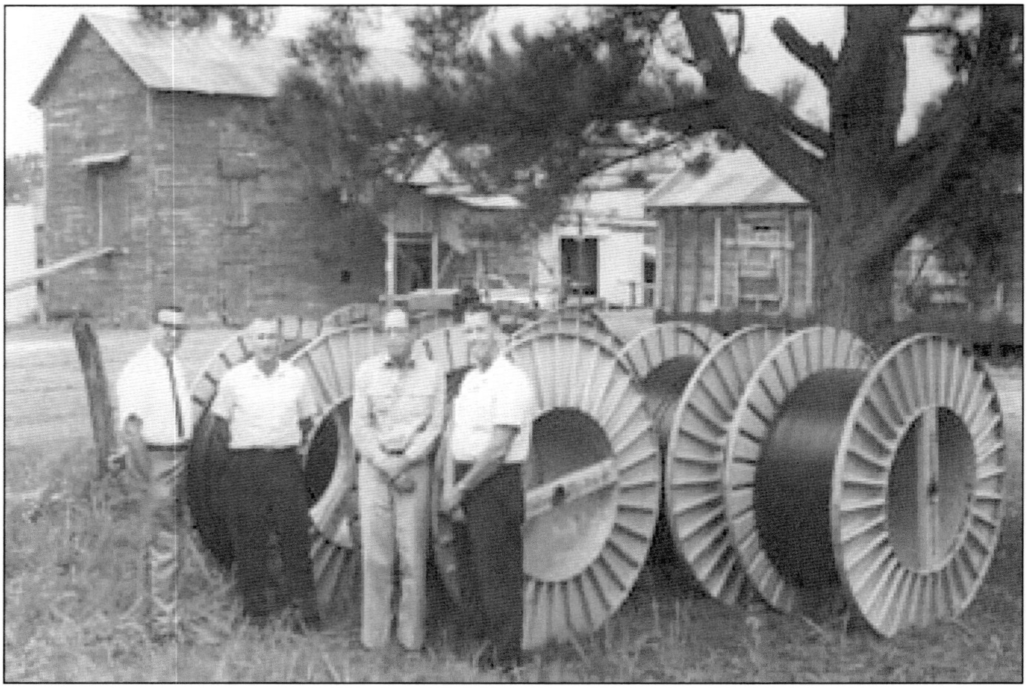

Pictured is Scotts Gin at Kingston, representing the importance of cotton in DeSoto Parish. Shown are Harold Cornet, James Burford, and Judson Scott and one unidentified man. (Photography by McPherson and courtesy of Raymond W. Powell.)

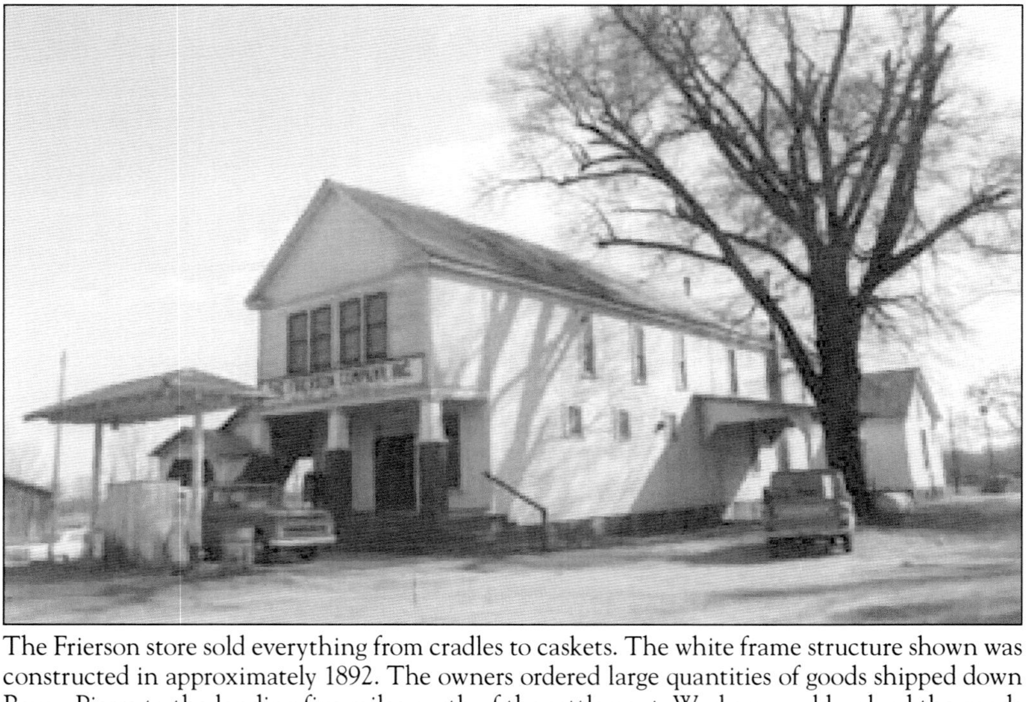

The Frierson store sold everything from cradles to caskets. The white frame structure shown was constructed in approximately 1892. The owners ordered large quantities of goods shipped down Bayou Pierre to the landing five miles north of the settlement. Workers would unload the goods off the barges and onto wagons for the remainder of trip to the store. (Courtesy Noel Memorial Library, Louisiana State University in Shreveport, Archives and Special Collections.)

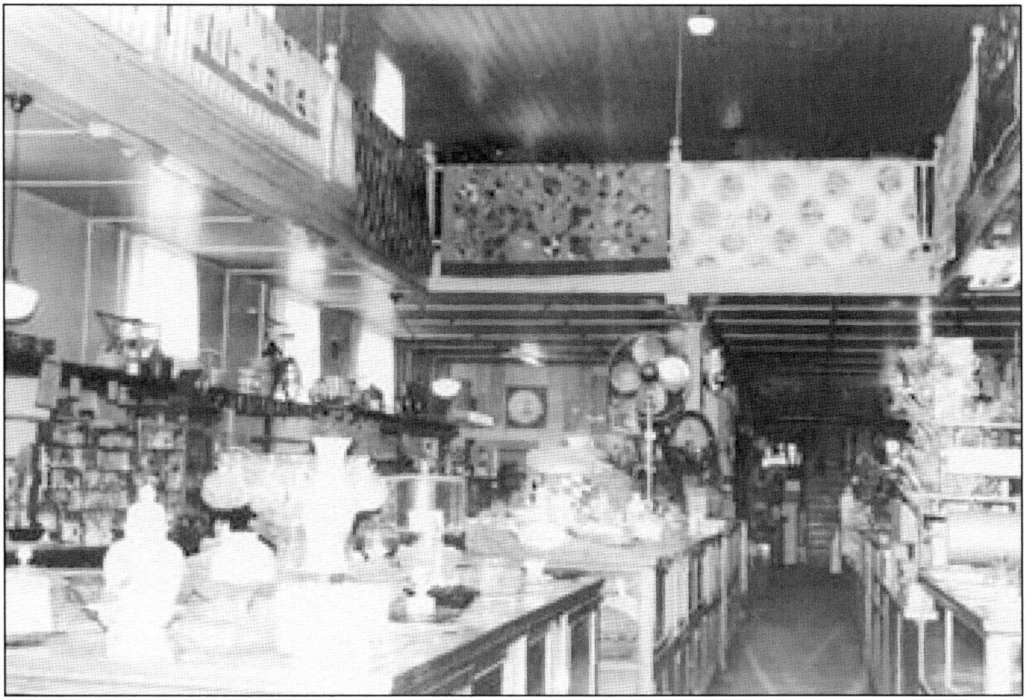

The Frierson Store, like other country stores, sold goods as varied as ham, pills, petticoats, corsets, and plows. Everything that was needed in this settlement was sold there, as shown by this picture of the interior. (Courtesy of Liz Chrysler.)

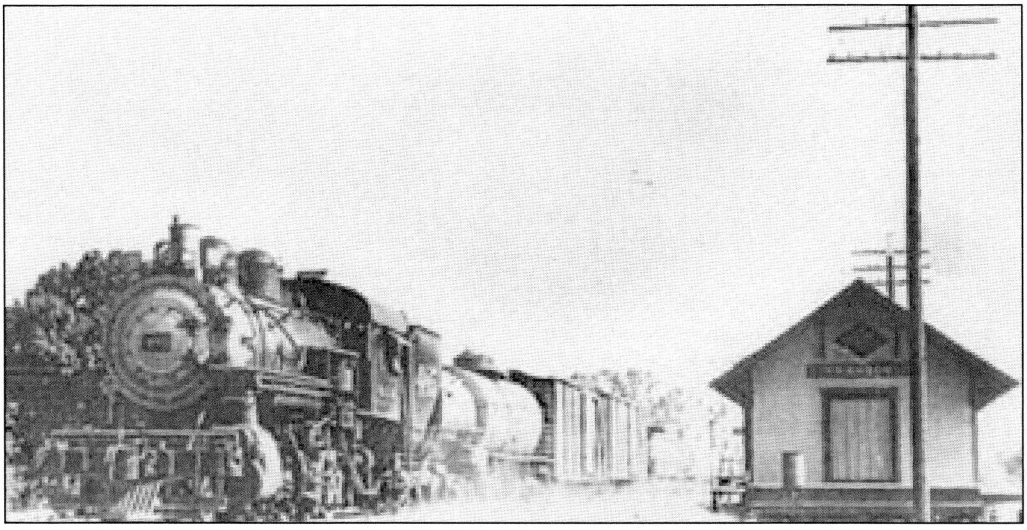

Coming through the town of Frierson as it passes the depot is Kansas City Southern Railway Company locomotive No. 485, Class E-3. The locomotive was built in January 1906 by the Pittsburg Locomotive Works. (Photograph by A. E. Brown, courtesy of Emilia Gay Griffith Means.)

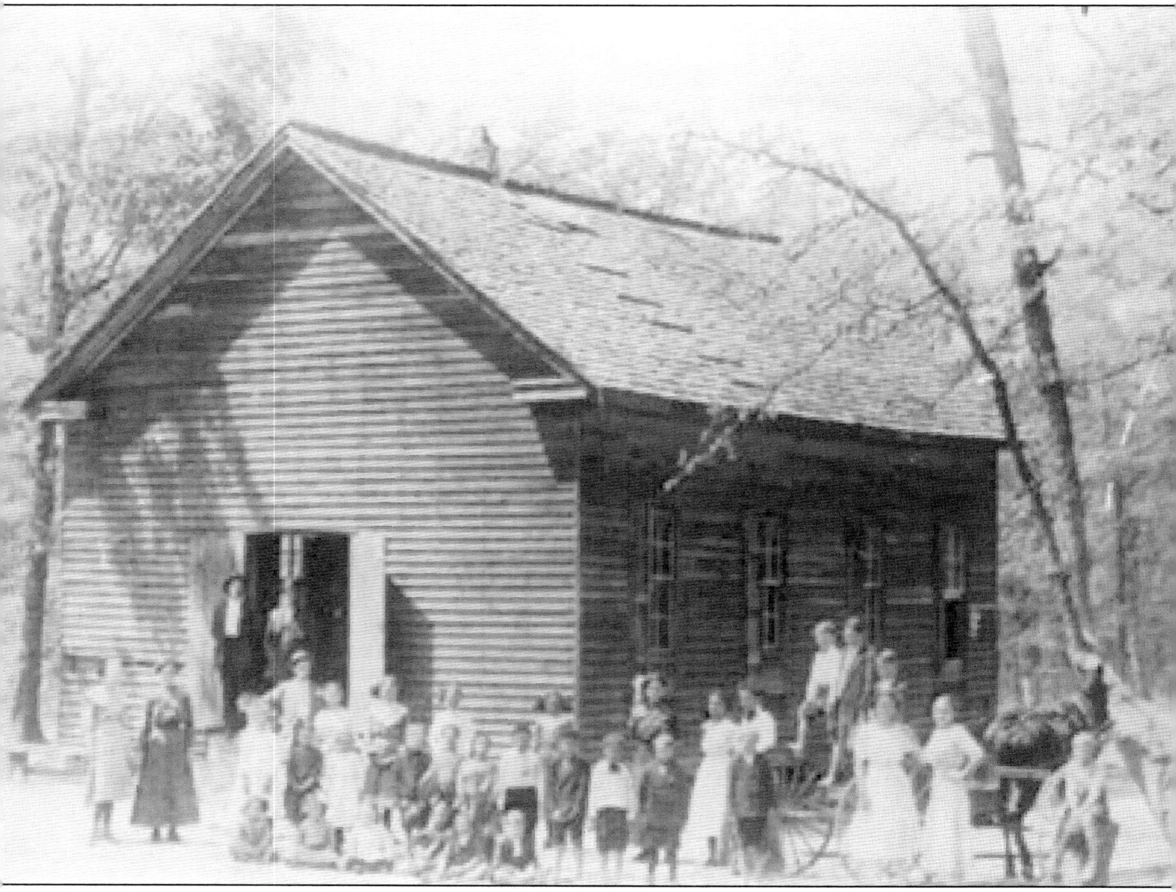

This is a picture of the entire Hunter School in front of the building. Of interest is that in the 1890s, school groups typically had dogs in their photographs. (Courtesy of Louisiana State University in Shreveport, Noel Memorial Library, Archives and Special Collections.)

Three

Farms, Dairies, and Early Lumber

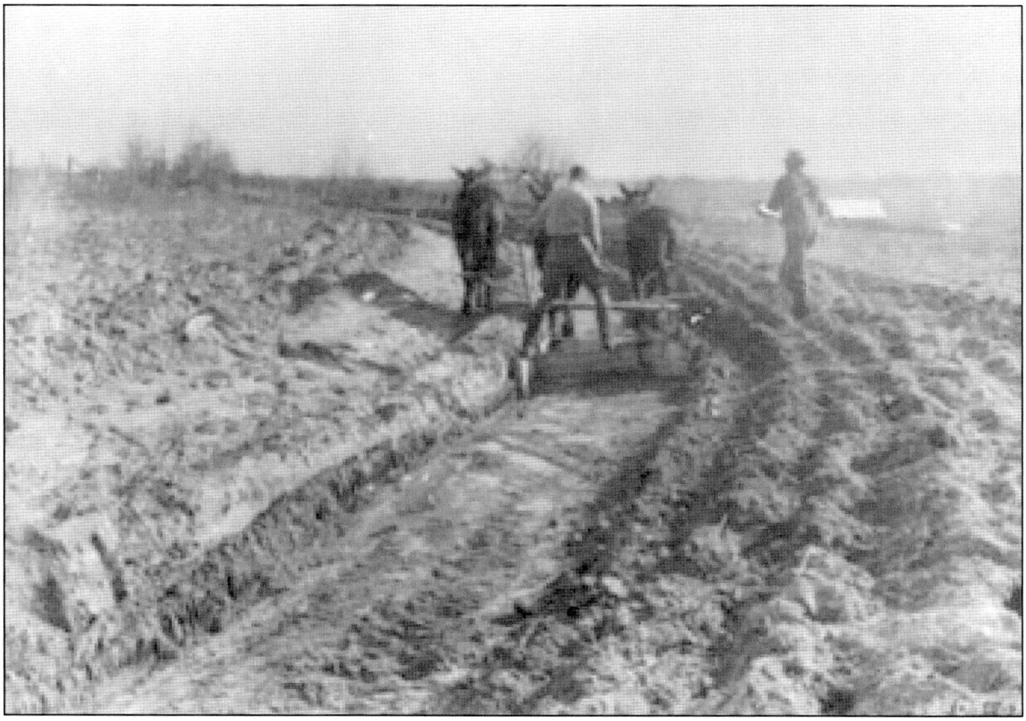

Shown here is the James and Roy Gamble farm in DeSoto Parish in 1940. (Courtesy of Louisiana State University in Shreveport, Noel Memorial Library, Archives and Special Collections.)

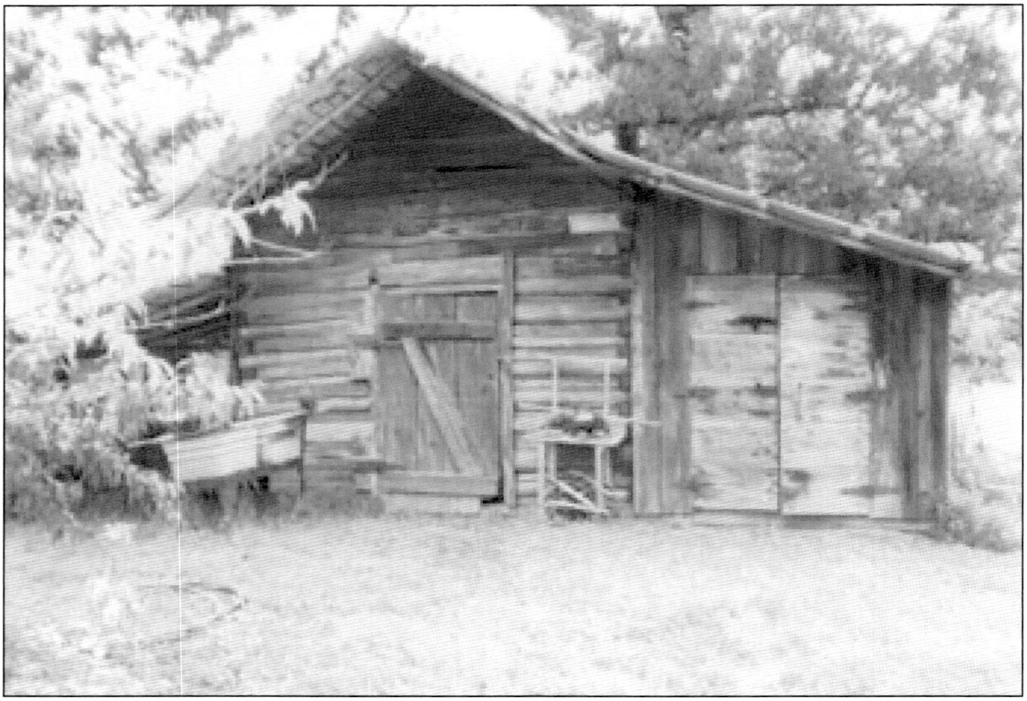

The old Taylor House, built by Walter Robinson about 1880, was originally a double pen dogtrot house with a detached kitchen and smokehouse. Before 1900, the kitchen was attached to the original structure and two "side shed rooms" were added. The home, located on Hunter Road, originally had 120 acres of land and was known as the Taylor dairy farm. (Courtesy of Raymond W. Powell.)

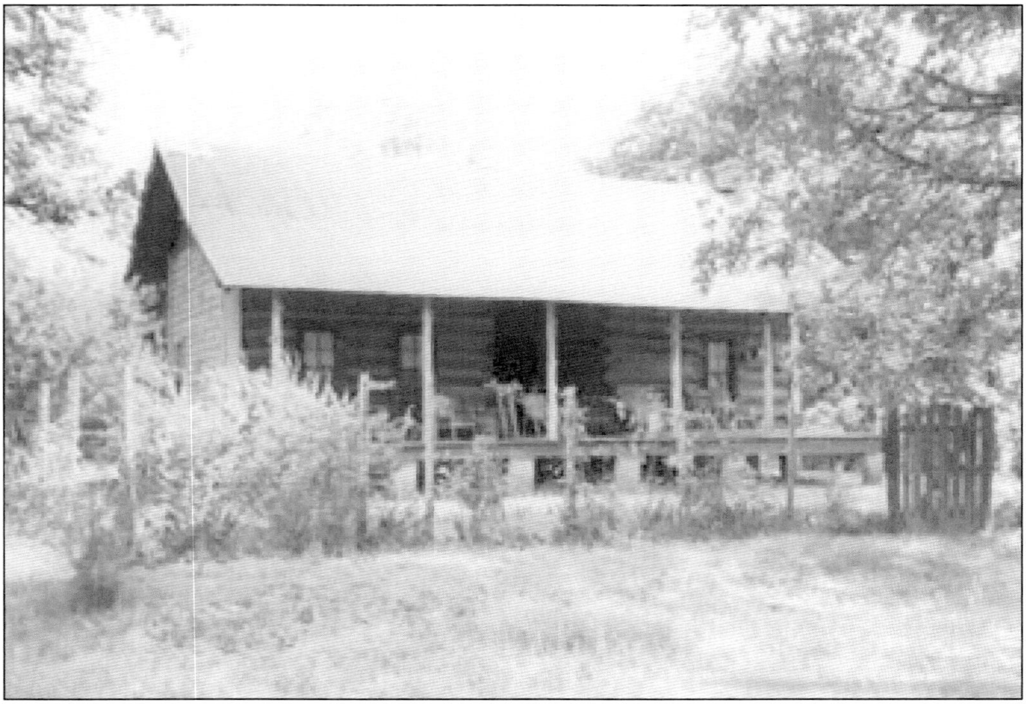

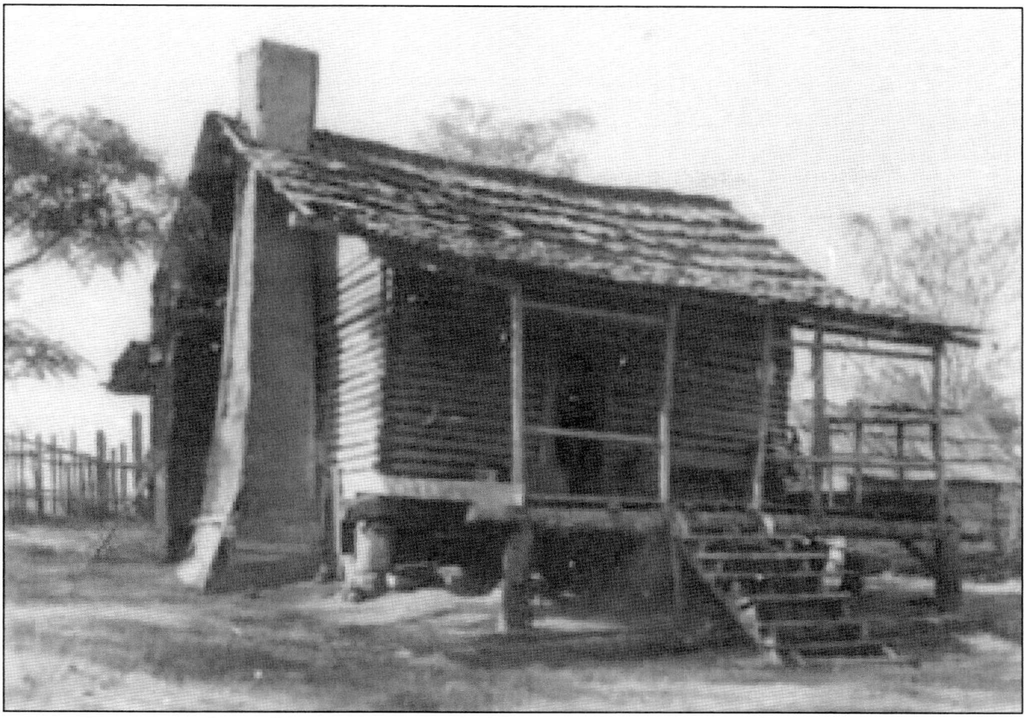

Pictured in 1938 is the Della Evans farm in DeSoto Parish. (Courtesy of Louisiana State University in Shreveport, Noel Memorial Library, Archives and Special Collections.)

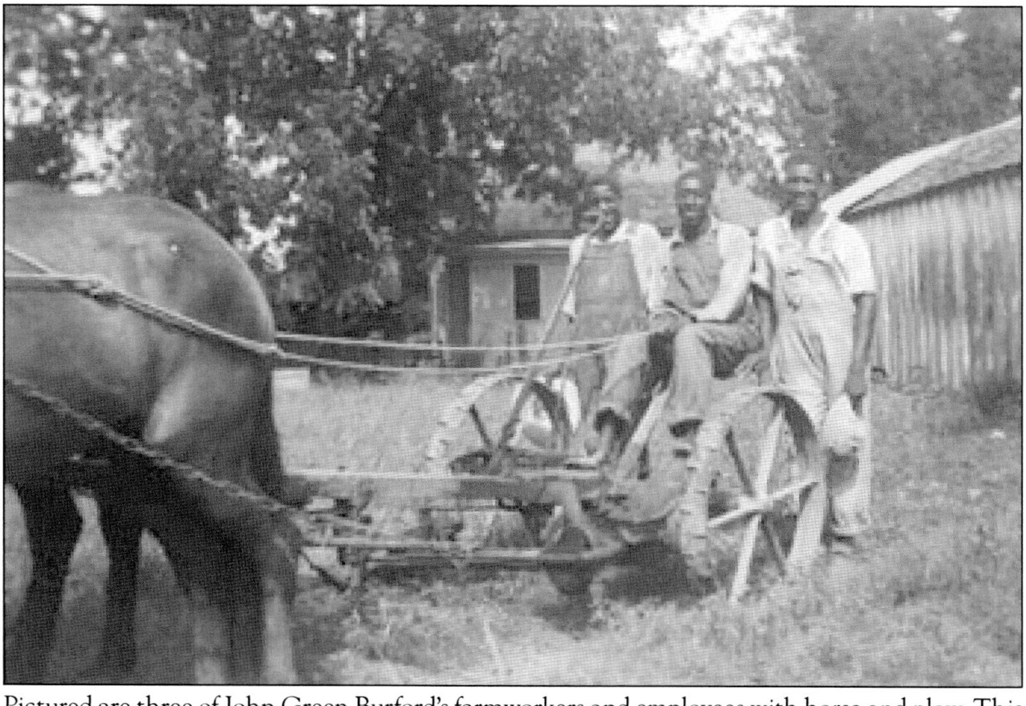

Pictured are three of John Green Burford's farmworkers and employees with horse and plow. This picture was taken across from his barn and behind his house around 1940. (Courtesy of Libby Dady Alcorn.)

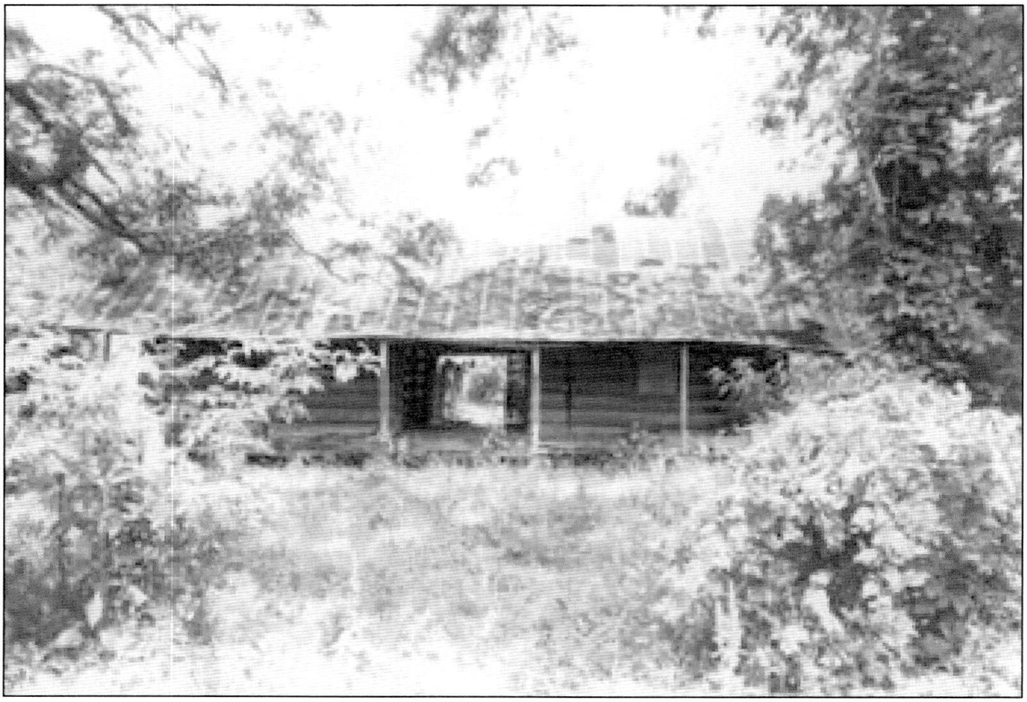

The John A. McMichael dogtrot home was built in 1885 on a farm of 7,500 acres. The double pen dogtrot is located on Louisiana Highway 191 about three miles south of Logansport. (Courtesy of Raymond W. Powell.)

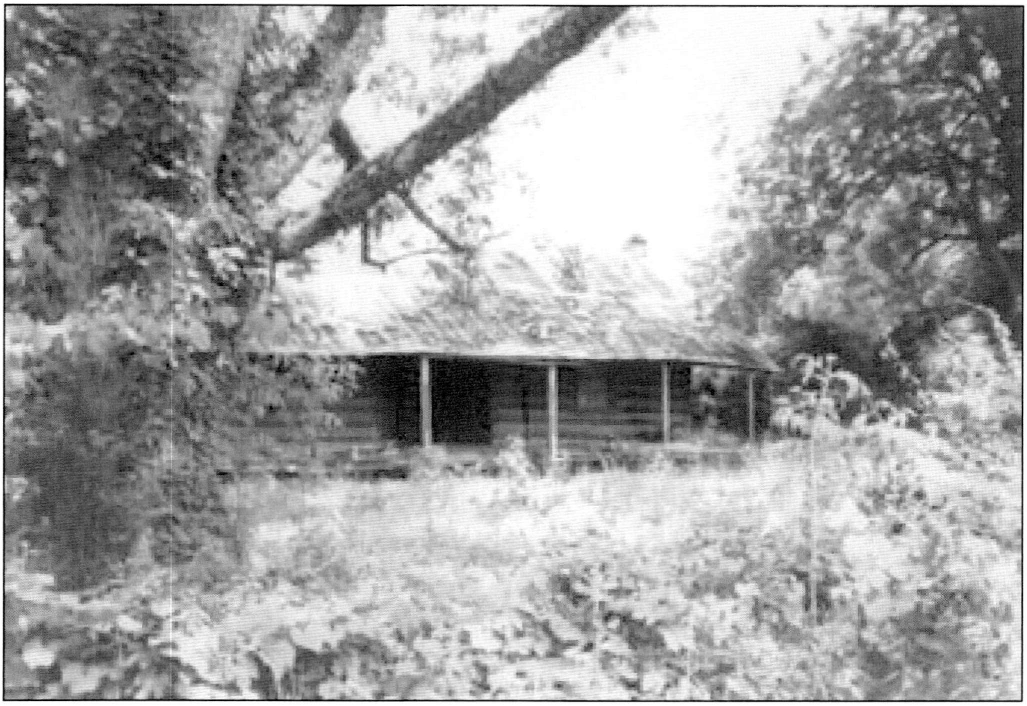

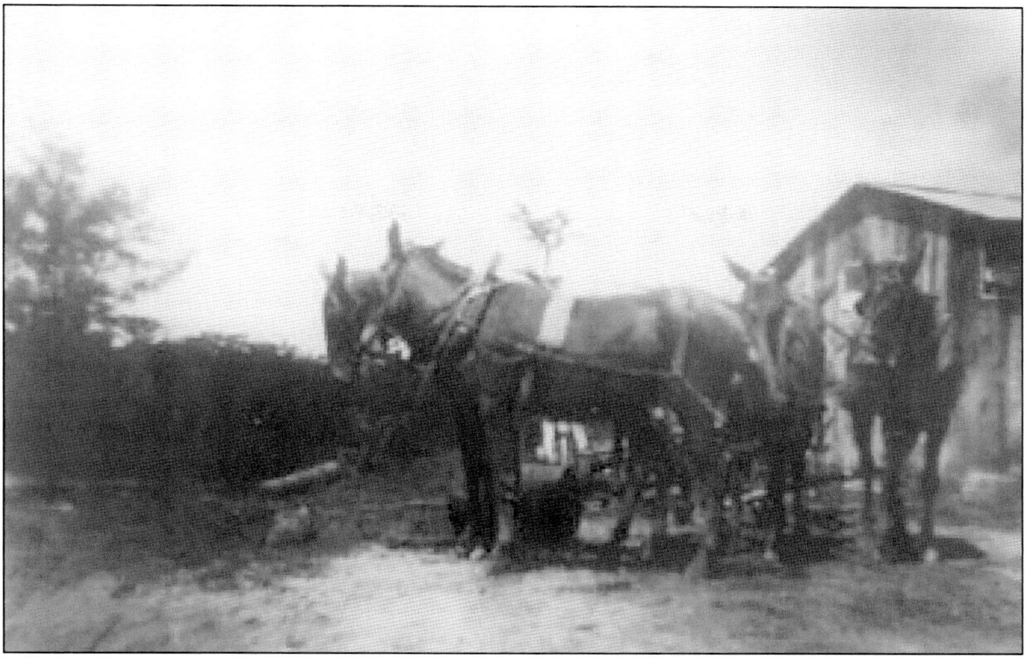

This picture is of a mule team at Clear Lake. A team of mules was considered very valuable in the 1890s. When an owner died, the mules were valued in the estate and passed to the children. Generally every mule had a name, such as "Ole Puss." A mule team was very useful in bringing in lumber from the woods. (Courtesy of W.J. Griffith family.)

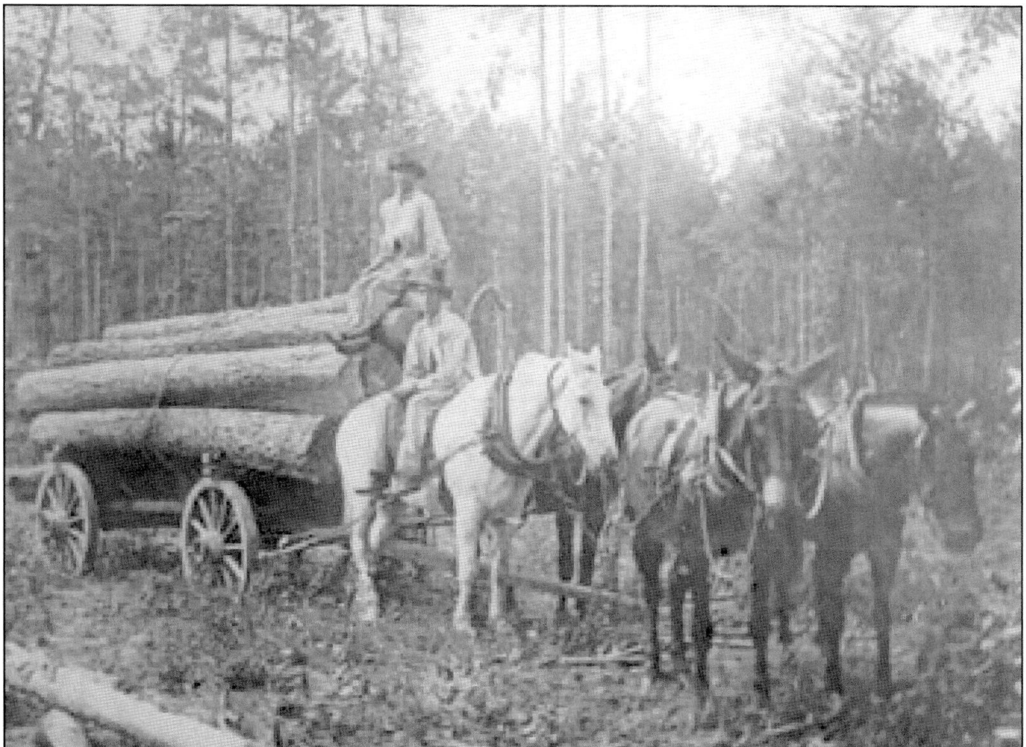

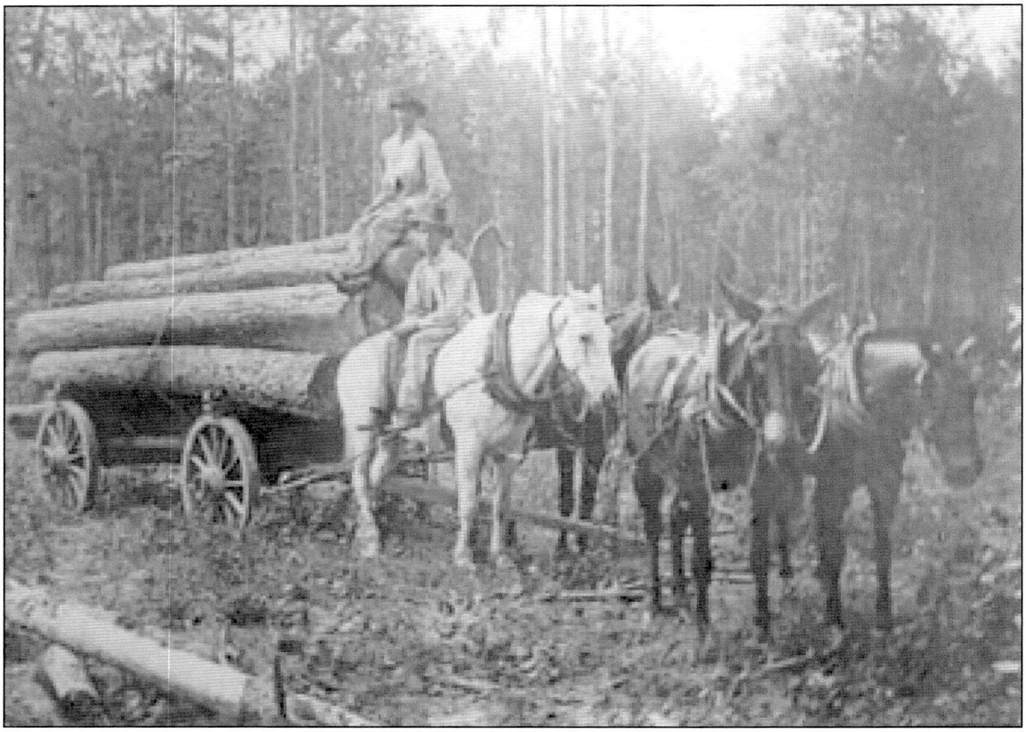

The Cedar Hill Dogtrot House was built around 1838 by George Provost, who came here that year from Alabama. The homestead was estimated to be 2,000 acres. The support beams of the double pen dogtrot house were handmade on the property by Provost himself. The property is known as Cedar Hill. (Courtesy of Raymond W. Powell.)

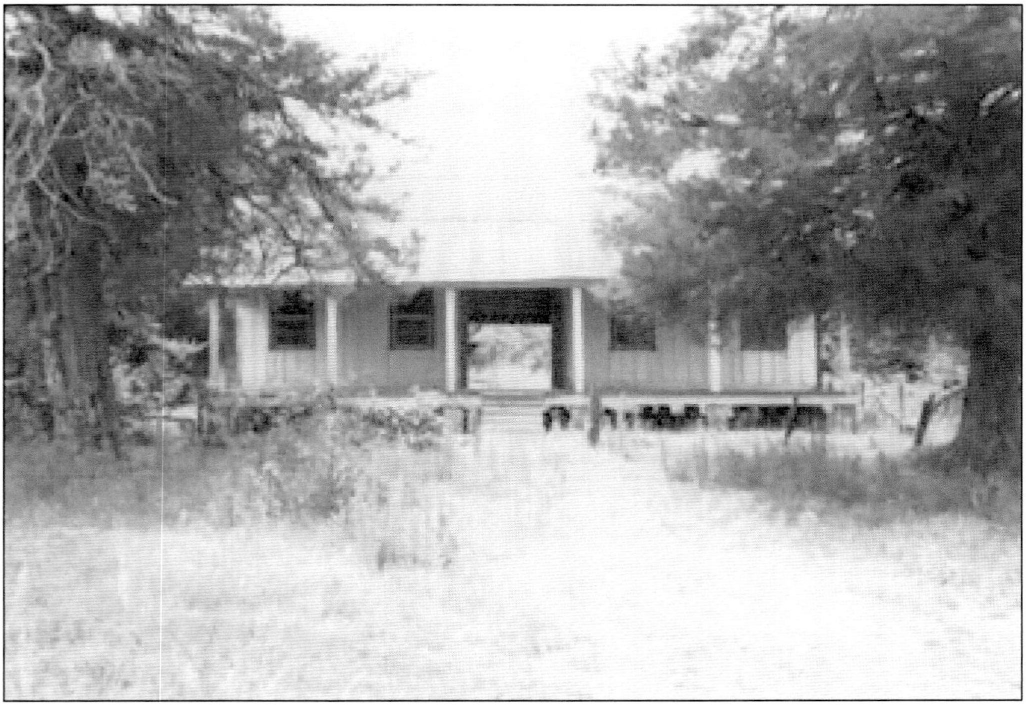

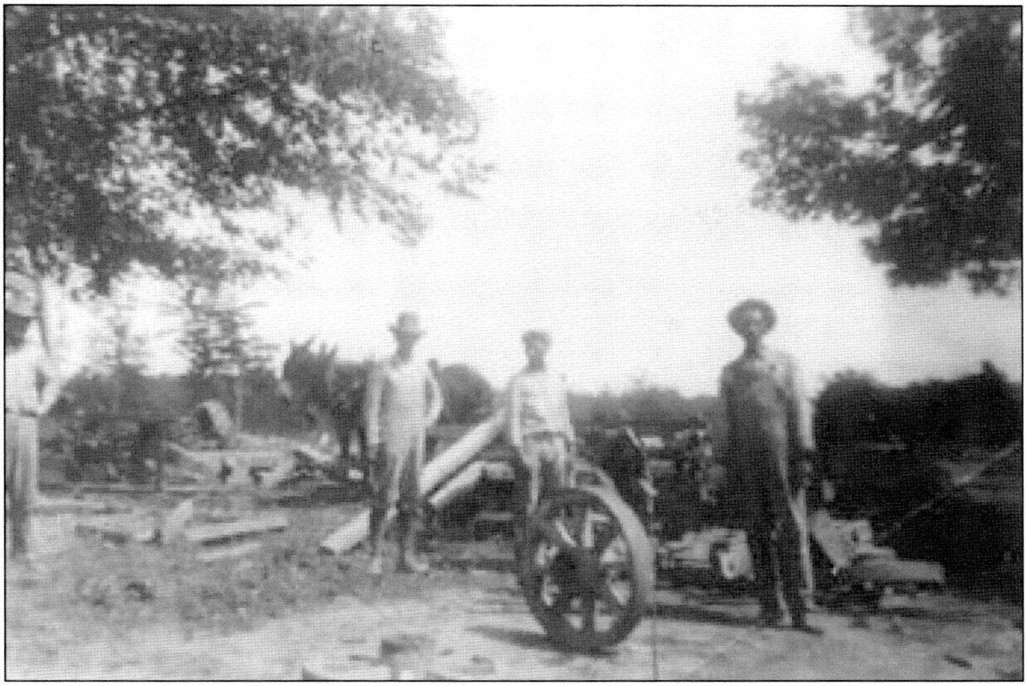

The W.J. Griffith Lumber Mill on Clear Lake can be seen in the background of the lake. The lumber mill sold cross ties, wood shingles, lumber for homes, and other wood products. Apparently nothing was wasted. (Courtesy of W.J. Griffith family.)

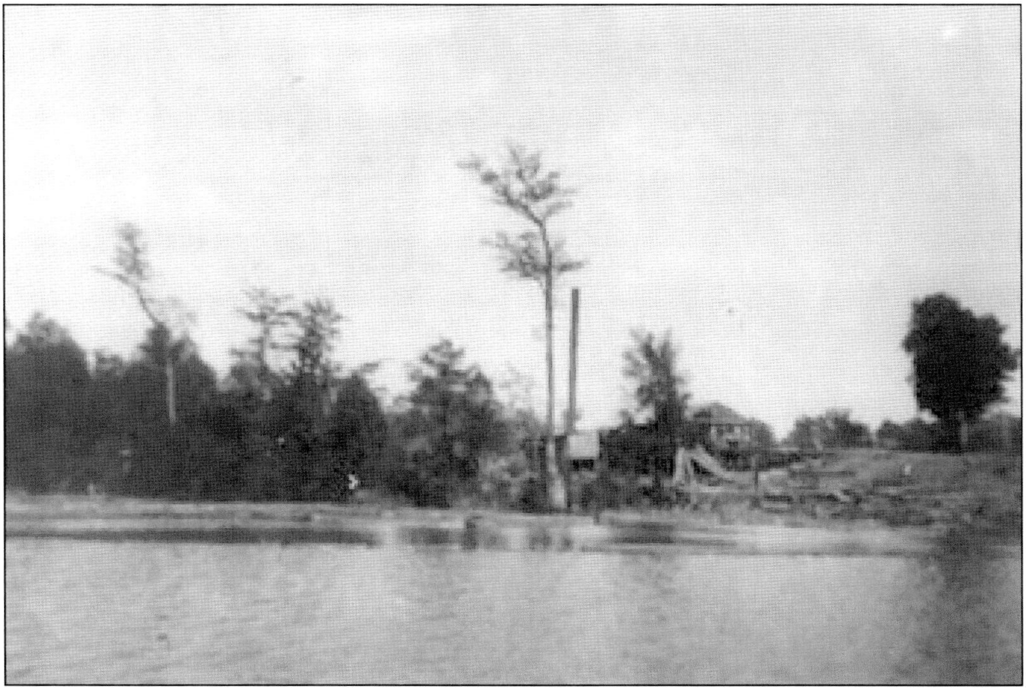

These men apparently are stranded in the woods with a broken down wagon and mule team. Most likely they were gathering in timber when their wagon broke down. This photograph would have been taken near Clear Lake. (Courtesy of W. J. Griffith family.)

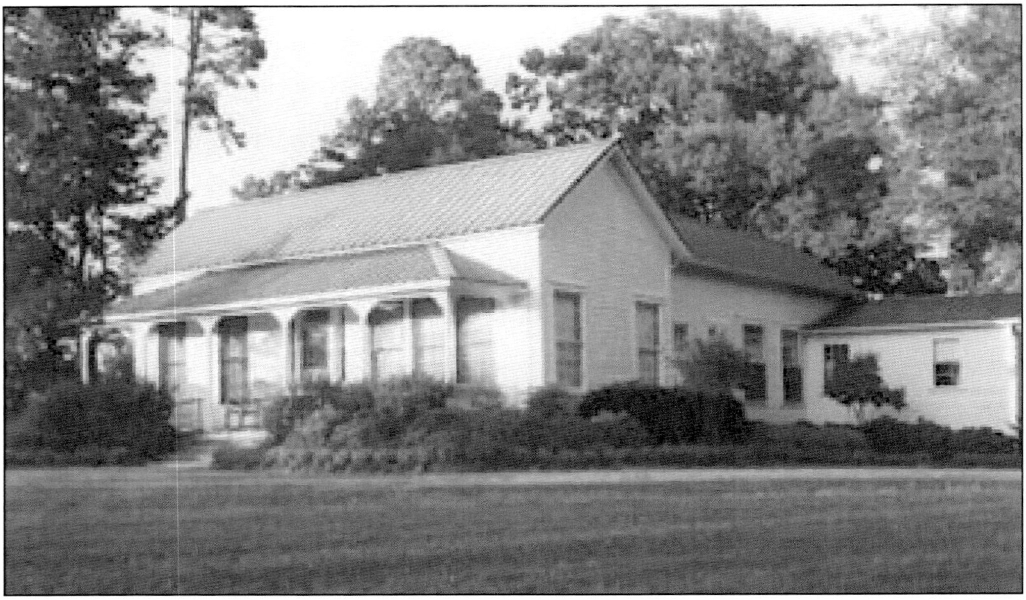

The Jones Home was built by Johnny Smith in 1897 in the True Vine community. T. Huel and Leah Evans Jones purchased the home in 1940. Due to coal mining, their son Don and wife JoAnn Jones moved the house to Highway 522 three miles north at True Vine Nursery. The house has been completely restored. Since 1999, their son, T. Huel Jones II, his wife, Christie, and son Christopher have made it their home and proudly continue the family farming tradition. (Courtesy of Raymond W. Powell.)

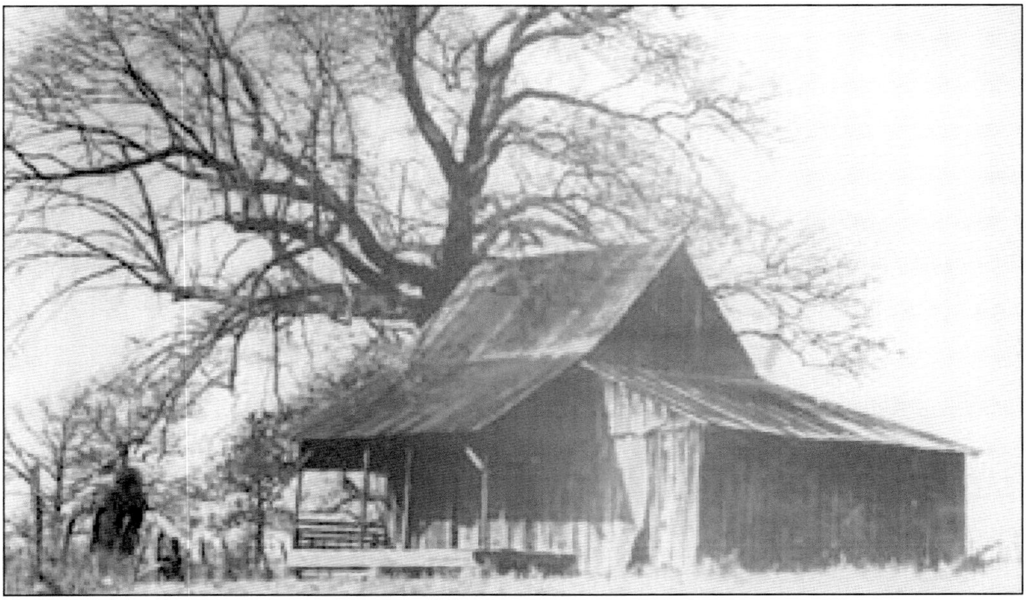

Mattie Marshall introduced the first registered Jersey cow into northwest Louisiana. She purchased it in 1886. A barn built to serve that 1880s dairy herd is still in use at Allendale for beef cattle. John James Marshall came to Louisiana from several plantations in operation in South Carolina and Florida. His brother Henry Marshall established a plantation in DeSoto Parish well-known as Land's End. Many other dairies grew in DeSoto Parish, earning it the reputation as dairy capital of Louisiana. Shown is the original barn at Allendale. (Courtesy of Liz Chrysler.)

Four

Plantations of Northern DeSoto Parish

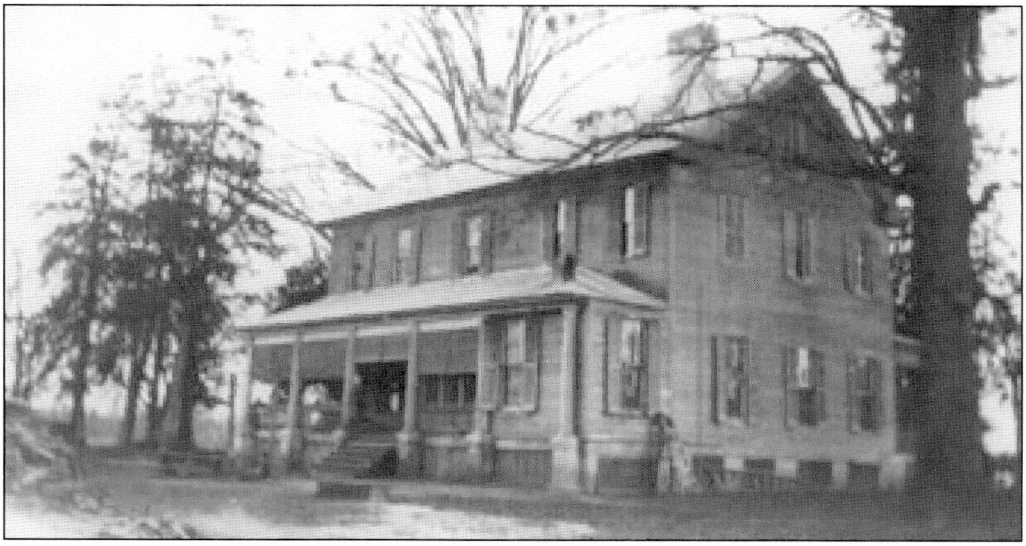

In 1837, Henry Marshall left Society Hill, South Carolina, on the Pee Dee River and located land about 20 miles south of Shreveport. He erected rudimentary buildings to serve the needs of his family. A year later in February 1837, his wife, Maria, joined him, along with her two small children and parents, Maj. Thomas and Mary Taylor. In 1857, Marshall completed their home, Lands End, which was designed by architect M. Robbins. He soon also accumulated 10,000 acres of land. (Courtesy of Louisiana State University in Shreveport, Noel Memorial Library, Archives and Special Collections.)

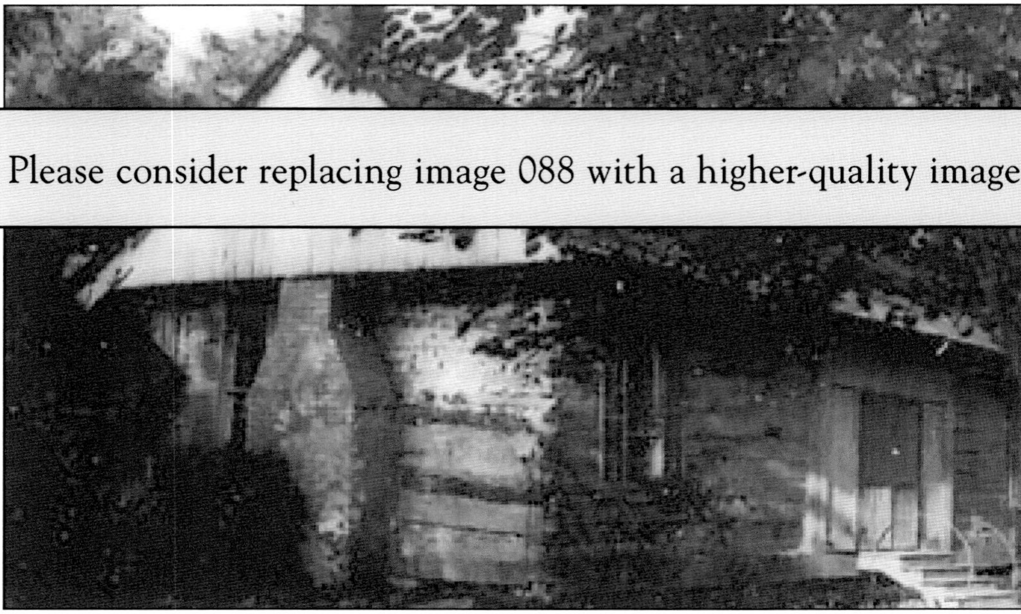

This is the log cabin where the Allendale plantation began. John James Marshall brought some slaves west to work his Louisiana acreage, located off what is now Linwood Avenue in DeSoto Parish. The name Allendale evolved from a later purchase of a 40-acre farm. John Marshall enlarged the one-room cabin to accommodate his large family, who were still living in Orange County, Florida. His wife died when he brought the family to Louisiana's frontier, and his oldest daughter, then about 18, came to help care for the younger children. Marshall continued to acquire acreage surrounding his farm until 1860, when he owned 3,040 acres, with 1,000 under cultivation. Allendale had 92 slaves, living in 23 slave dwellings on the plantation. (Courtesy of Liz Chrysler.)

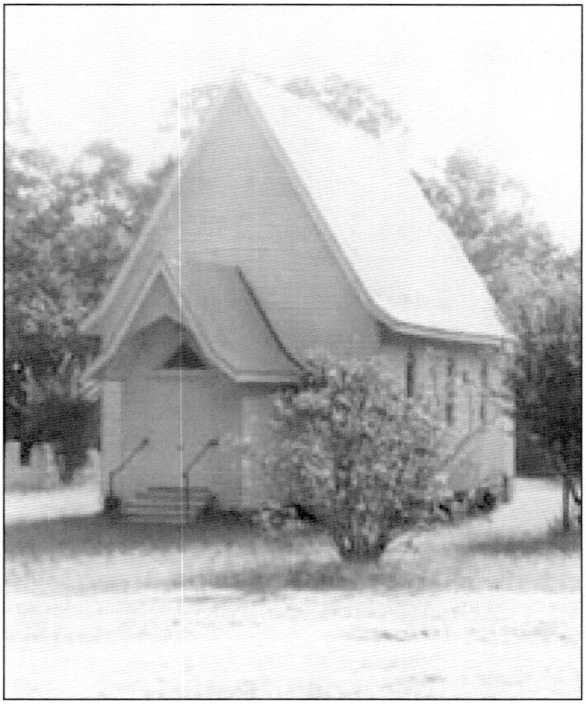

In 1887, John Julian Marshall donated four acres of Allendale for construction of All Saints Episcopal Chapel, located on the Stonewall-Frierson Road less than a mile from the Allendale home. Over the chapel altar is a stained glass window, a memorial to John James Marshall and his oldest daughter, Margaret Olivia Marshall, the first two people buried in the graveyard adjoining the chapel. That site had been selected as a family burial ground before the donation of the acreage to the church, and five of the six sons of John James Marshall are buried there. Much of the chapel's original stained glass is intact. Behind the altar is a communion rail hand carved from a single pine board. The sturdy chapel has walls of solid virgin pine. Benches were tooled of virgin pine with imported mahogany trim. (Photograph by Liz Chrysler.)

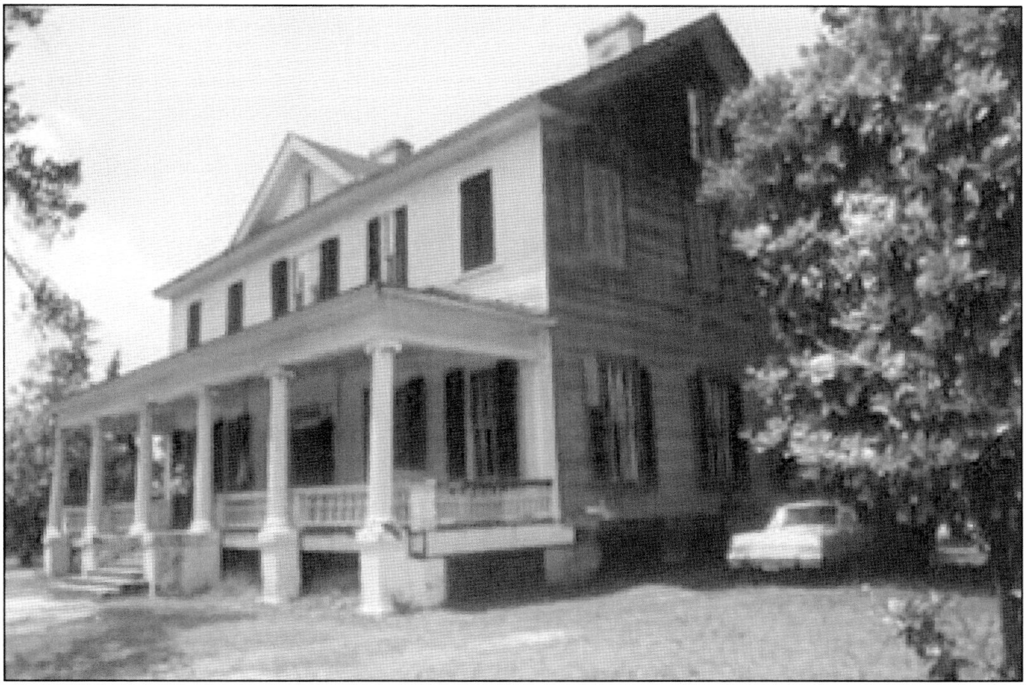

Shown is a later view of Lands End from the front in around the late 1970s. One can tell the decadent condition of the home. (Photograph by W. Conway Link)

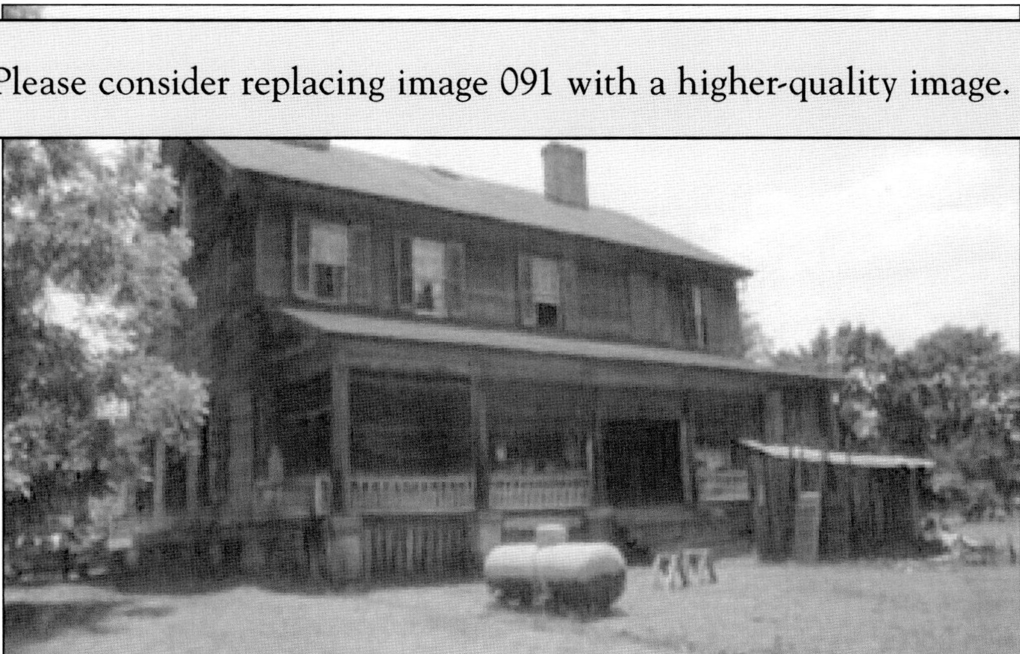

This view of the back of Lands End was taken at the same time. It appears that the front of the house was the only part that was painted. (Photograph by W. Conway Link.)

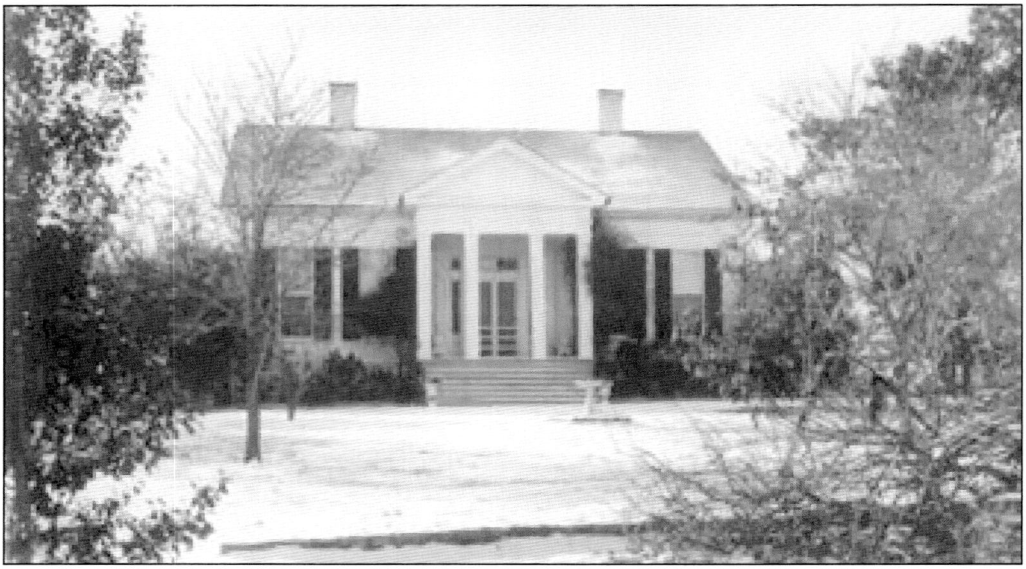

In the small community of Gloster lies the Greek Revival plantation house built in 1852 by Edward Riggs. The house passed through several generations of the Means and Marshall family. Finally, in the 1930s in the midst of the Great Depression the house and 750 acres of land fell into the hands of John Burford. The house had fallen into disrepair. A fire had badly damaged some walls and flooring around a fireplace, and were it not for the foresight and interest in historical preservation of Ray P. Oden the house would not have long remained standing. (Photograph by Robert Menasco, courtesy of Nathaniel Means.)

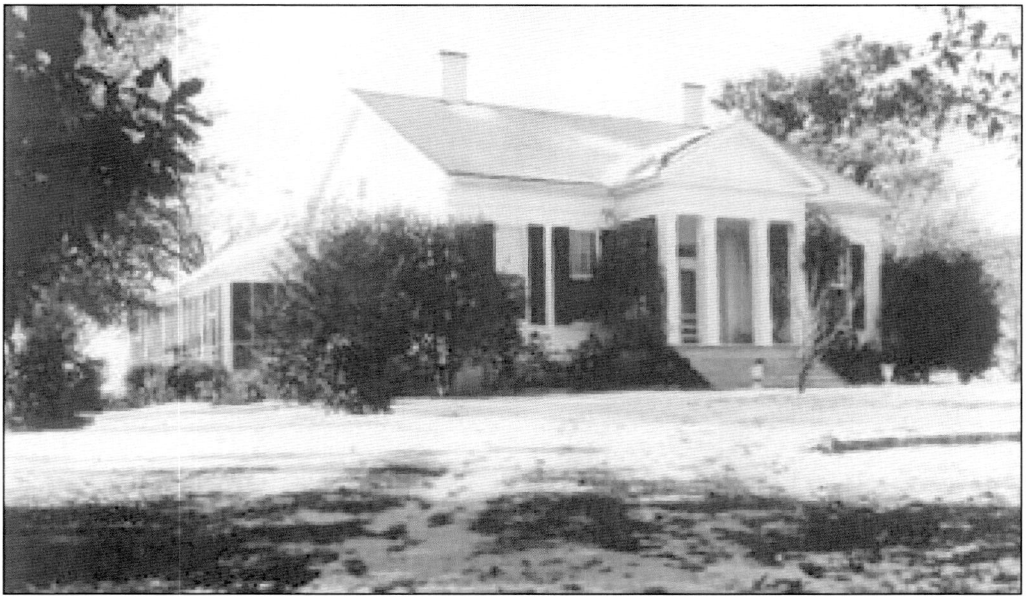

Shreveport banker Ray P. Oden and his wife, Vera Taylor Oden, both expressed a lifelong interest in buying houses and furnishing them. Over the course of their lives, they bought over 15 houses in Louisiana, restored them, and moved on. When Ray P. Oden heard about the status of Myrtle Hill, he offered to assume the mortgage on the house and 750 acres. In 1937, the Prudential Insurance Company willingly let him have it. (Photograph by Robert Menasco, courtesy of Nathaniel Means.)

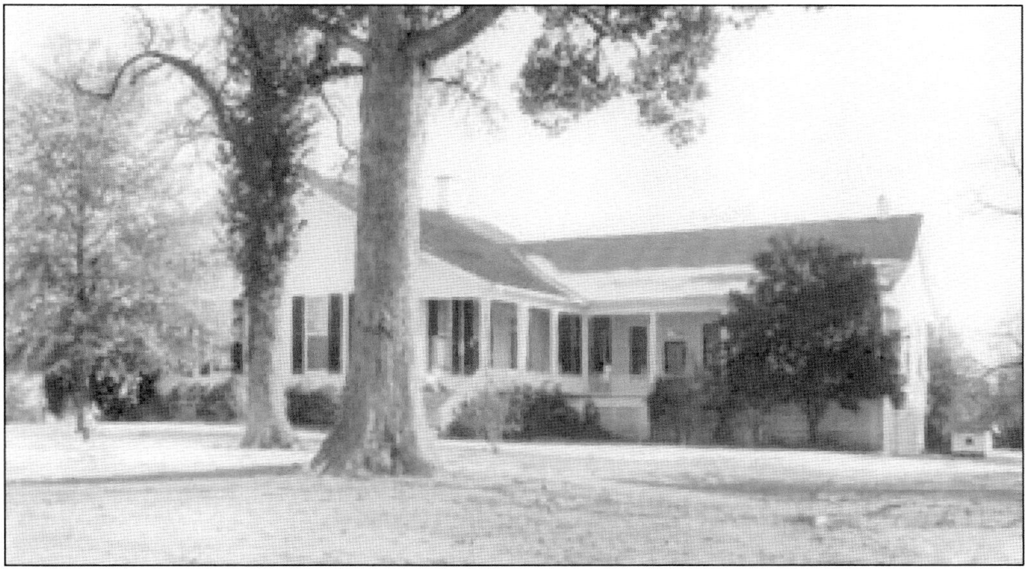

Immediately, the Odens replaced a tin roof with a more historically accurate roof of wooden shingles. Always keen on maintaining the exact historical integrity of the house, while allowing for modern conveniences, Ray added bathrooms in the bedroom closets, which were original, but rare in antebellum houses. Over time, they furnished the home with antebellum furniture acquired during their frequent trips to New Orleans to add to Vera's collection of bedroom furniture from her family in Arcadia, Louisiana. (Photograph by Robert Menasco, courtesy of Nathaniel Means.)

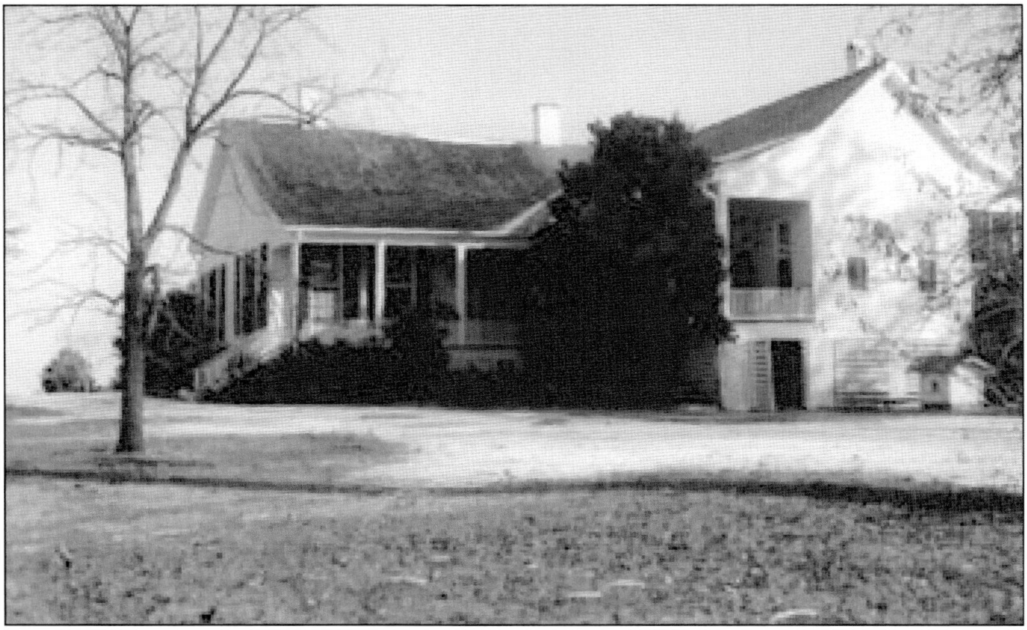

Originally named Oaklawn for the numerous oak trees that once surrounded the house, Ray P. Oden renamed the place Myrtle Hill after the crepe myrtles that he and his wife planted on the sloping lawn. It became for the Odens a hobby and a weekend house for the whole family. By the time Ray P. Oden died in 1978, he and his wife had accomplished a magnificent feat in historical preservation. (Courtesy of Nathaniel Means.)

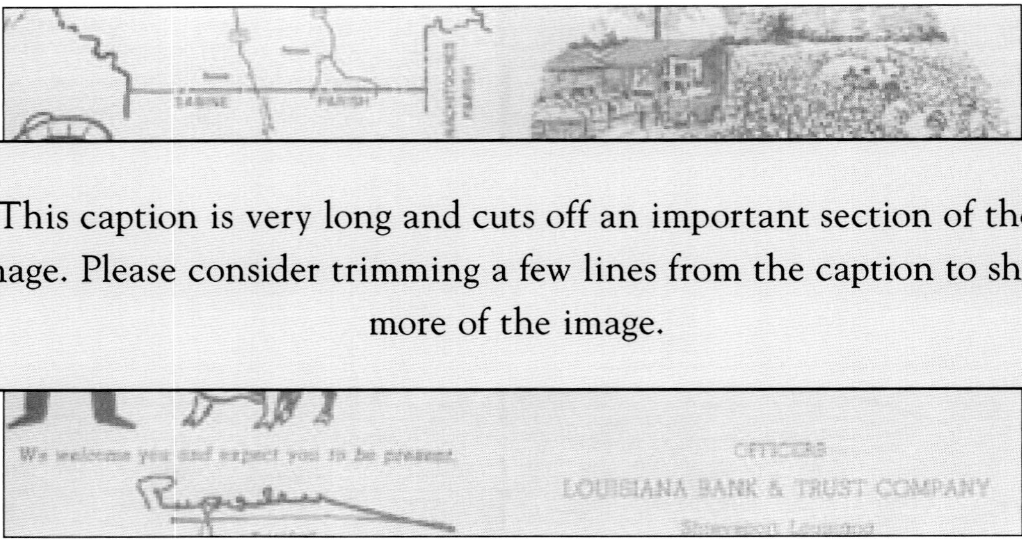

In spite of the fact that Oaklawn had been occupied by various members of the Means, Marshall, and Furman families, who are normally associated with Lands End and Roseneath Plantations, it was still originally a dogtrot house. Ray Oden added an enclosure to the dogtrot which could still be opened and did nothing to destroy the integrity of the home. He also added a shotgun house which was already on the land to the back of the home with an outside connection to serve as a kitchen and dining room. The Odens restored Myrtle Hill into a self-sufficient farm and place to entertain family and friends. In their invitations, the Odens created a plantation image, and he was given an original plantation bell by a good friend. Since he was president of Louisiana Bank & Trust, he would entertain employees, stockholders, and customers. (Courtesy of Nathaniel Means.)

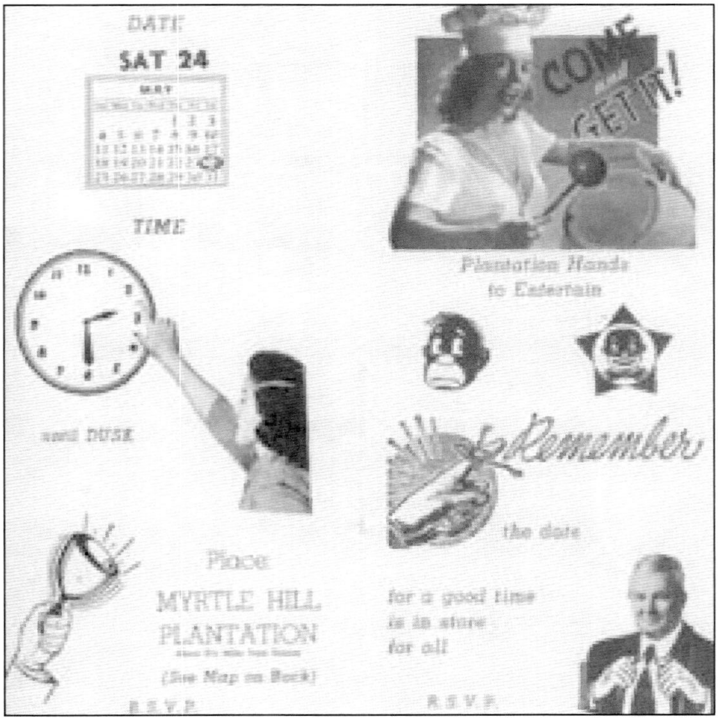

The Odens would entertain outside for the evening meal and serve fried fish, steak, corn, sweet potatoes, and fresh tomatoes. Ray Oden would proudly say, "Now remember that everything you are eating was grown on this place." He grew a large vegetable garden, made use of the smokehouse on the property, and raised Hereford cattle. There were seven spring-fed ponds. (Courtesy of Nathaniel Means.)

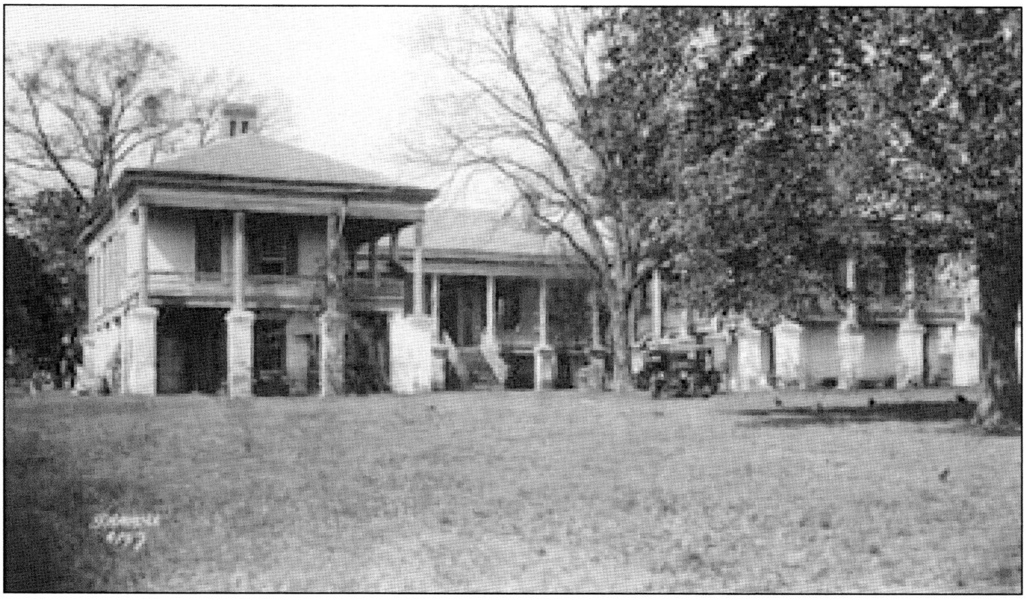

Welcome Hall was built by Col. Charles P. Edwards, who came from South Carolina to northern DeSoto Parish. He did not begin building Welcome Hall until 1851, finishing the central portion in 1853, the first wing in 1855, and the second in 1857. Robbins, the master contractor, was given free reign to design and build. Robbins had a penchant for large brick piers, from which he carried 44 columns to an entablature with a horizontal beaded molding topped with dentils. (Photograph by Birch Grabill, courtesy of Spring Street Historical Museum.)

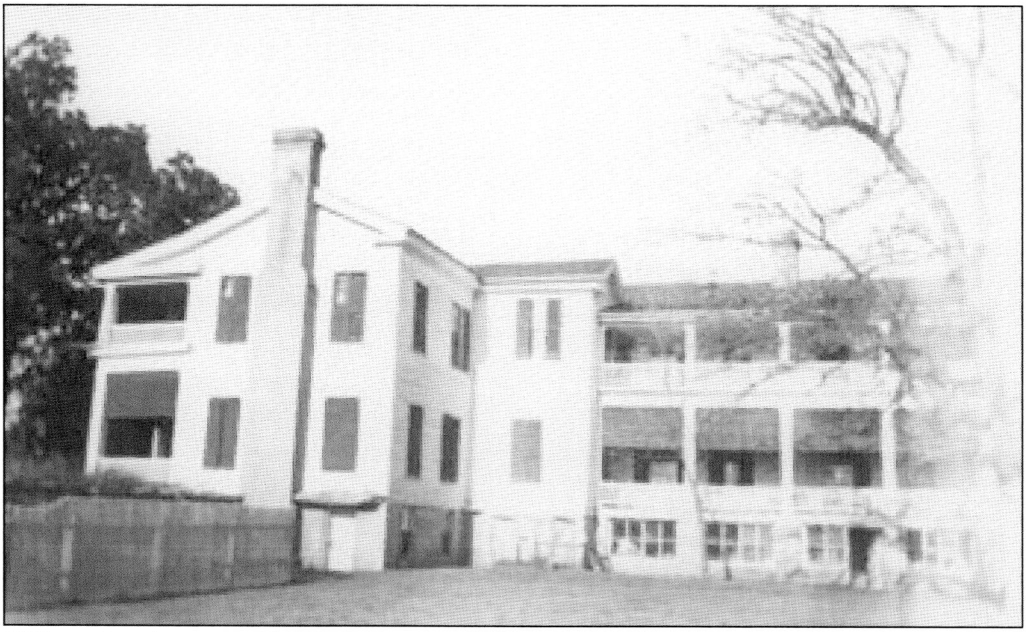

William Bundy Means, from a prominent South Carolina family, came in 1844 to the fertile lands of North Louisiana between the Red River and the Texas border. He built the first large plantation house in the newly acquired Indian lands. His slaves grew their crops and worked on construction of the house for three years. (Courtesy of Louisiana State University in Shreveport, Noel Memorial Library, Archives and Special Collections.)

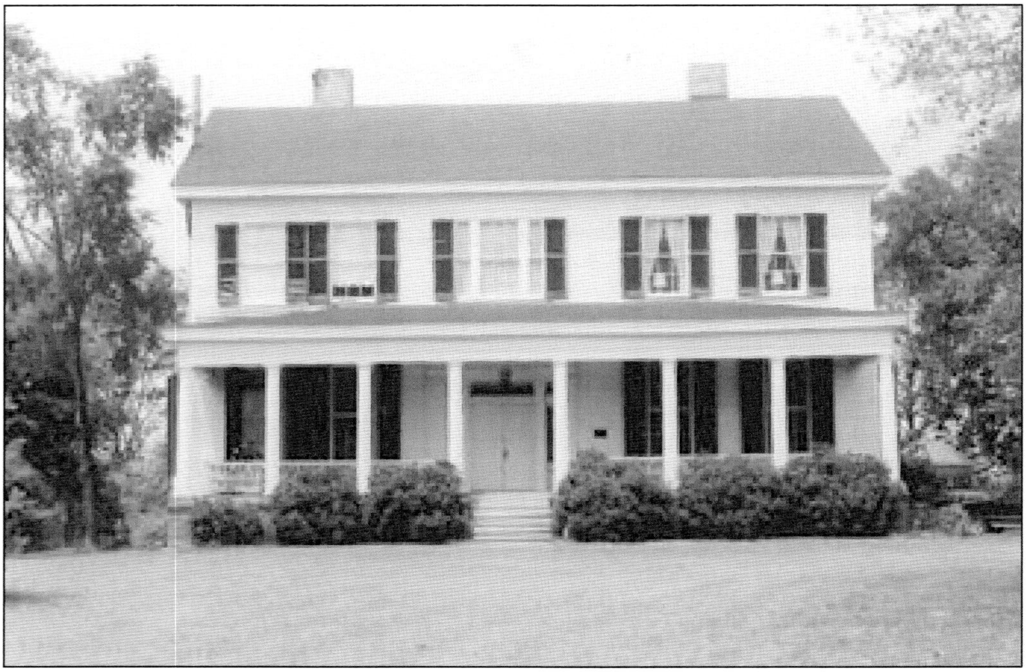

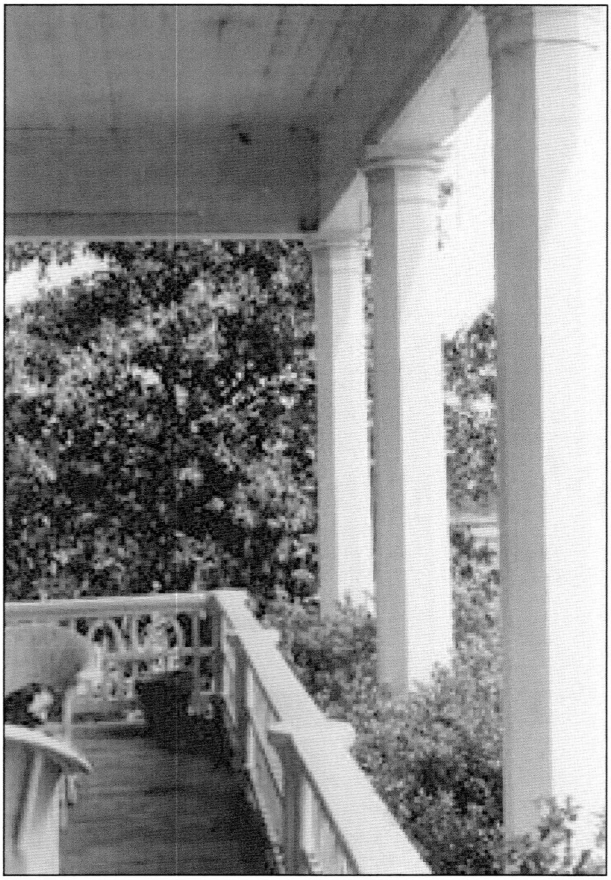

Buena Vista Plantation, in northern DeSoto Parish, Louisiana, was established by Boykin Witherspoon, a planter who came overland from South Carolina. Construction on the plantation home itself began in 1859, five years after Witherspoon moved his family to Louisiana. The house was built under the supervision of popular area architect and builder M. Robbins. Robbin's trademark, tall columns set on brick and offset from the edge of the gallery, is evident. (Photograph by Vicky C. Gourley.)

Five

Creation of the Parish and Mansfield

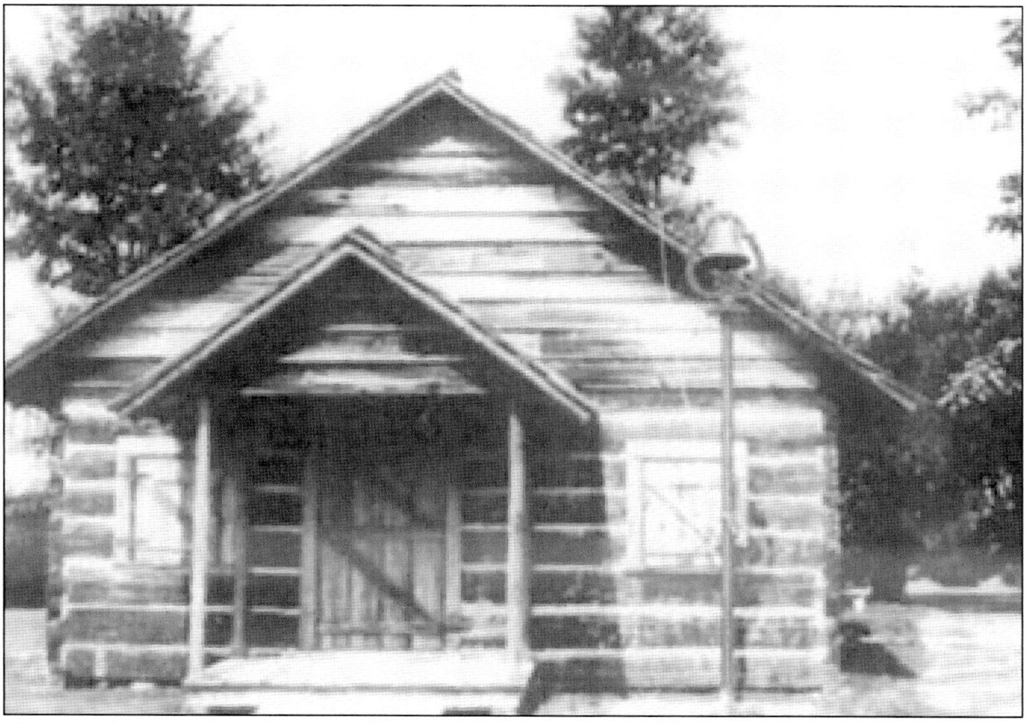

This is a photograph of the original log courthouse in Mansfield. It was erected about 1843. After Nabors Trailers purchased the Hewitt home the log courthouse was found and reassembled on a mini city park on the corner of Polk and Jefferson under the guidance of DeSoto Historical Society, Inc.. (Courtesy of Liz Chrysler.)

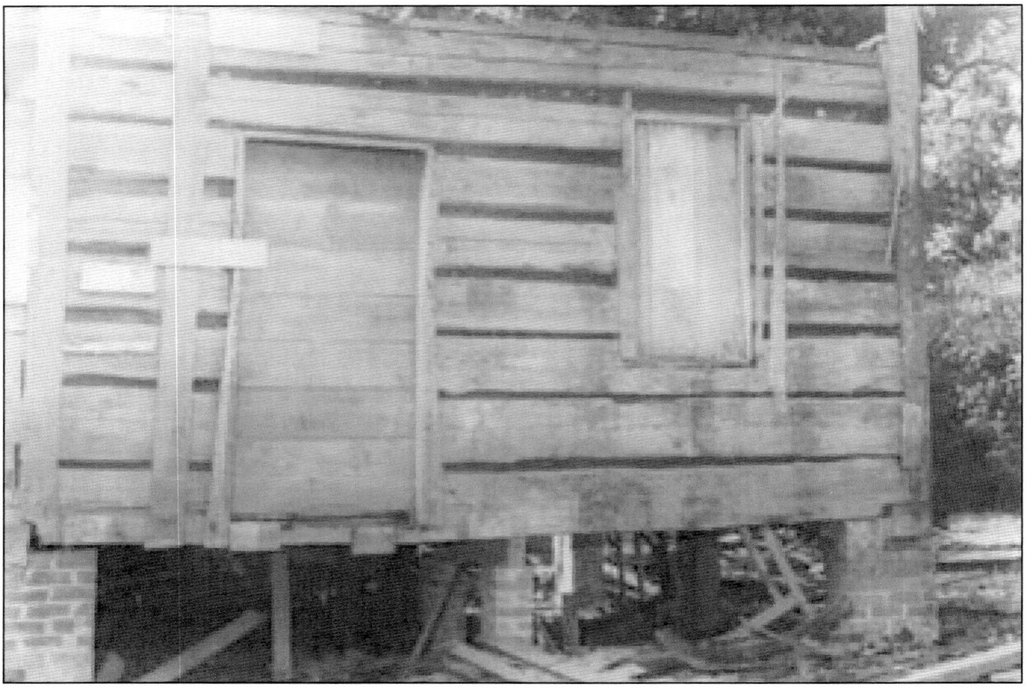

This original old courthouse was taken down when the second courthouse was built. The log courthouse was encased in the William Beall Hewitt home for 129 years. It served as the first courthouse in DeSoto Parish and today is the only log courthouse known to exist in the state of Louisiana. (Courtesy of Liz Chrysler.)

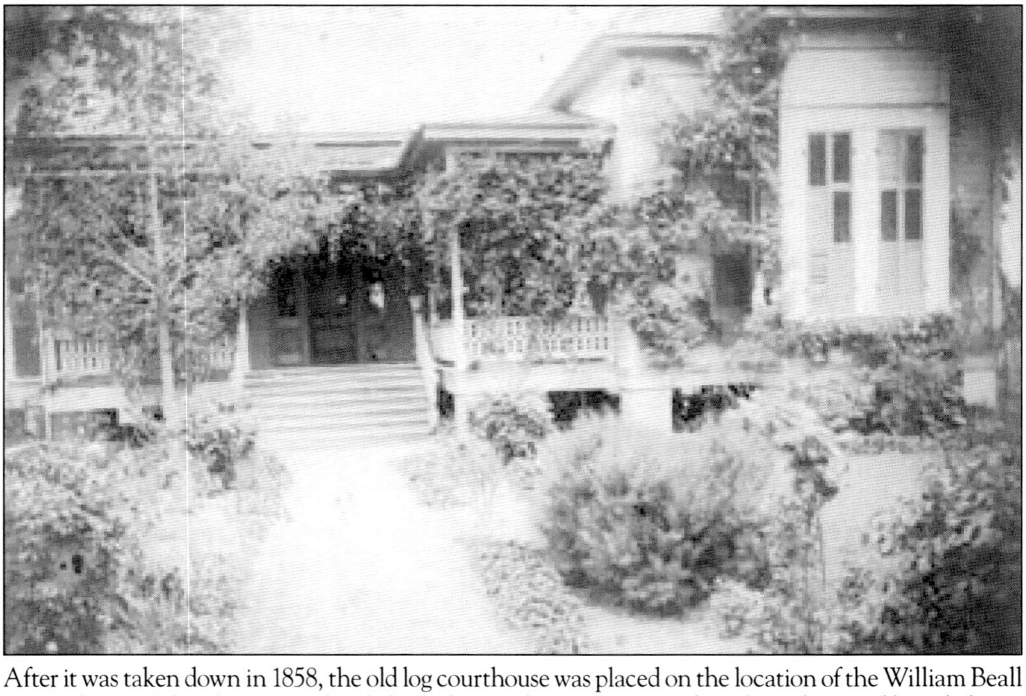

After it was taken down in 1858, the old log courthouse was placed on the location of the William Beall Hewitt home. After the Hewitt family built the new home, it was used as a basis for it and boarded over so it could not be seen. (Photograph by McPherson Studios, courtesy of Raymond W. Powell.)

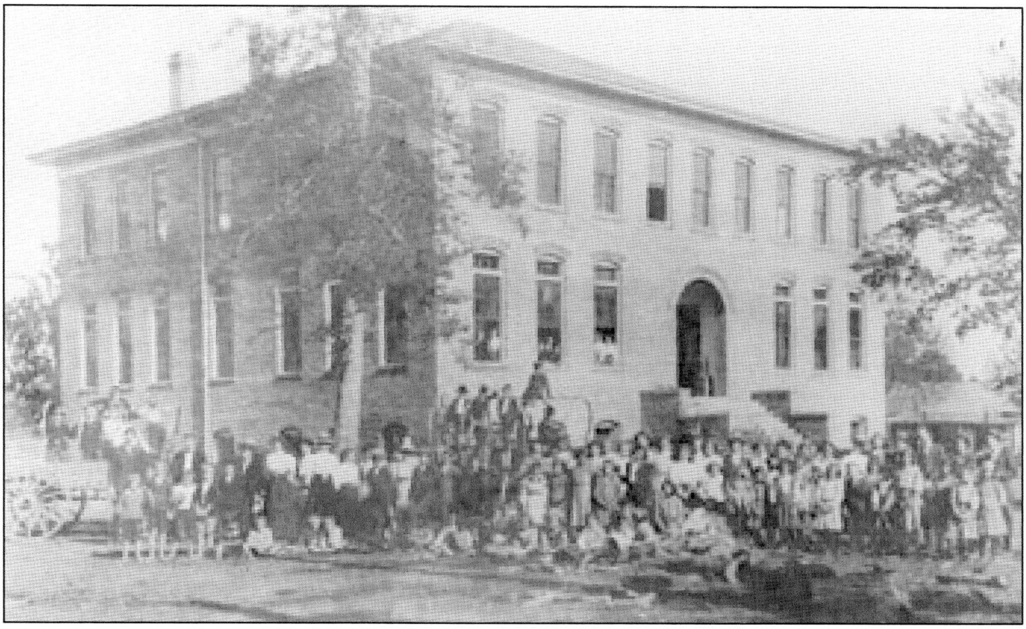

The second courthouse, built of brick, is shown in this illustration. It was completed around 1854. Pictured around the building are a group of Mansfield School children. It was taken down prior to the erection of the current courthouse in 1908. (Courtesy of Louisiana State University in Shreveport, Noel Memorial Library, Archives and Special Collections.)

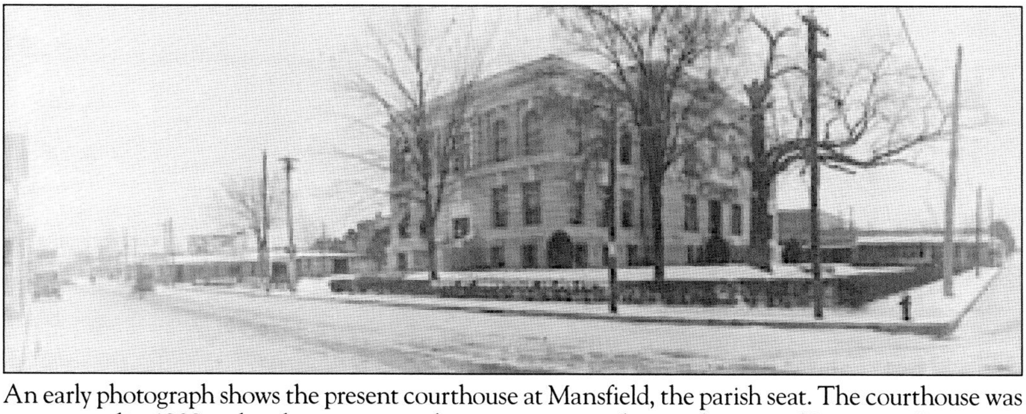

An early photograph shows the present courthouse at Mansfield, the parish seat. The courthouse was constructed in 1908 and underwent a complete restoration in the past few years. (Courtesy of Louisiana State University in Shreveport, Noel Memorial Library, Archives and Special Collections.)

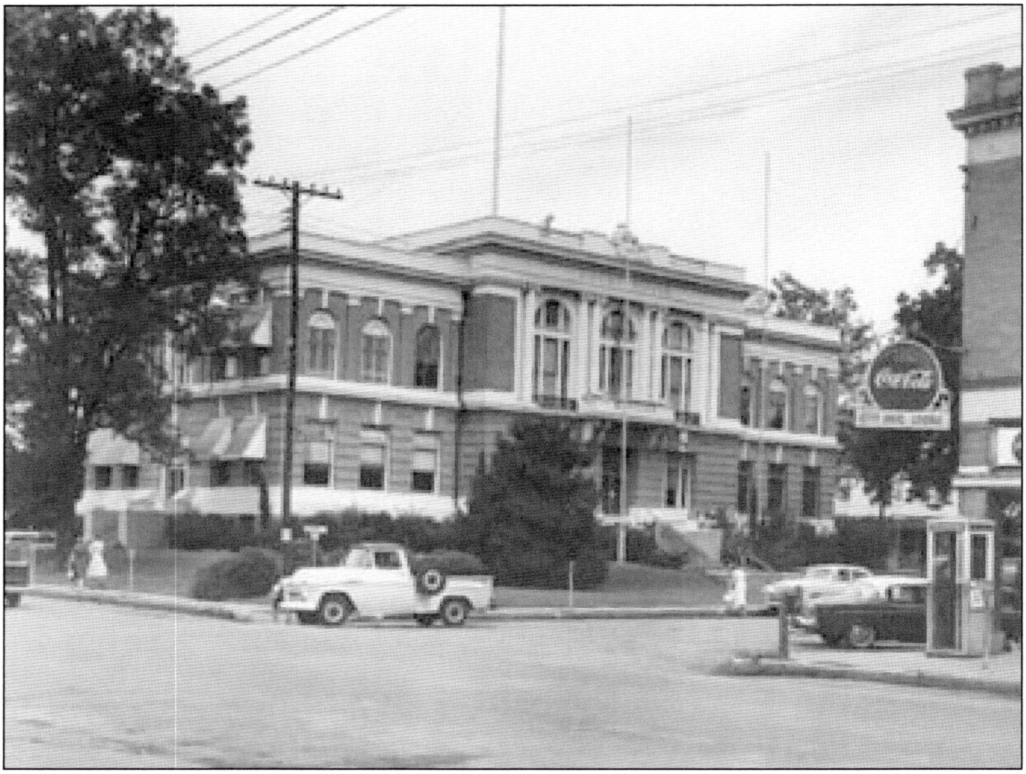

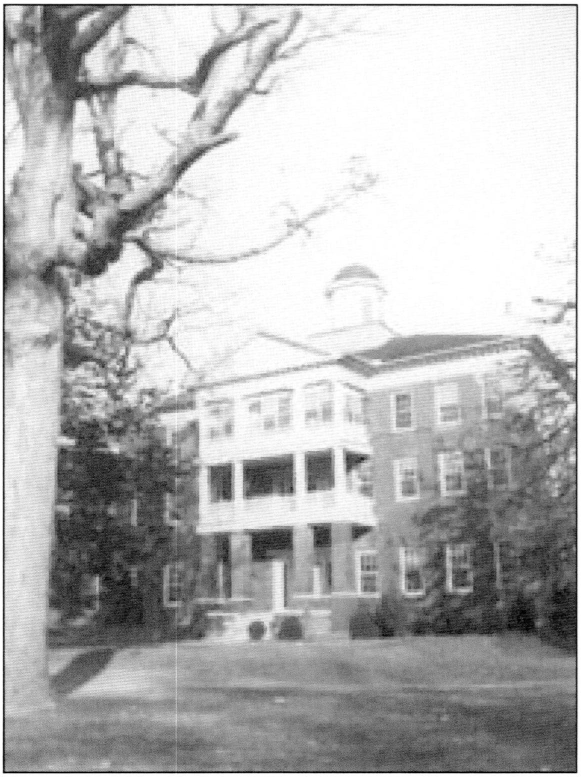

Another early photograph displays the present courthouse during business hours on a weekday. In these busy times today with land men and women coming and going one can stand in front of the office of the *Mansfield Enterprise* and envision another time and place in this busy and traditional southern town. (Courtesy of Louisiana State University in Shreveport, Noel Memorial Library, Archives and Special Collections.)

Mansfield Female College, pictured in 1934, was the oldest college for women west of the Mississippi River. Accepted by the Louisiana Conference of the Methodist Episcopal Church, the college's first commencement was in July 1858. The college was a major center of learning for Mansfield and the surrounding area until it closed in the late 1930s. (Courtesy of Louisiana State University in Shreveport, Noel Memorial Library, Archives and Special Collections.)

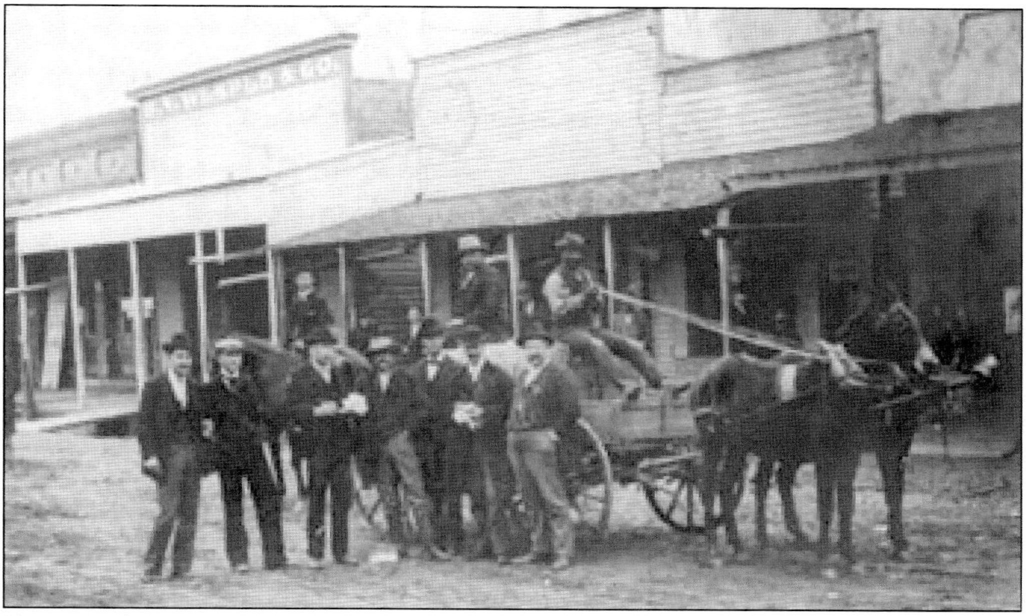

Shown in this 1898 picture is the second storefront of Wemple & Co., owned by B.Y. Wemple in Mansfield. Pictured from left to right are (first row) L.R. Pryer Stone, S.G. Sample, Jobe Wemple, Pomp Williams, M.K Neilson, and an English cotton buyer by the name of Mr. Baker; (second row) Dr. H.C. Stokes (on horse), Sike Simpson (rear of wagon), and Tony Tapp (driver). (Courtesy of DeSoto Historical Society.)

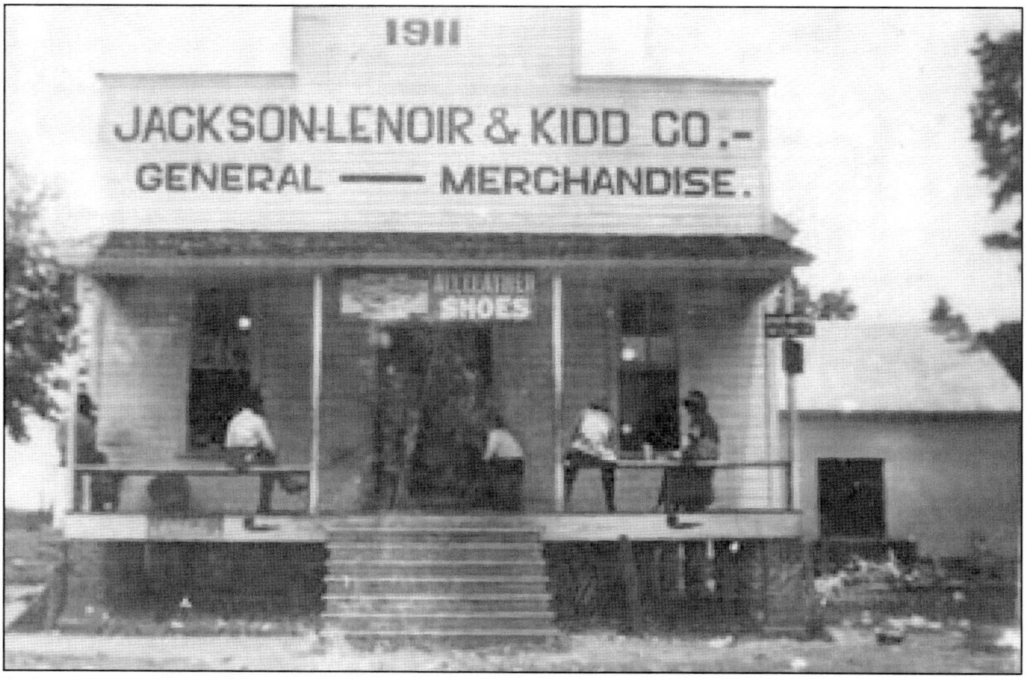

Jackson-Lenoir & Kidd Co. General Merchandise located in Mansfield in a store built in 1911. However, the business was started in Mansfield in the late 19th century by Adolphus Franklin Jackson under the original name Jackson & Kidd General Merchandise. (Courtesy of Louisiana State University State University-Shreveport, Noel Memorial Library, Archives and Special Collections.)

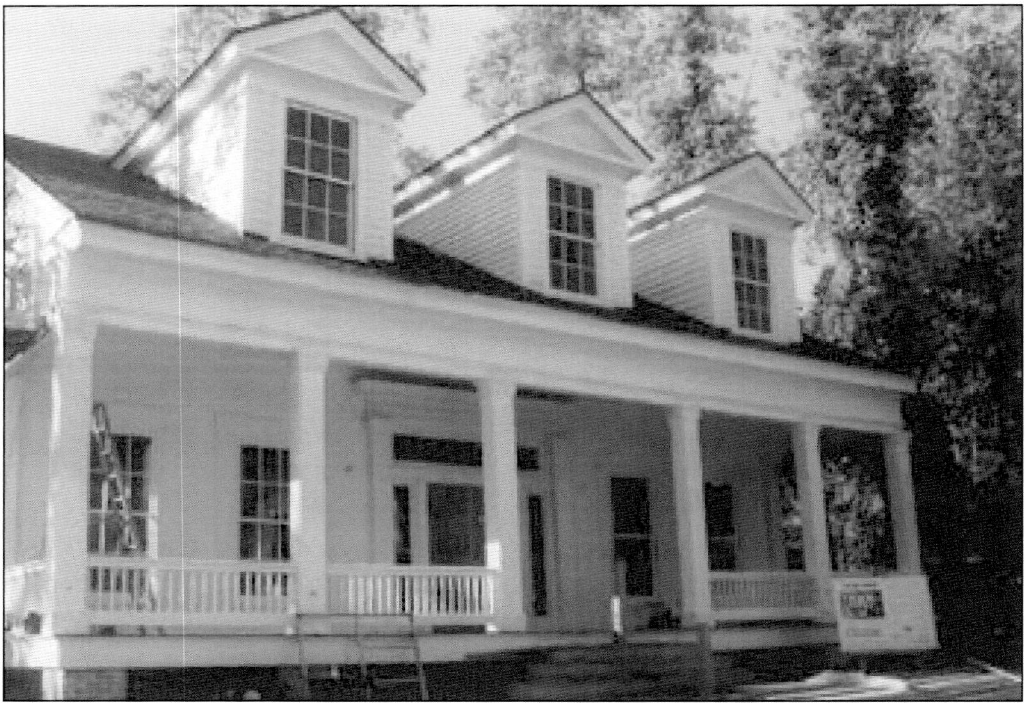

The Samuel Guy House at 309 Pine Street in Natchitoches, Louisiana, is an excellent example of Greek Revival architecture. In 1849, the widow Mary Whitehead Greening Guy moved with her sons Thomas and Samuel to the Mansfield area. They settled five miles south of Mansfield on a farm on Oxford Road (also Highway 513). Samuel continued to live on Oxford Road, where he built his Greek Revival plantation home about 1850. (Photograph by Monica Pels.)

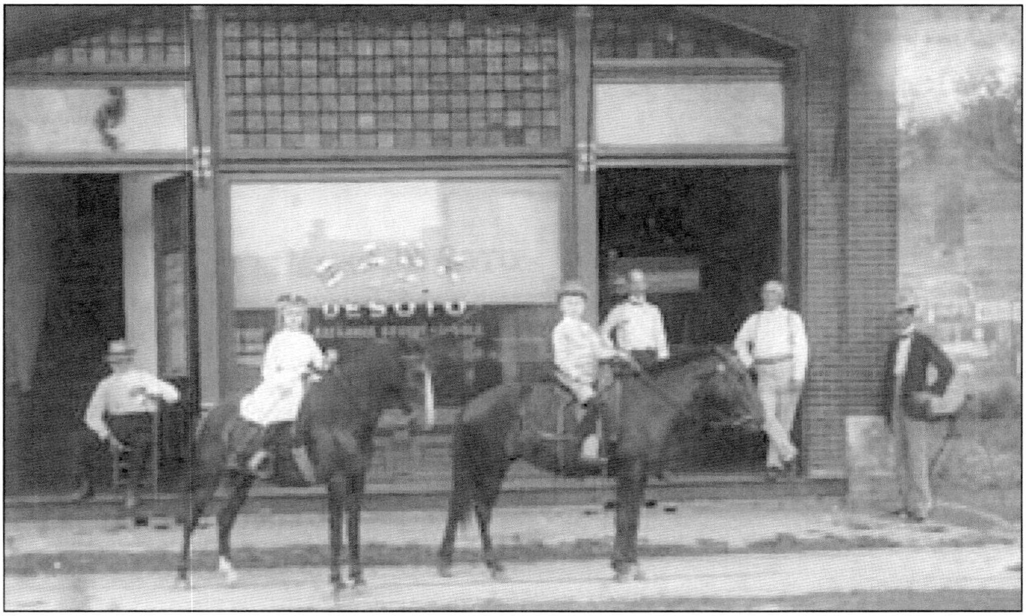

An image of the Bank of DeSoto with people on horseback, many others standing around, and a dog in the foreground. Note most early photos had a dog in the picture. (Courtesy of Louisiana State University in Shreveport, Noel Memorial Library, Archives and Special Collections.)

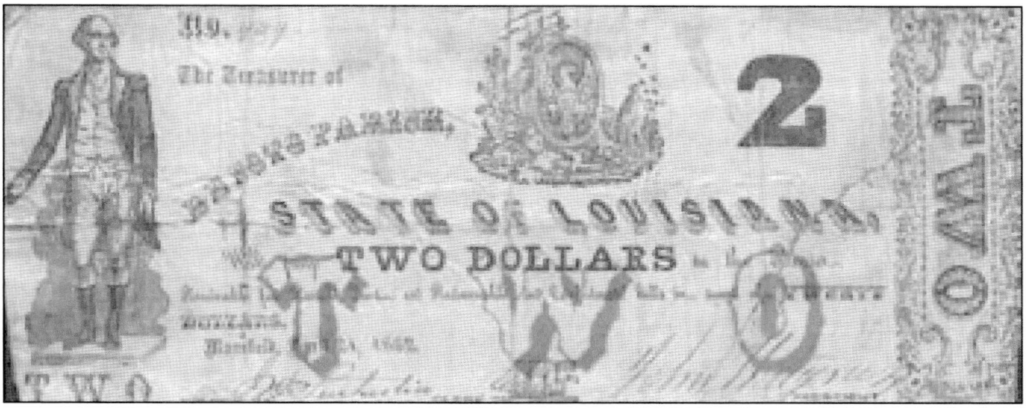

Pictured here is a $2 DeSoto Parish note. The central vignette depicts an oval seal bearing an American eagle, surrounded by such items as a cornucopia, a beehive, a bust, an artist's palette, and the masts of a sailing ship. The note states that the "the treasurer of DeSoto Parish, state of Louisiana, will pay two dollars to the bearer" and that the note was "receivable for parish dues or redeemable in Confederate bills in sums of twenty dollars". The note was issued at Mansfield and bears the pre-printed date of April 21, 1862. The signatures of J. H. Sutherlin (clerk) and John Wagner (president) appear. (Courtesy of Richie Self Collection.)

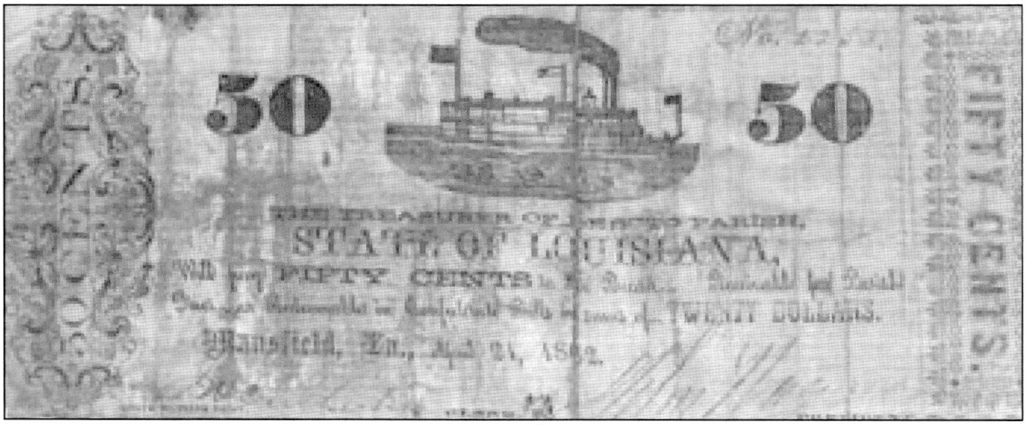

This is an image of a 50¢ DeSoto Parish note. The central vignette depicts a period riverboat proceeding across the note from left to right, flanked by denomination presented in numerical format. The note was issued at Mansfield and bears the pre-printed date of April 21, 1862. The signatures of J. H. Sutherlin (clerk) and John Wagner (president) appear. The verso, as with many notes of the era, was left blank. (Courtesy of Richie Self.)

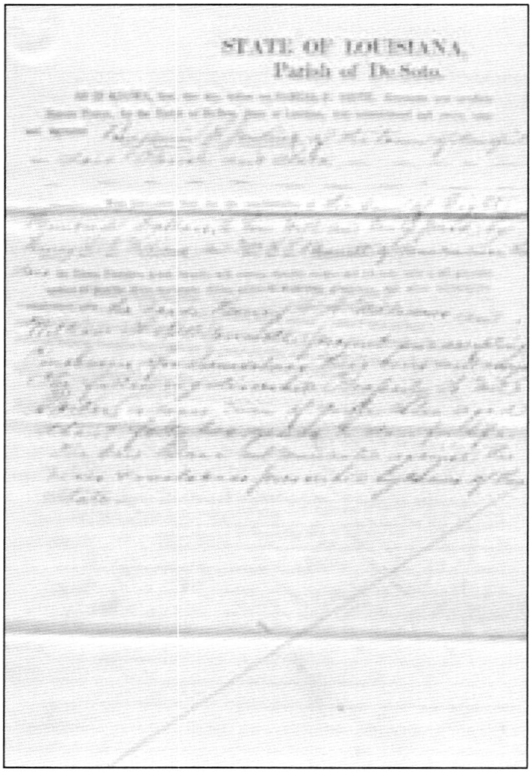
STATE OF LOUISIANA,
Parish of De Soto.

Shown is a pre-printed slave bill of sale. This document is headlined "State Of Louisiana, Parish of De Soto" and was signed in the presence of Samuel F. Smith, recorder and ex-officio notary public. It details the sale of "Parker, a negro man of griffe color, aged about forty two years old" for the payment of $800. Parker is listed as " a slave for life," but interestingly the document notes, " The said slave is not warranted against the vices and maladies prescribed by the laws of this state." (This is unusual, as most slaves were sold with a warranty). According to the document, the purchaser was Benjamin F. Jenkins and the sellers were Henry L. N. Williams and William F. T. Bennett, all of Mansfield. Thomas J. Williams and Jones Persons signed as the witnesses. (Courtesy of Richie Self.)

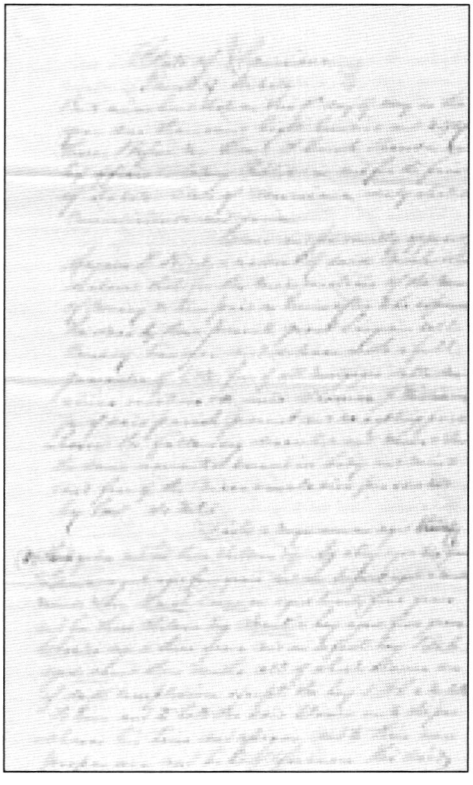

Shown is a manuscript slave bill of sale. It details the sale of "Lish, a Negro woman aged twenty (23) three years and her three children viz: Sy a boy aged Six years, Laura a girl aged four years, and an Infant aged 8 months named Lou, Marsh a woman aged twenty five years, and her three children viz Frank a boy aged five years, Charles aged three years, and an infant boy Bob aged about three months," all for the sum of $4,500. All of the slaves were of "dark complexion, except the boy Bob, a mulatto" and all were "warranted sound in body and mind and free of the vices and maladies prescribed by law." (It would be interesting to know how they certified the two infants as sound in mind.) (Courtesy of Richie Self.)

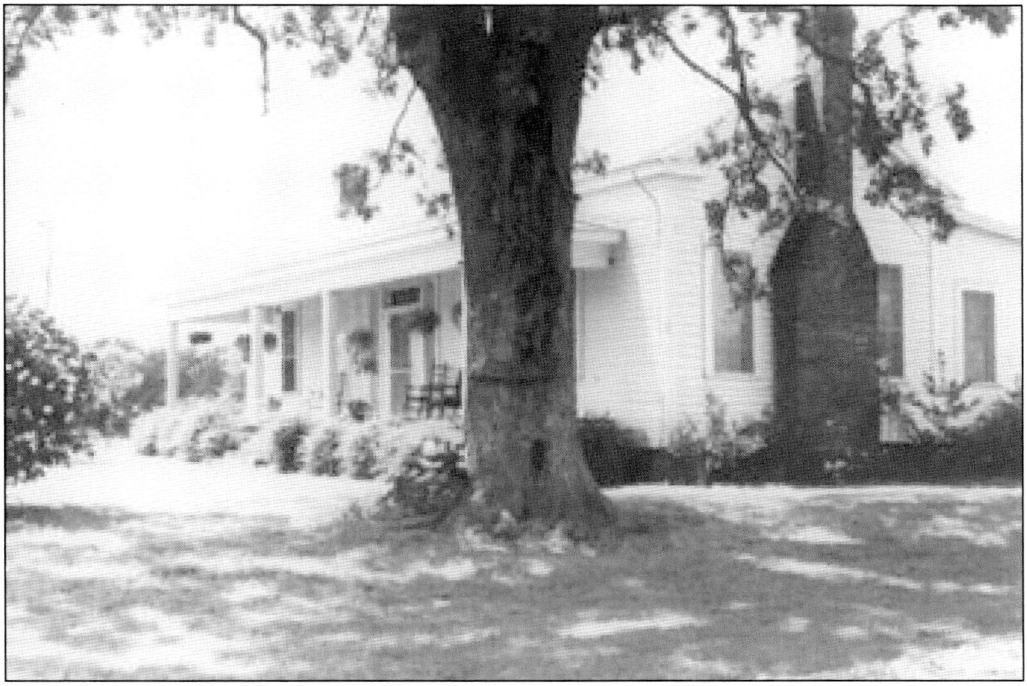

The Williams dogtrot was built by Wess Williams in 1870 from logs and wooden boards. On the roof were lightning rods to attract lightning in hopes that it would not strike animals or people. The house was later purchased by Mary and Jerry Decelle, who, after numbering the logs, moved the house to Bernice, Louisiana for restoration. (Courtesy of Raymond W. Powell.)

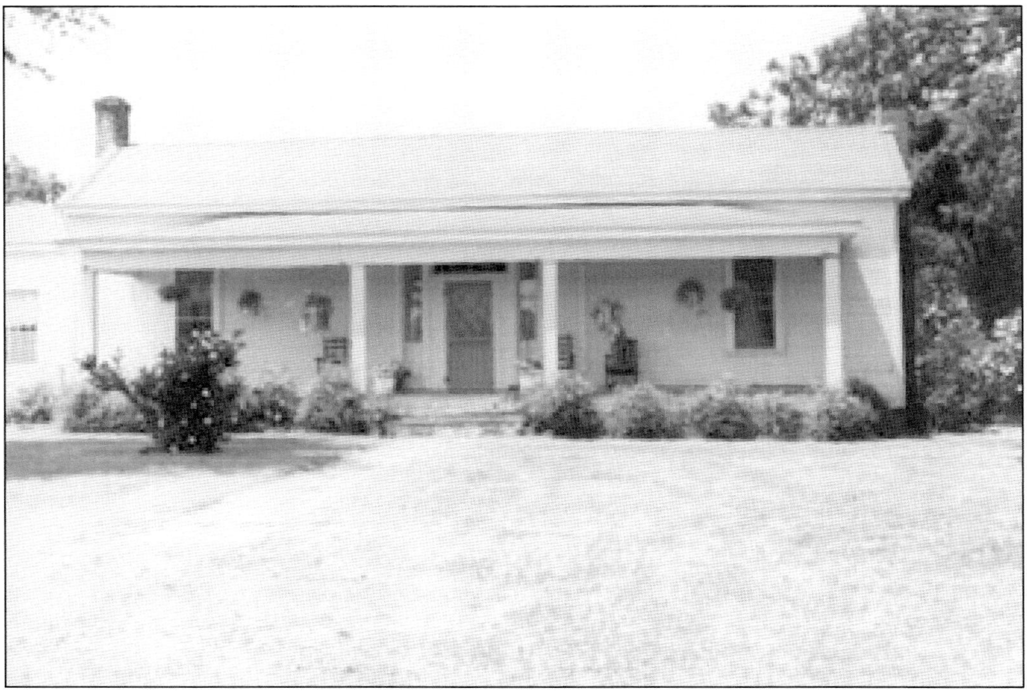

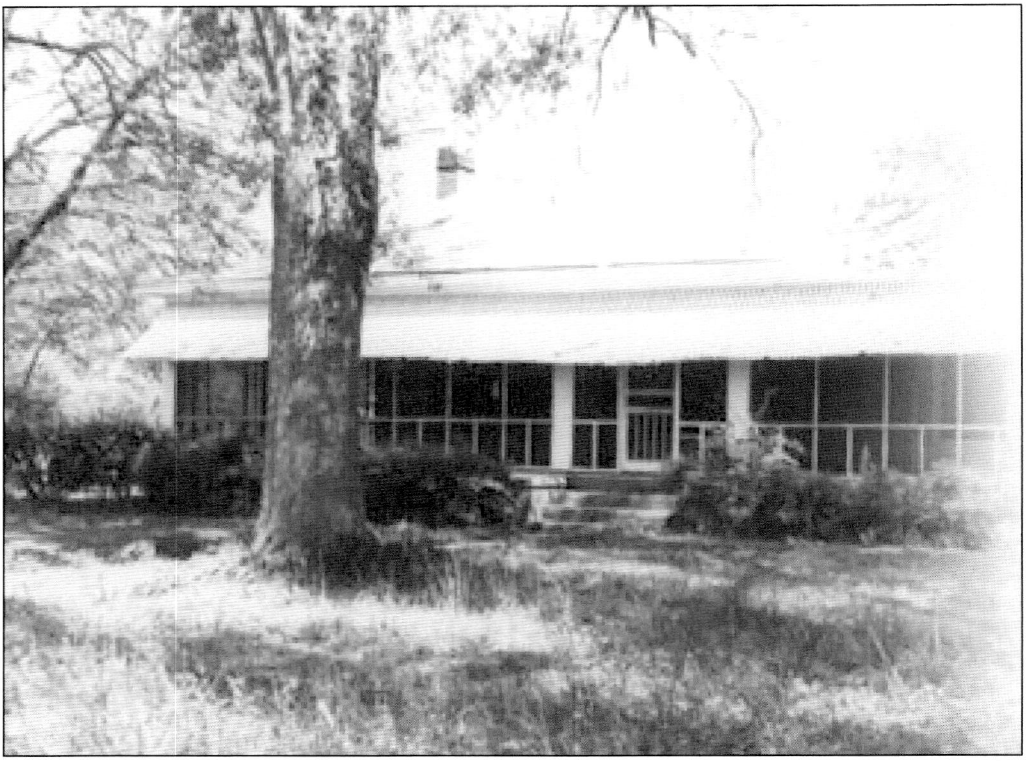

Little is known about the Pegues home in Mansfield. It was built sometime around 1880 by William T. Pegues, former sheriff of Mansfield. The house contains eight rooms. The last owner was William Pegues of Mansfield. (Courtesy of Raymond W. Powell.)

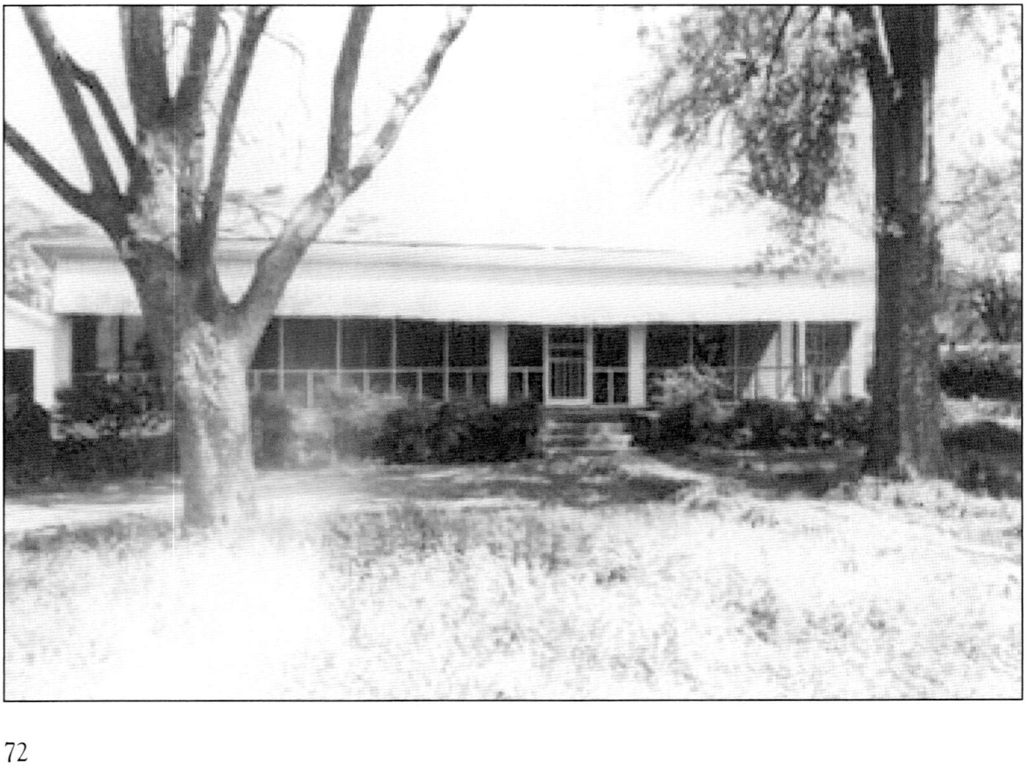

The first Episcopal services were held in Mansfield sometime in 1849. DeSoto Parish Episcopalians renamed their parish church Christ Memorial in memory of both Union and Confederate dead. The building pictured was constructed in 1881. One side of the altar commemorates the Union dead and the other side commemorates the Confederate dead. (Courtesy of Raymond W. Powell.)

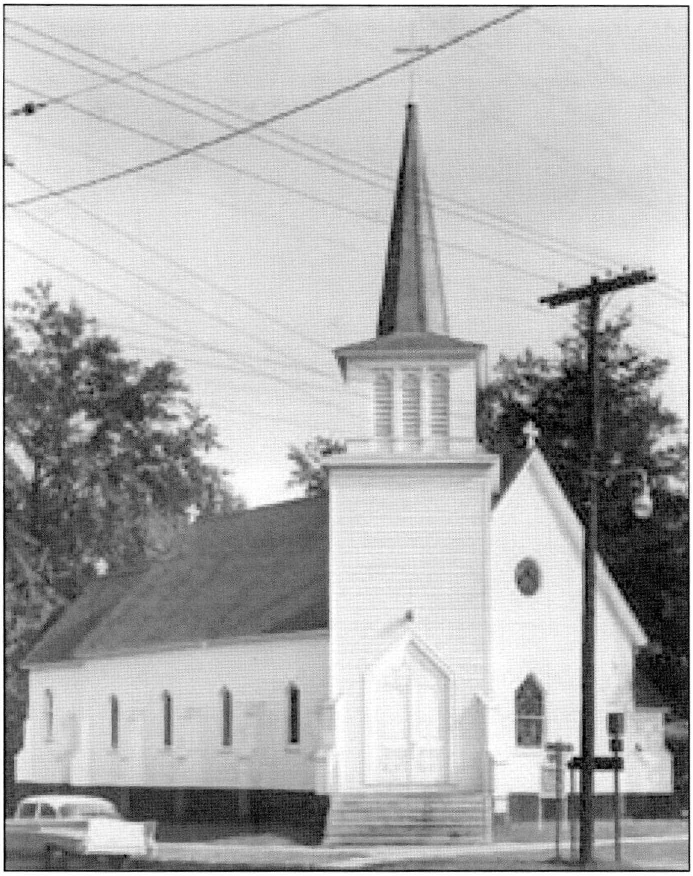

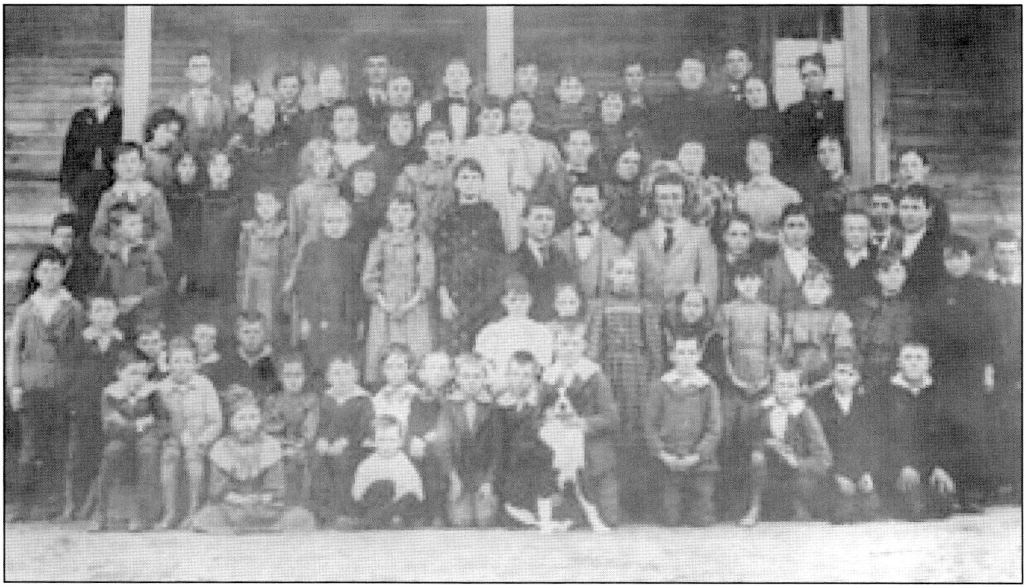

An 1897 image of an older Mansfield school is shown with all of the schoolchildren in front. (Courtesy of Louisiana State University in Shreveport, Noel Memorial Library, Archives and Special Collections.)

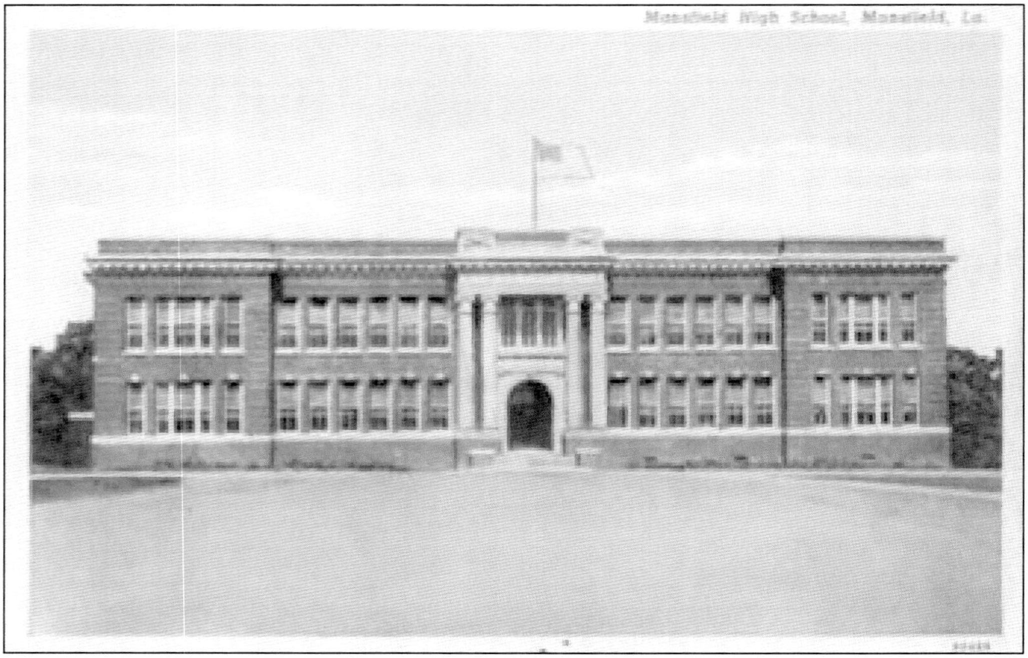

Mansfield High School, shown here on a postcard, was built around 1910. Many students remember happy years spent there, and it still has a strong alumni association. (Courtesy of Ina Larkin Young.)

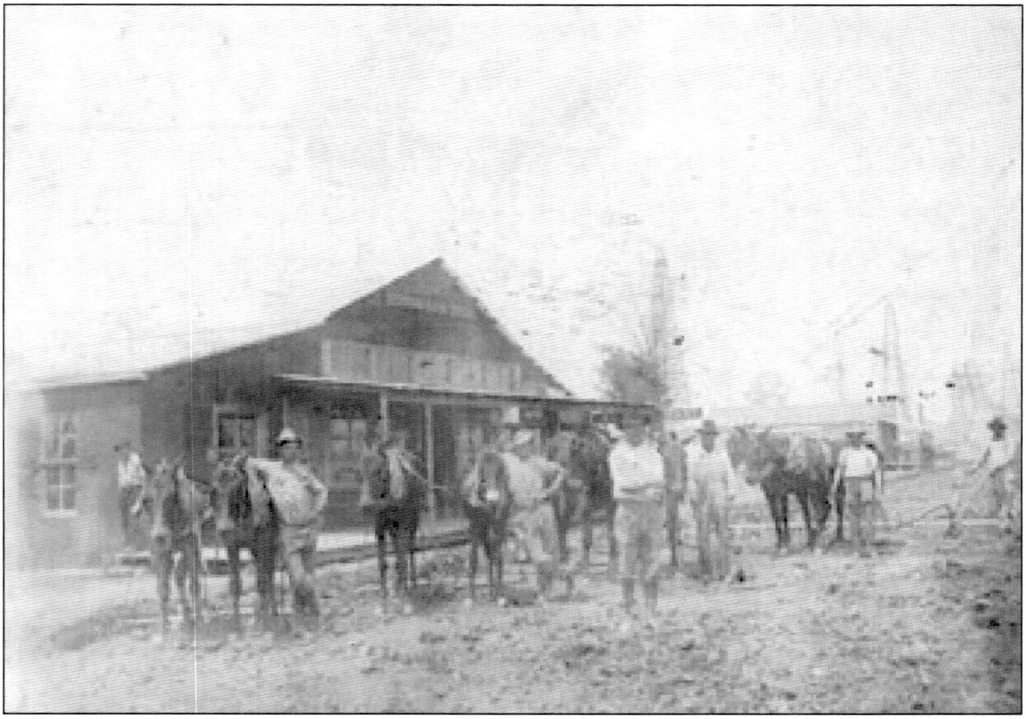

Lenzburg Cash Store was located in the heart of the business district in Mansfield. This photograph was made in 1913. (Courtesy of Louisiana State University in Shreveport, Noel Memorial Library, Archives and Special Collections.)

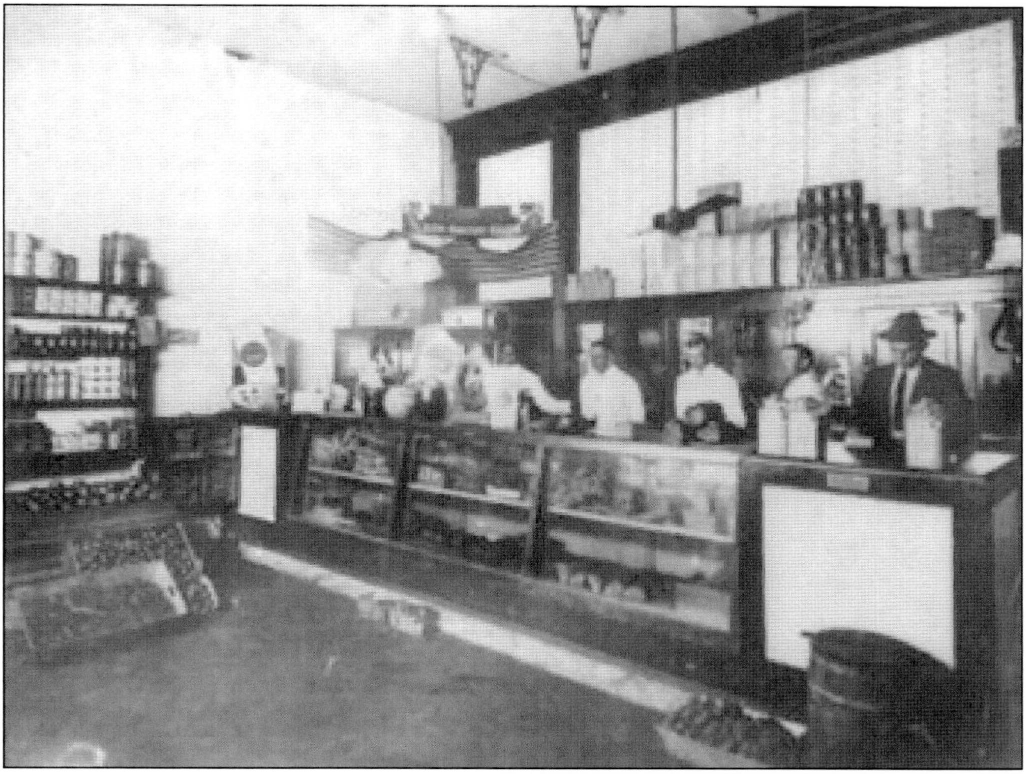

The Cold Storage House in Mansfield was located on Water Street in Mansfield in a tin building. The city of Mansfield uses it presently for the maintenance department. (Courtesy of Louisiana State University in Shreveport, Noel Memorial Library, Archives and Special Collections.)

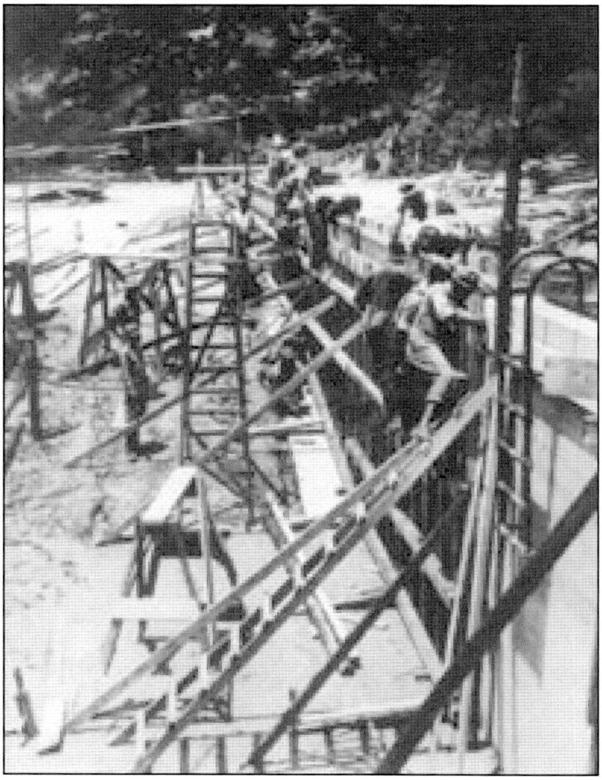

The Mansfield recreational center was a Works Progress Administration (WPA) project in the 1930s. The WPA provided jobs during the Great Depression of the 1930s. Many contributions were made, such as guidebooks to the various states, which captured an era, a time, and a place. (Courtesy of Louisiana State University in Shreveport, Noel Memorial Library, Archives and Special Collections.)

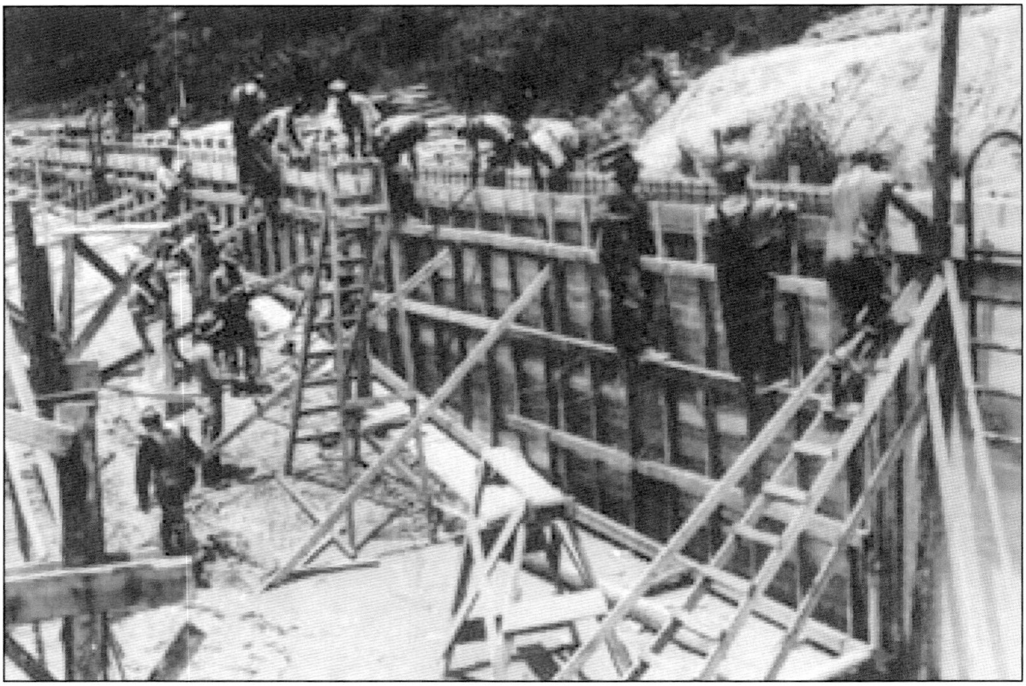

This is a view of the construction of the Mansfield swimming pool by the WPA in the 1930s. (Courtesy of Louisiana State University in Shreveport, Noel Memorial Library, Archives and Special Collections.)

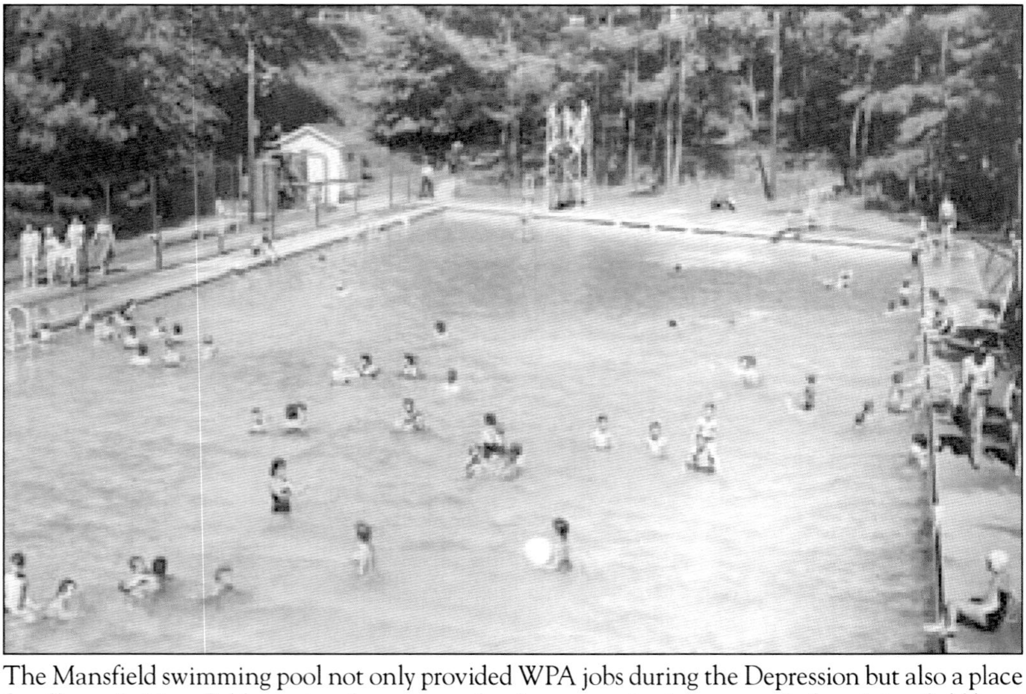

The Mansfield swimming pool not only provided WPA jobs during the Depression but also a place for all ages in Mansfield to enjoy the water and to learn to swim. Many people from Mansfield have fond memories of the swimming pool. Furthermore, it provided jobs for lifeguards and swimming instructors. (Courtesy of George Meriwether Gilmer Jr.)

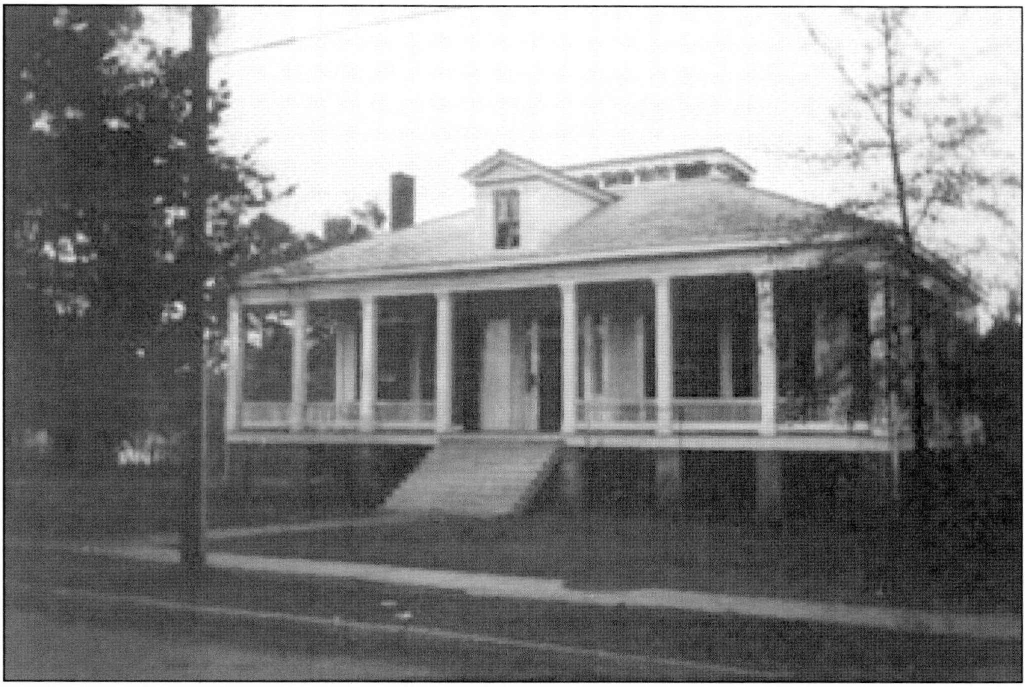

Here is the antebellum Mundy-McFarland home, located in the town of Mansfield, as it was photographed in 1934. (Courtesy of Louisiana State University in Shreveport, Noel Memorial Library, Archives and Special Collections.)

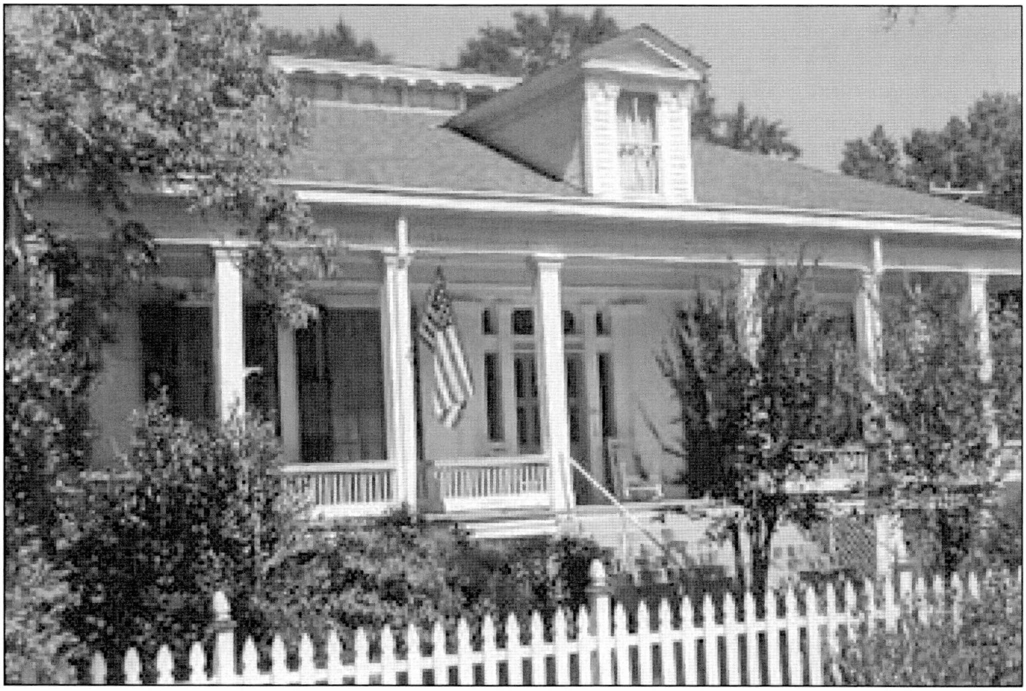

Here is a more recent photograph of the Munday-McFarland home after a restoration. The home is in excellent condition. It is on the corner of Welsh and Water Streets off of Washington Avenue in Mansfield. (Courtesy of George Meriwether Gilmer Jr.)

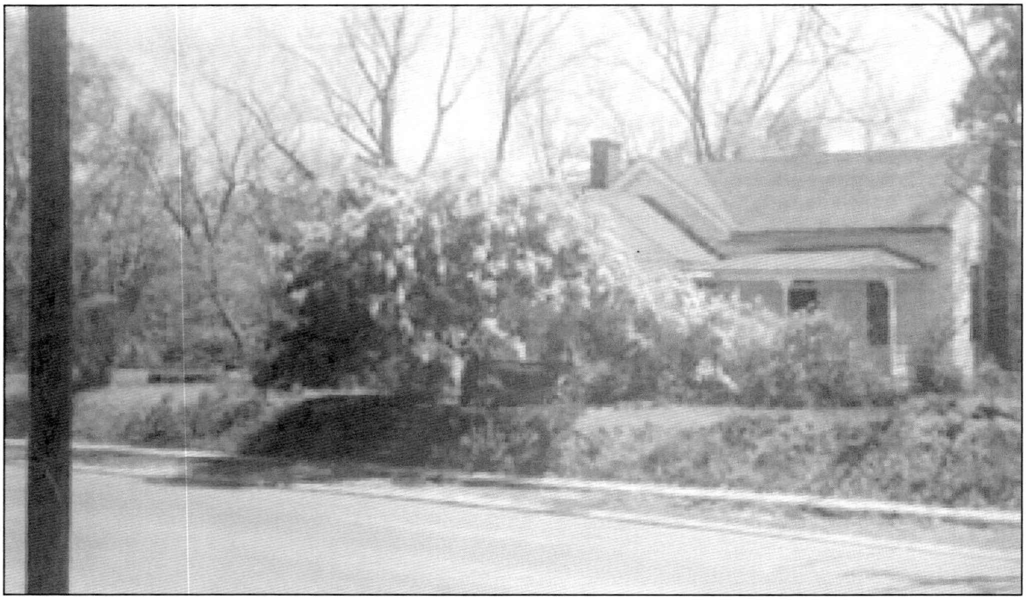

Shown in March 1971 is the home of McHenry Nabors, one of the oldest homes in Mansfield. It is located on an extension of Washington Avenue north of the courthouse. (Courtesy of Louisiana State University in Shreveport, Noel Memorial Library, Archives and Special Collections.)

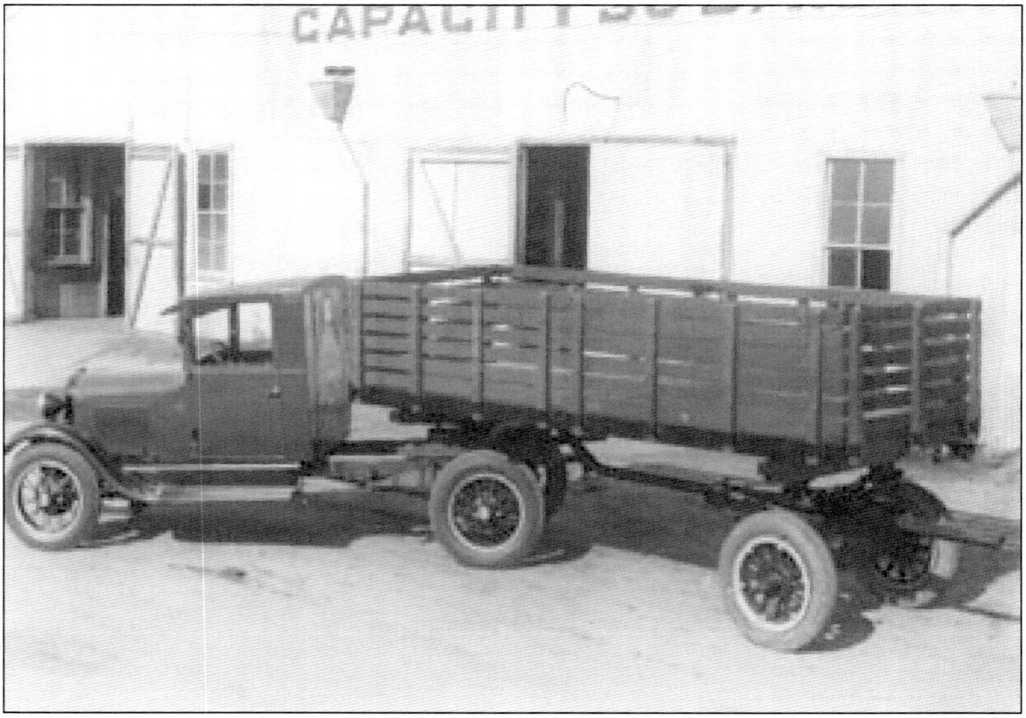

Nabors Trailors, photographed around 1926, was one of the most important local industries. It provided numerous jobs for welders and others, not only in Mansfield but in the surrounding area. The business was known throughout the region, if not nationwide, and many wondered how a small town such as Mansfield could have an important industry.. (Courtesy of Louisiana State University in Shreveport, Noel Memorial Library, Archives and Special Collections.)

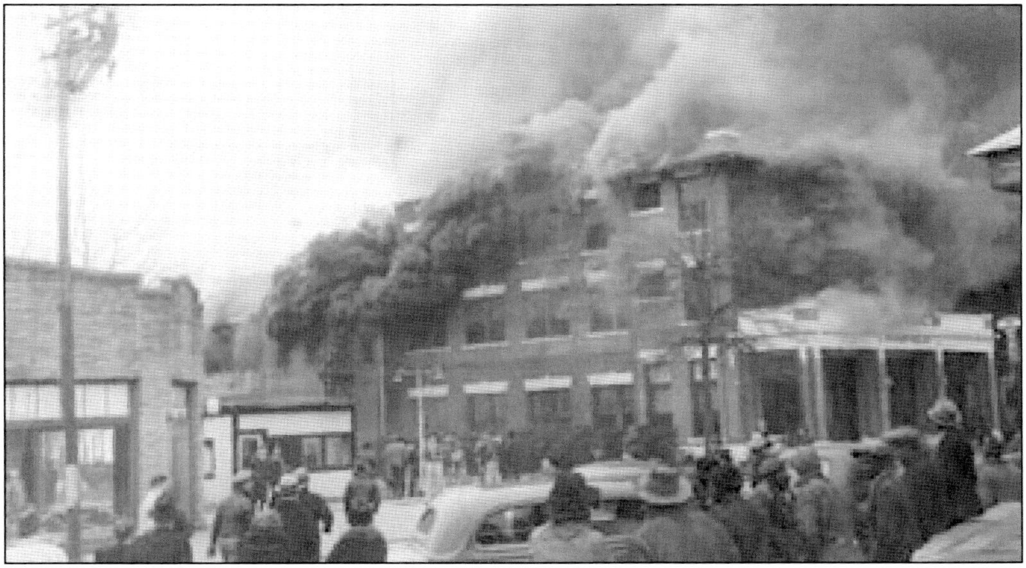

The Mansfield hotel fire occurred in the 1940s and was a major loss to the town. The hotel was in the 200 block of Washington Avenue and almost directly across the street from the current Capital One Bank. (Courtesy of Louisiana State University in Shreveport, Noel Memorial Library, Archives and Special Collections.)

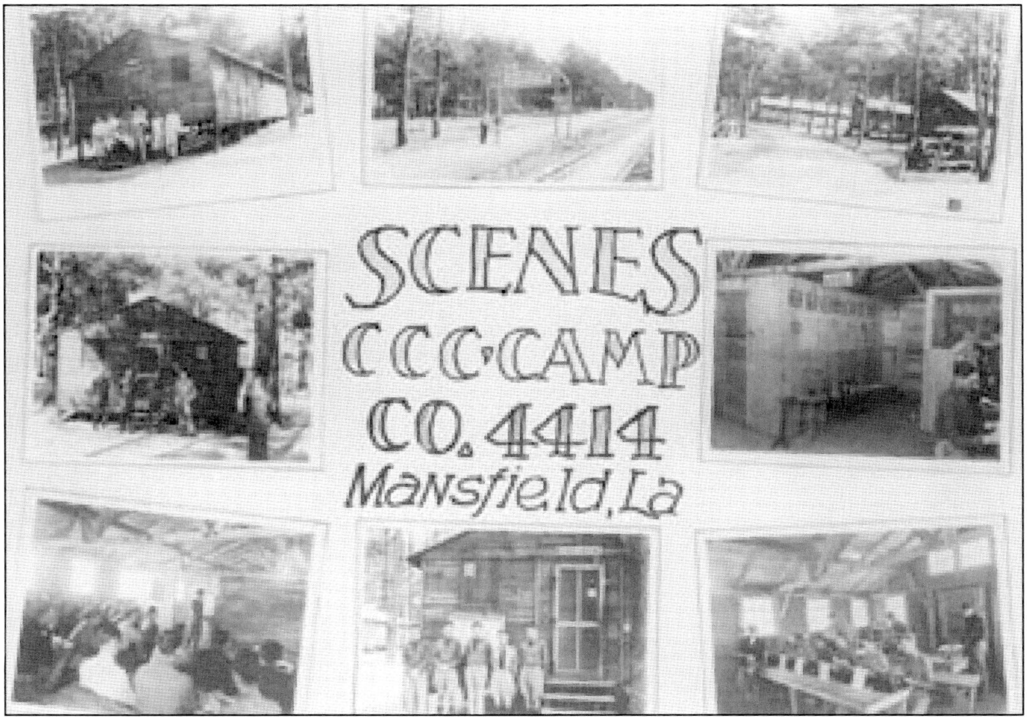

The Civilian Conservation Corps (CCC) was another way to put young men to work during the Great Depression. Numerous contributions were made in Mansfield and many others places. Many larger cities such as Dallas, are proud of their CCC structures, such as those around White Rock Lake. (Courtesy of Louisiana State University in Shreveport, Noel Memorial Library, Archives and Special Collections.)

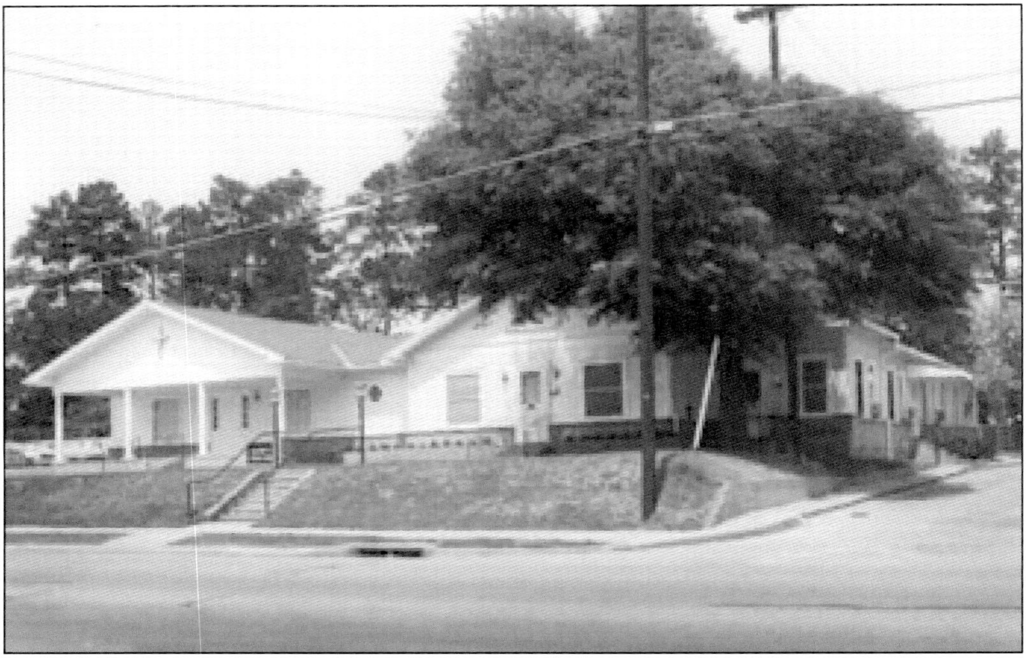

Pictured is Drewett Funeral Home, which was located on Gibbs Street and was the first funeral home in the town. The Drewett family came to DeSoto Parish in approximately 1908 and operated out of their home originally. Drewett functioned as the only funeral home in Mansfield until the early 1990s. (Photograph by McPherson Studios, courtesy of Raymond W. Powell.)

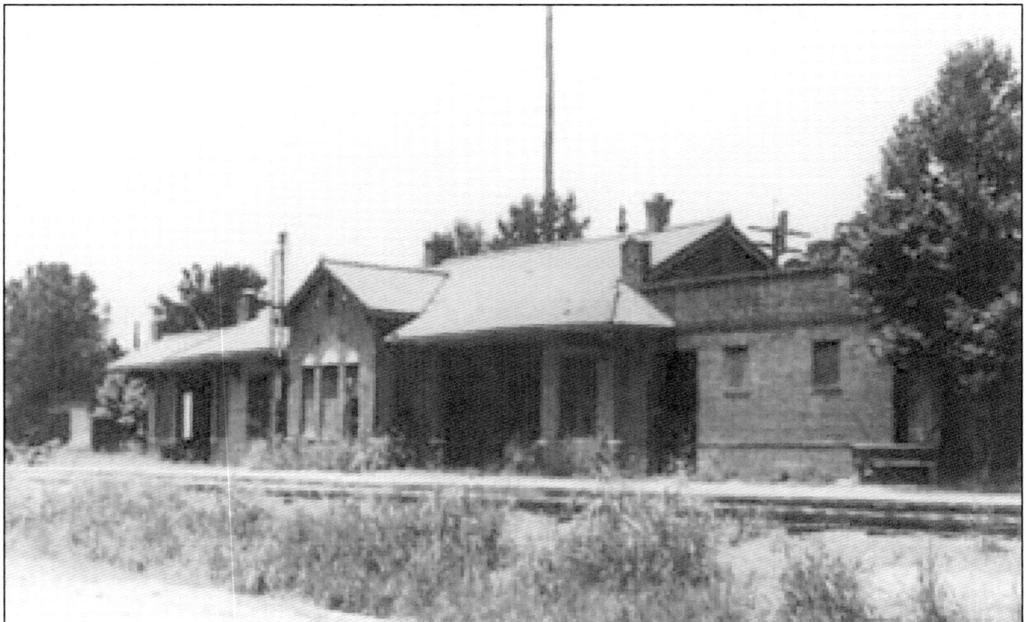

This photograph shows the newest of the Kansas City Southern Railway stations in Mansfield. There one could board a passenger train and travel south to either Beaumont or Port Arthur, or north Friarson, Shreveport, and as far as Kansas City. It is listed on the National Register of Historic Places but is in a decadent condition. (Courtesy of Liz Chrysler.)

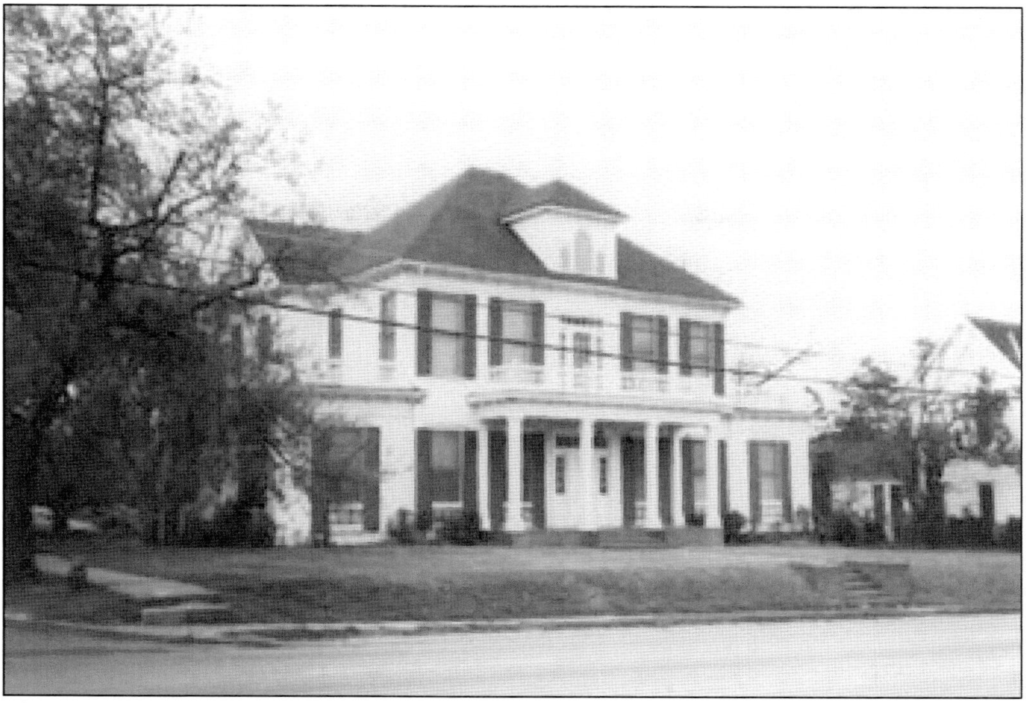

The Fraser home was built after the Civil War by Israel Brown (1819–1885) on Polk Street in Mansfield. The home remained in the same family and never changed hands. When the house was first built, hand-hewn sells, square nails, and wooden pegs were used. When the house was completed, it contained eight rooms and six fireplaces. When it was torn down in the late 1990s, it contained 19 rooms and four fireplaces. (Courtesy of Raymond W. Powell).

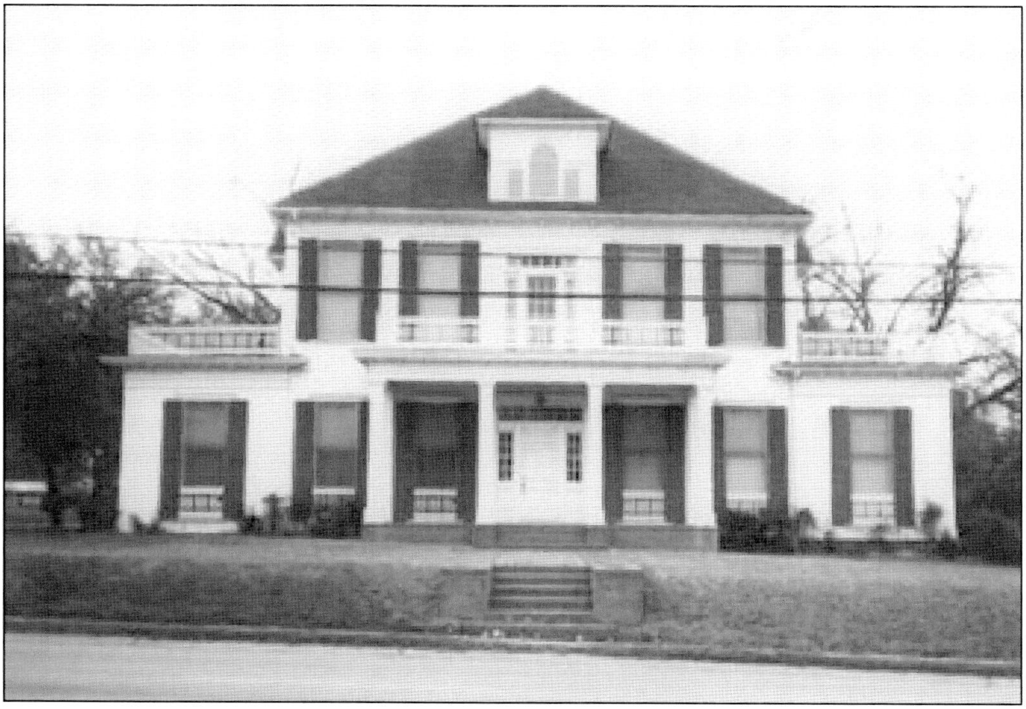

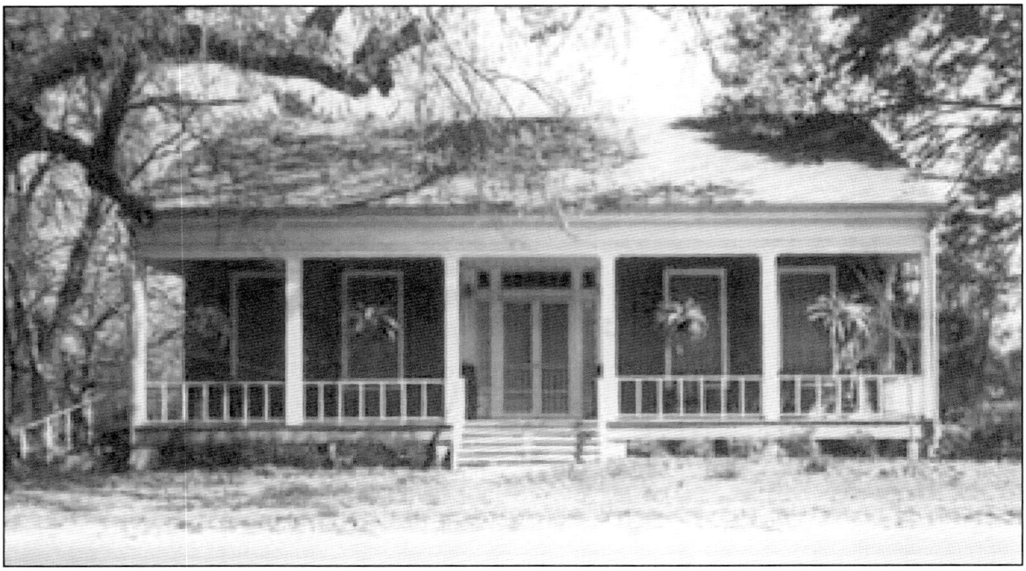

The Dillon House was built around 1882 by the Dillon family on Oxford Road. The house was constructed with wooden pegs and hand-hewn boards. Most of the woodwork has been plastered over, and the inside of the house has been refurbished. Oifilya Dillon was the last of the Dillons to live in the house. The house has had several owners since. Among them are Myron D. Walker and Hall Peyton. (Courtesy of Raymond W. Powell.)

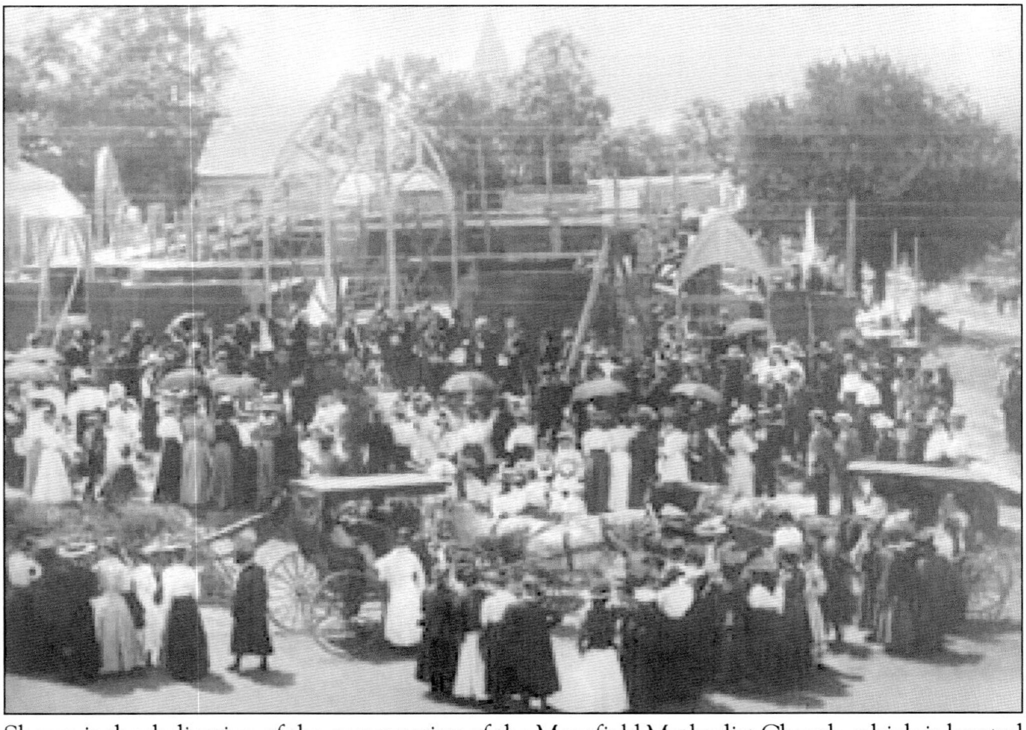

Shown is the dedication of the construction of the Mansfield Methodist Church, which is located on the corner of Polk and Monroe Street and is so close to the Mansfield Female College that one can only speculate that there would have been a close relationship between the two. (Photograph by McPherson Studios, courtesy of Raymond W. Powell.)

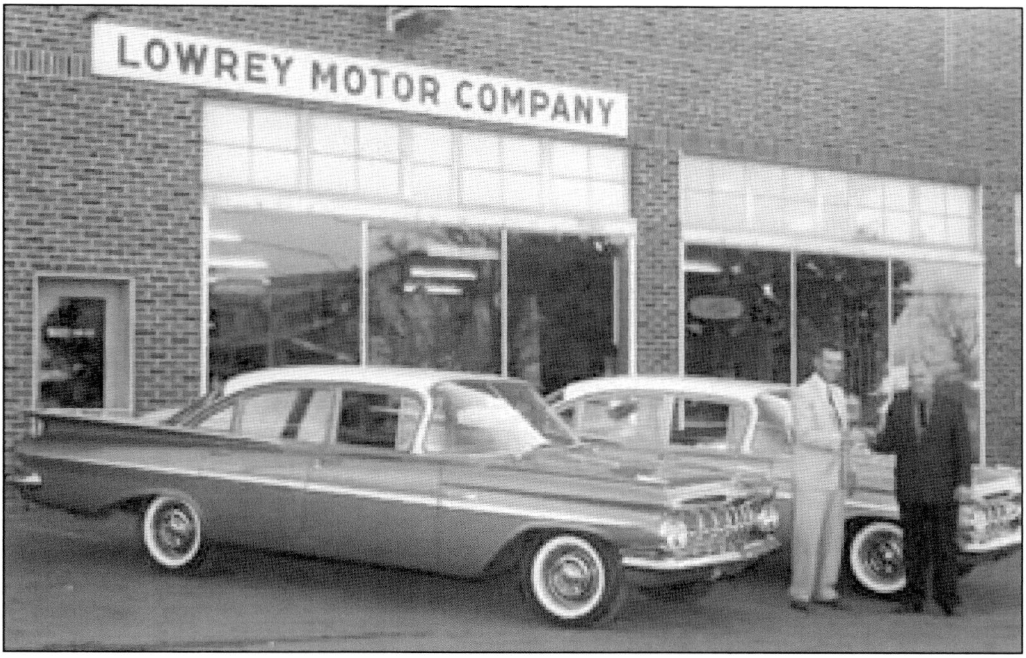

Lowery Motor Company in Mansfield was the only car dealership in the town. Shown here is a salesman who appears to be delighted to have just made a sale and a customer happy to have purchased a new car. The dealership was in operation until recent times at this location. (Photograph by McPherson Studios, courtesy of Raymond W. Powell.)

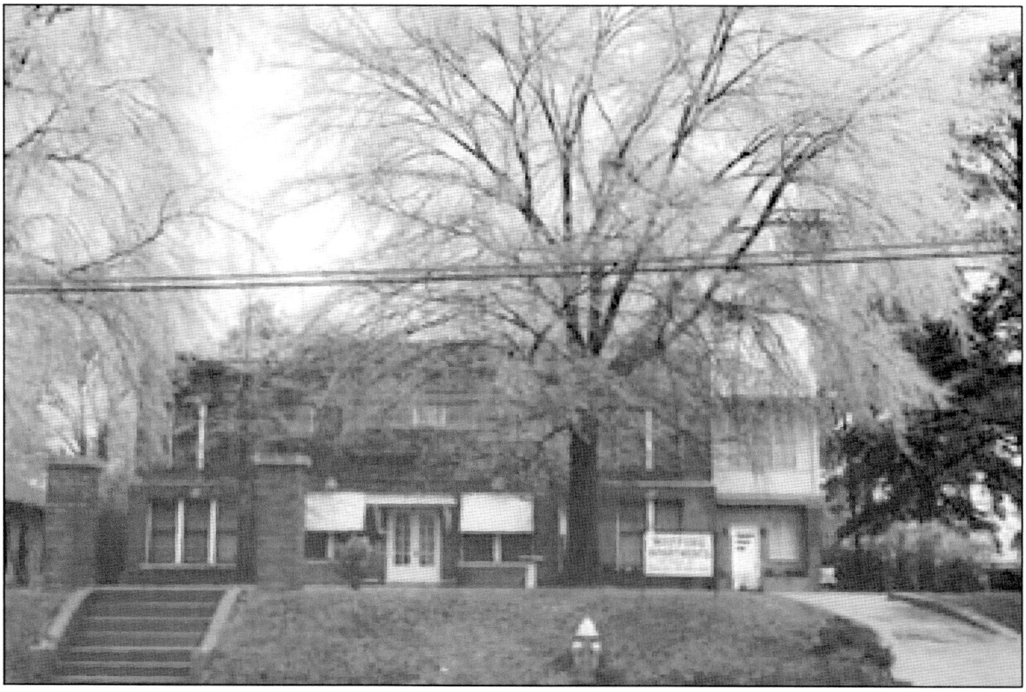

Here is an older Mansfield hospital building, which was of extreme significance to the town, as one can imagine. A much newer facility exists at the present and provides complete hospital facilities. (Photograph by McPherson Studios, courtesy of Raymond W. Powell.)

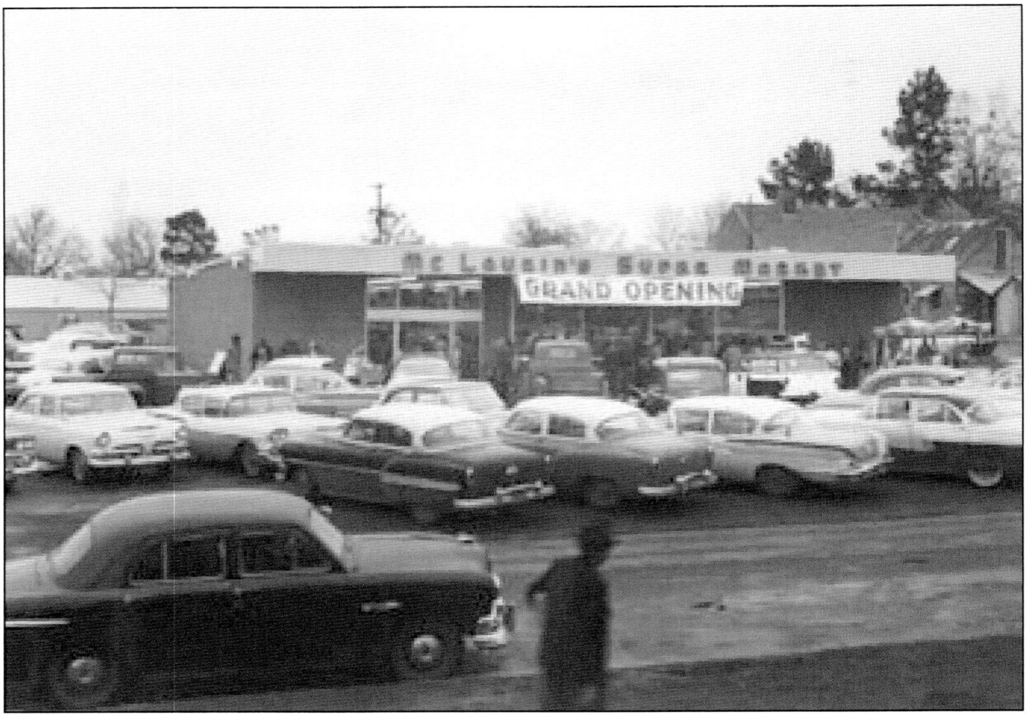

A grocery store opening, like a bank opening, was a grand affair. Pictured here is the opening day of McLaurin's Super Market on Polk Street. (Photograph by McPherson Studios, courtesy of Raymond W. Powell.)

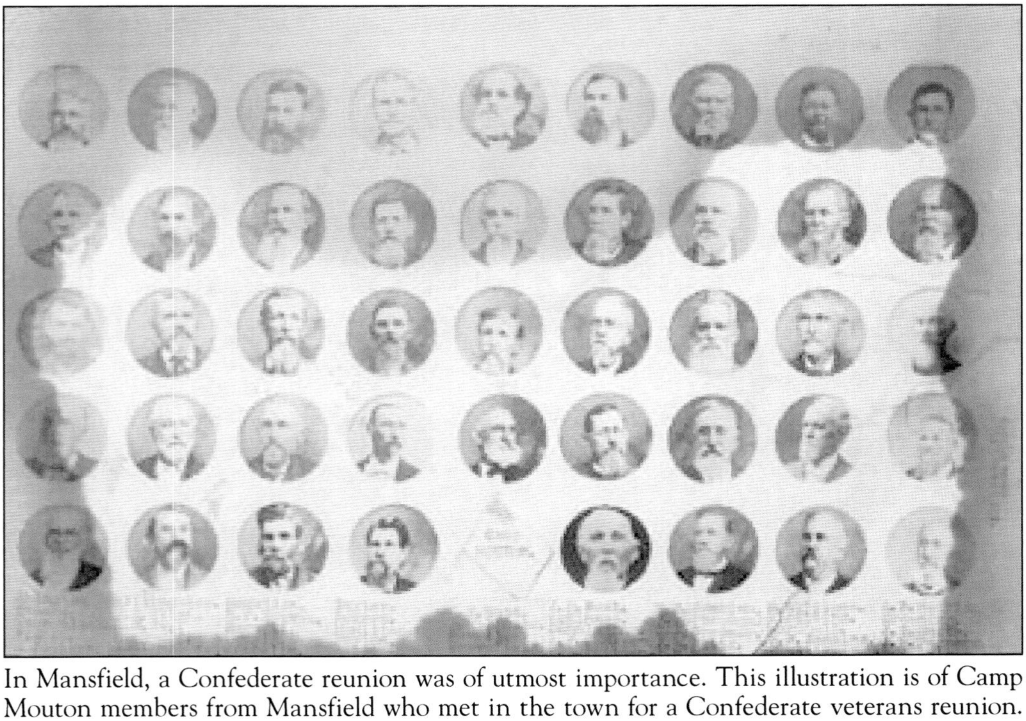

In Mansfield, a Confederate reunion was of utmost importance. This illustration is of Camp Mouton members from Mansfield who met in the town for a Confederate veterans reunion. (Photograph by McPherson Studios, courtesy of Raymond W. Powell.)

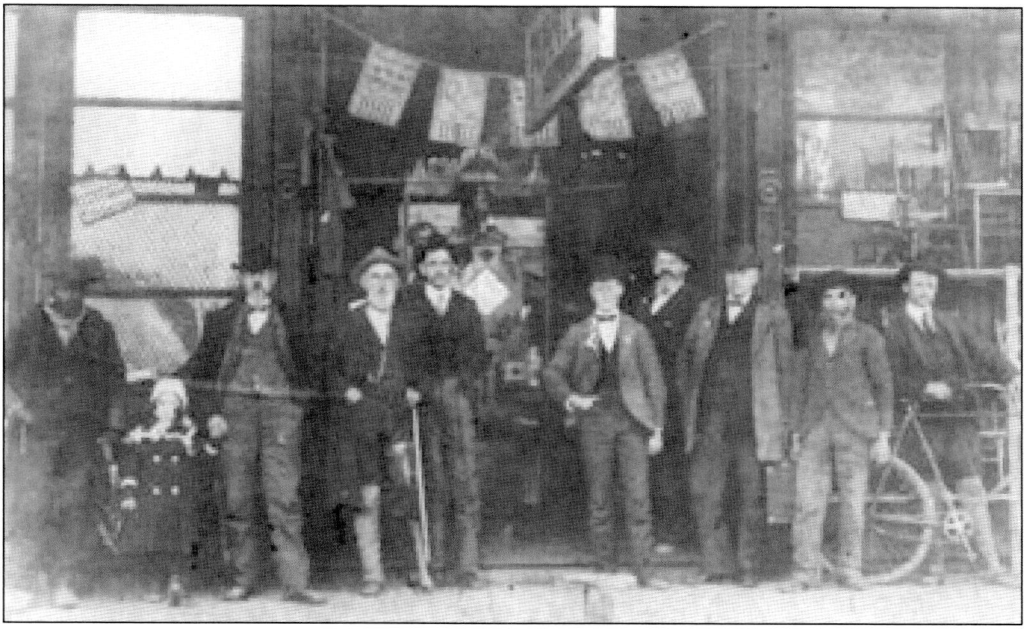

Apparently Jackson & Kidd Hardware in Mansfield, shown in the 1890s, had constructed a new building. From the looks of the merchandise in this illustration, the store sold just about everything, as did all small town stores. If they did not have it in stock, they would easily order it. (Courtesy of Louisiana State University in Shreveport, Noel Memorial Library, Archives and Special Collections.)

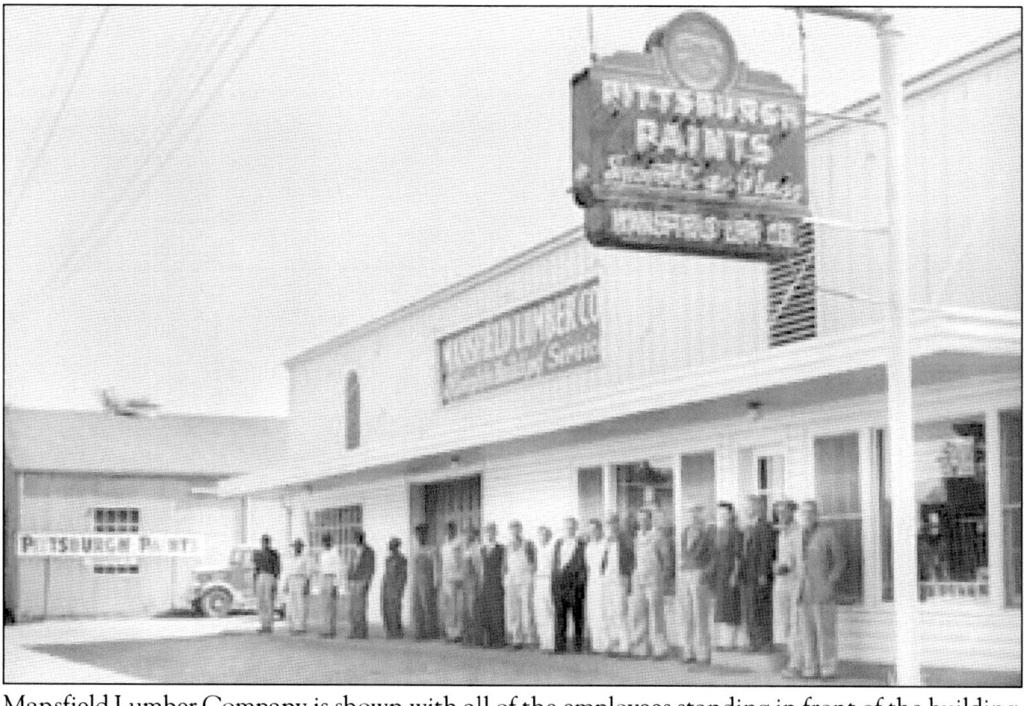

Mansfield Lumber Company is shown with all of the employees standing in front of the building. The Mansfield Lumber was in the 1100 block of Polk Street where Dr. Rew's (dentist) office is currently located. (Photograph by McPherson Studios, courtesy of Raymond W. Powell.)

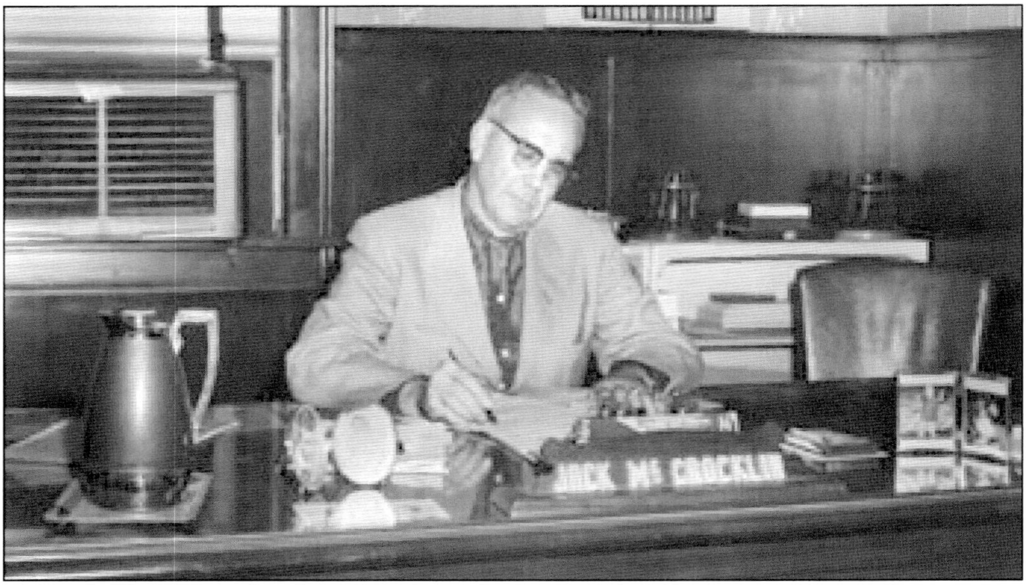

Jack McCrocklin, president of Mansfield Lumber Company, is shown at his desk. He was originally from South Mansfield. (Photograph by McPherson Studios, courtesy of Raymond W. Powell.)

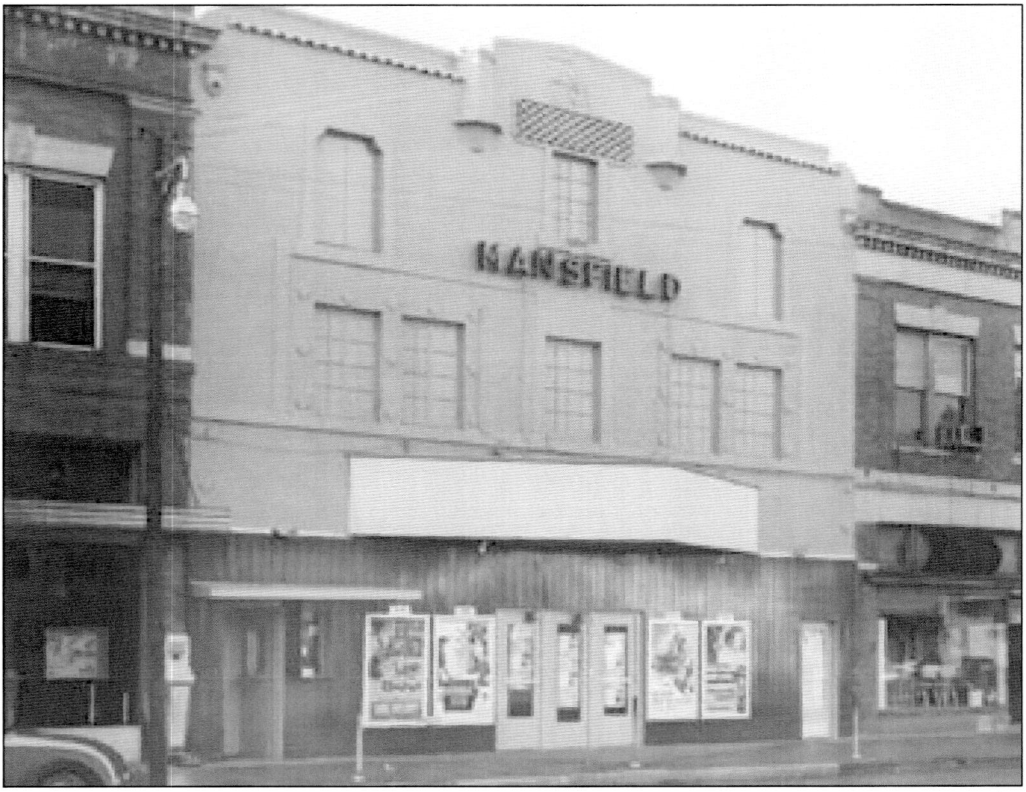

The Mansfield Theatre, the town movie theater, is shown in this photograph. It is located on the southern side of Texas Street across from the courthouse and still stands. Many citizens today have fond memories of the one movie theater in the town. (Photograph by McPherson Studios, courtesy of Raymond W. Powell.)

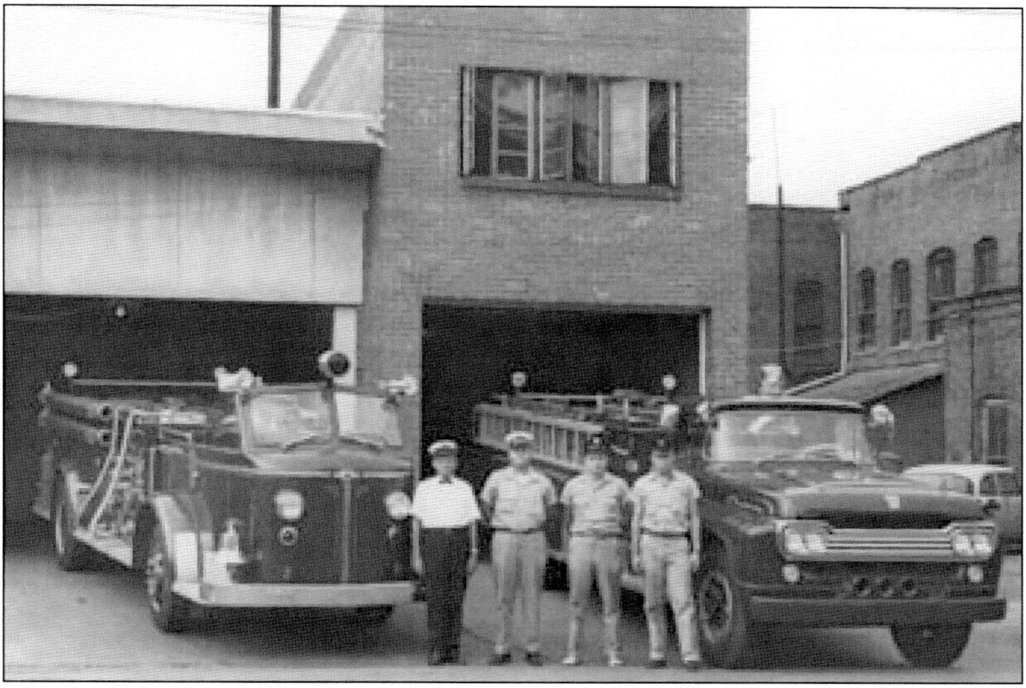

The Mansfield Fire Department is shown in this image, perhaps during an event for the purpose of displaying their engines and station. It was located on Texas Street behind the city hall. (Photograph by McPherson Studios, courtesy of Raymond W. Powell.)

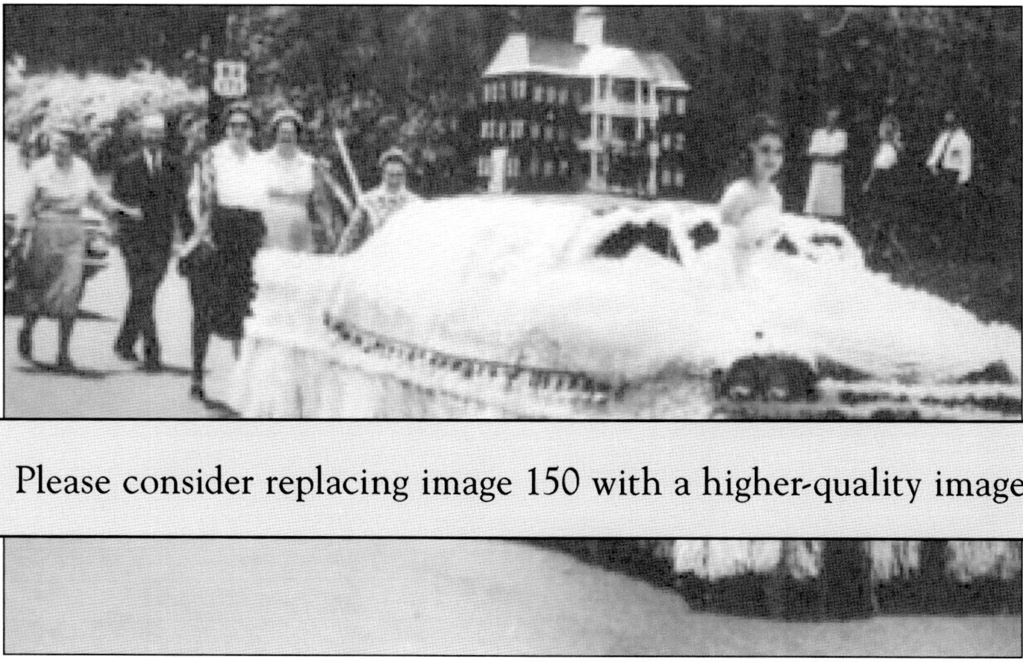

A parade was always a big event in any small town. Shown here is a group of ladies, probably graduates of Mansfield Female College, which had closed in 1934, keeping alive the memories of their college. They had constructed a model of the college for this float. (Photograph by McPherson Studios, courtesy of Raymond W. Powell.)

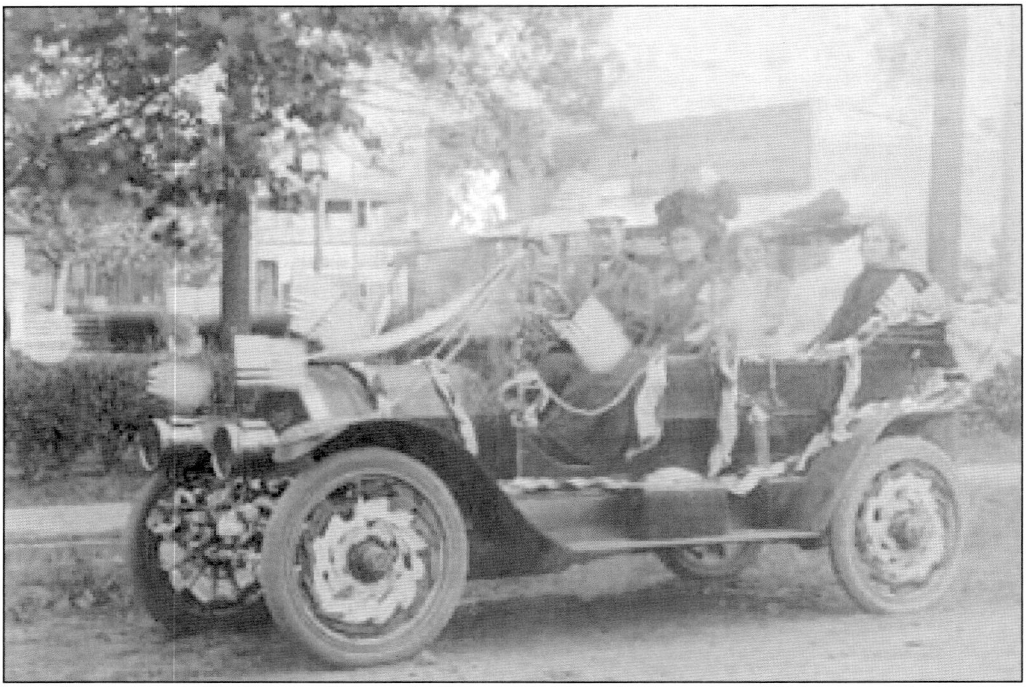

Mansfield ladies and gentlemen decorated their car for the Fourth of July and drove around town. They are Walter Anderson, Mary Lizzie Pegues Storey, India Cook Enloe, Cora Pegues, and Carolyn Nabors. This appears to be near the courthouse square. (Courtesy of Raymond W. Powell.)

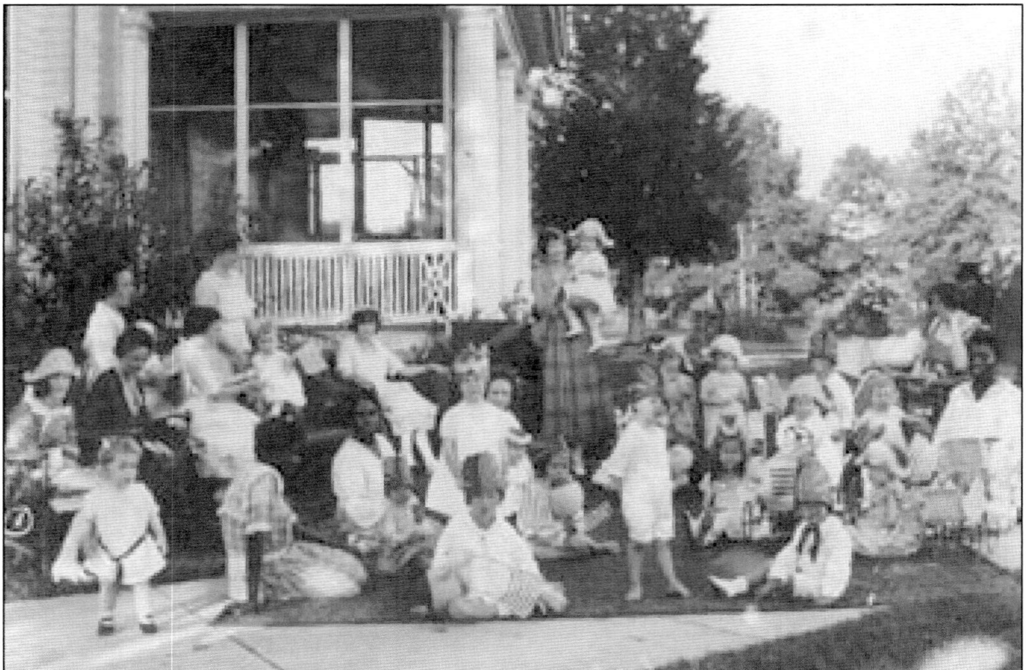

These residents of Mansfield dressed their children for the Fourth of July party in a town always ready to celebrate the occasion in a big way. Fortunately, the occasion was of enough importance that this photograph was taken in front of the party givers' home. (Courtesy of Raymond W. Powell.)

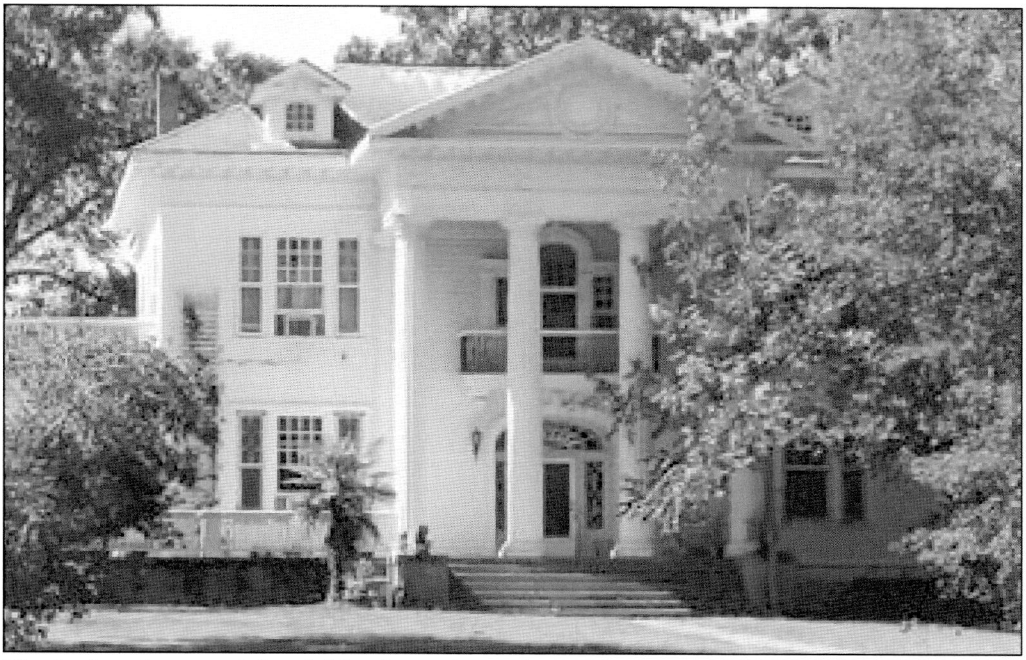

The Jenkins home in Mansfield is located on a large spacious area of land, almost like a town park. It was built by Ned Walter Jenkins in the 1890s. Mrs. Ned Walter Jenkins was one of the organizers of the Mansfield chapter of the United Daughters of the Confederacy, an organization very active in the establishment of the Mansfield Battle Park and responsible for the erection of several of the monuments there. One time the Princess and Prince de Polignac were returning to the site of the Battle of Mansfield, and all of the magnolia trees had died. Mrs. Jenkins, afraid that they would notice this, sent her husband out into the woods to cut down some magnolia trees and stick them in the ground. That evening, the Princess and Prince de Polignac were entertained at the Jenkins home. A descendant, Right Reverend Charles Jenkins, recently retired as bishop of the Episcopal Diocese of Louisiana. (Courtesy of George Meriwether Gilmer Jr.)

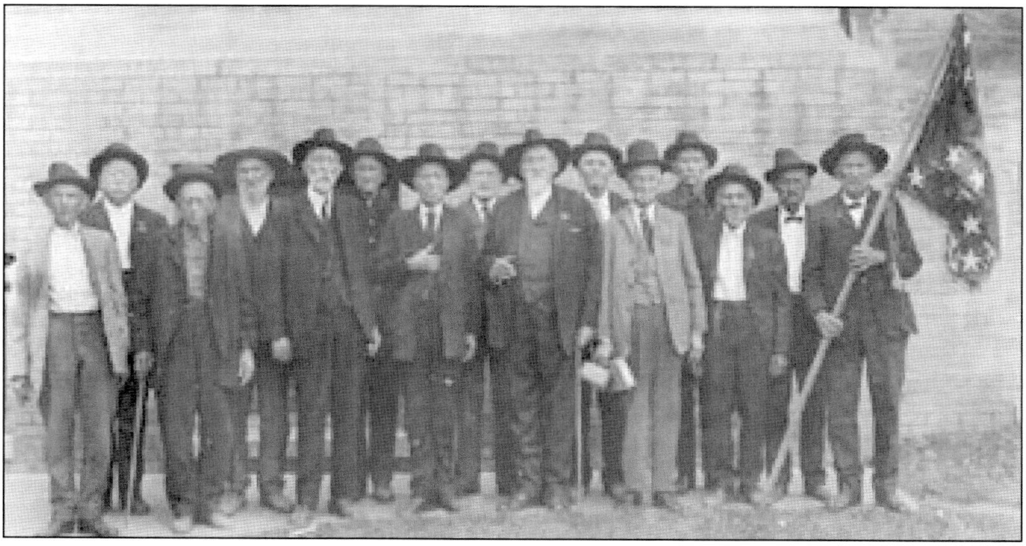

Pictured is another Confederate veterans reunion at Mansfield. These were very important occasions for the veterans. (Photograph by McPherson Studios, courtesy of Raymond W. Powell.)

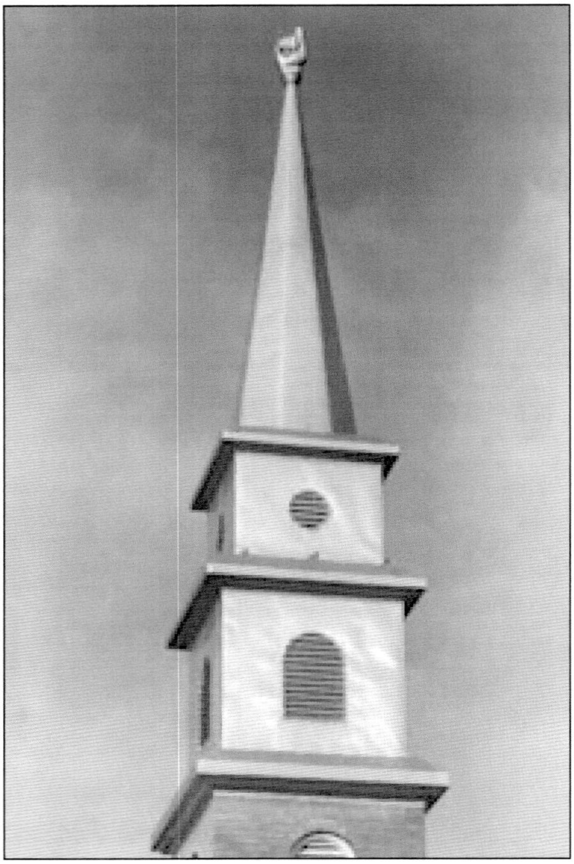

Shown is the steeple on the Southside Baptist Church in Mansfield, similar to the popular church steeple in Port Gibson, Mississippi, with hand and finger pointing to the sky. (Photograph by McPherson Studios, courtesy of Raymond W. Powell.)

Here is a signboard advertising Ruffin Brothers Grocery Store, which was located in downtown Mansfield on Polk Street. (Photograph by McPherson Studios, courtesy of Raymond W. Powell.)

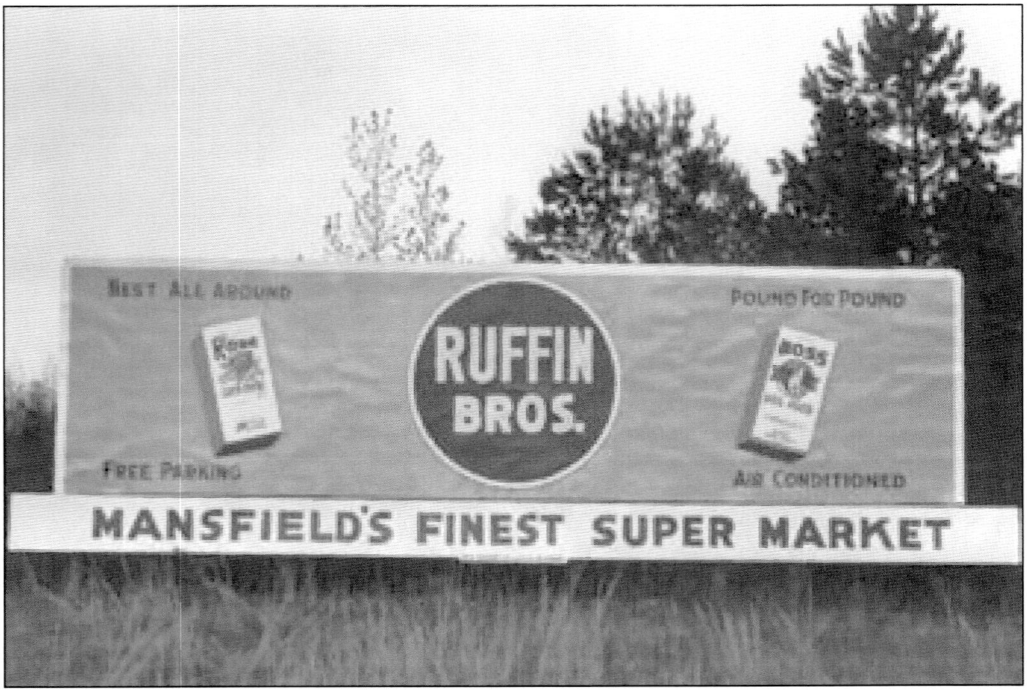

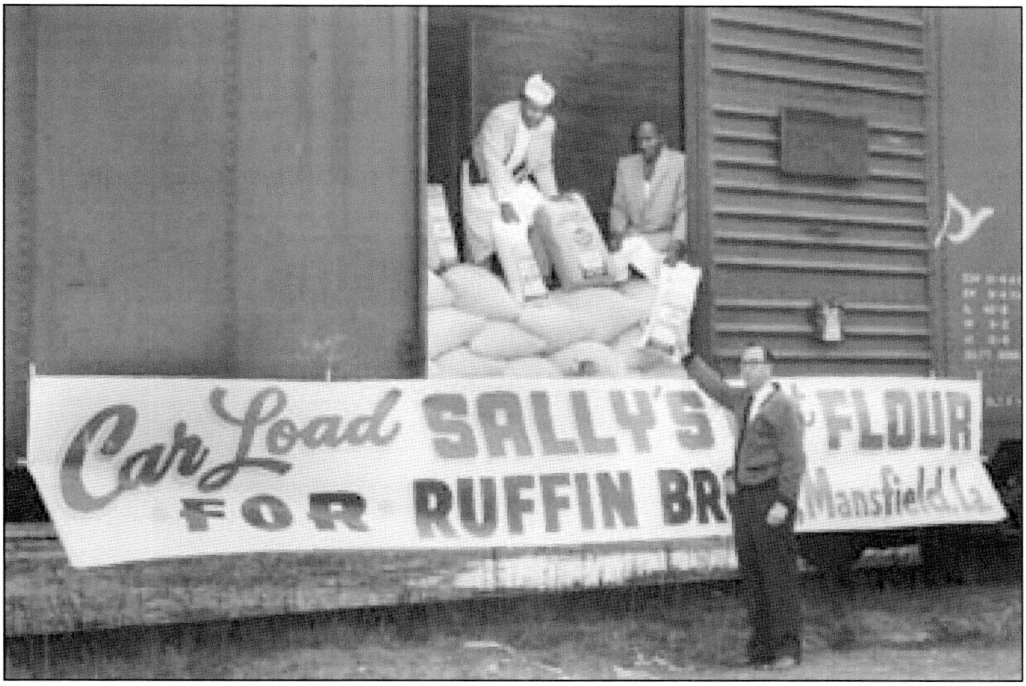

A carload of Sally's Flour for Ruffin Brothers Grocery Store is shown being unloaded from the boxcar. (Photograph by McPherson Studios, courtesy of Raymond W. Powell.)

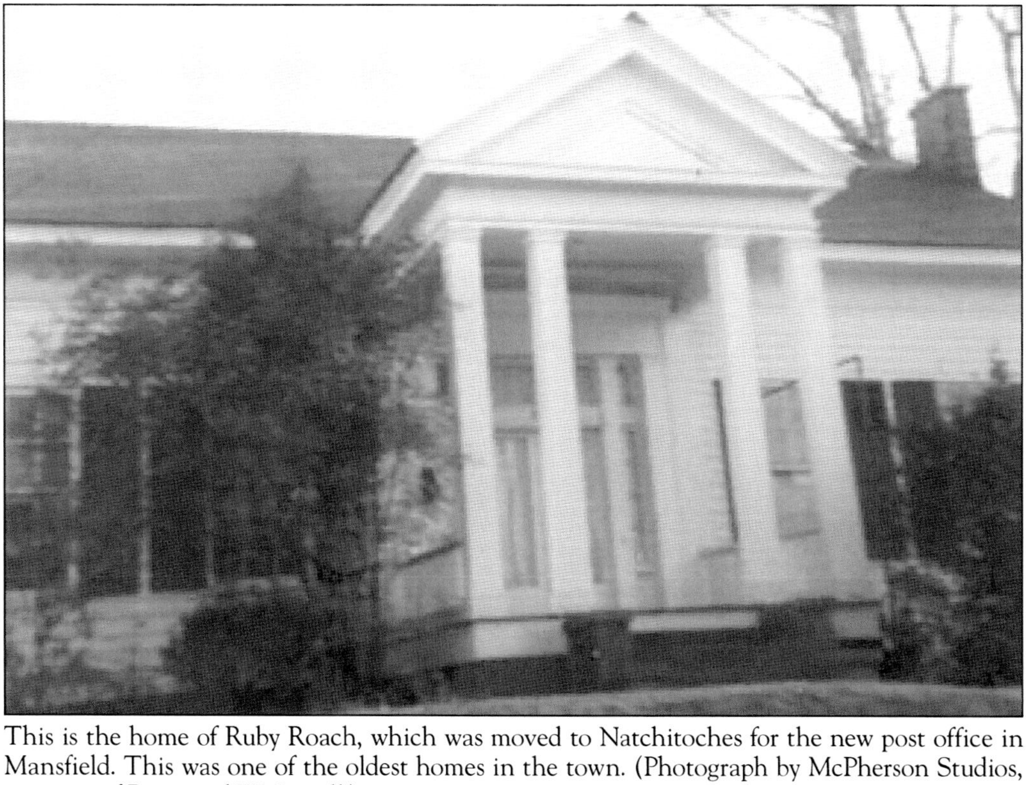
This is the home of Ruby Roach, which was moved to Natchitoches for the new post office in Mansfield. This was one of the oldest homes in the town. (Photograph by McPherson Studios, courtesy of Raymond W. Powell.)

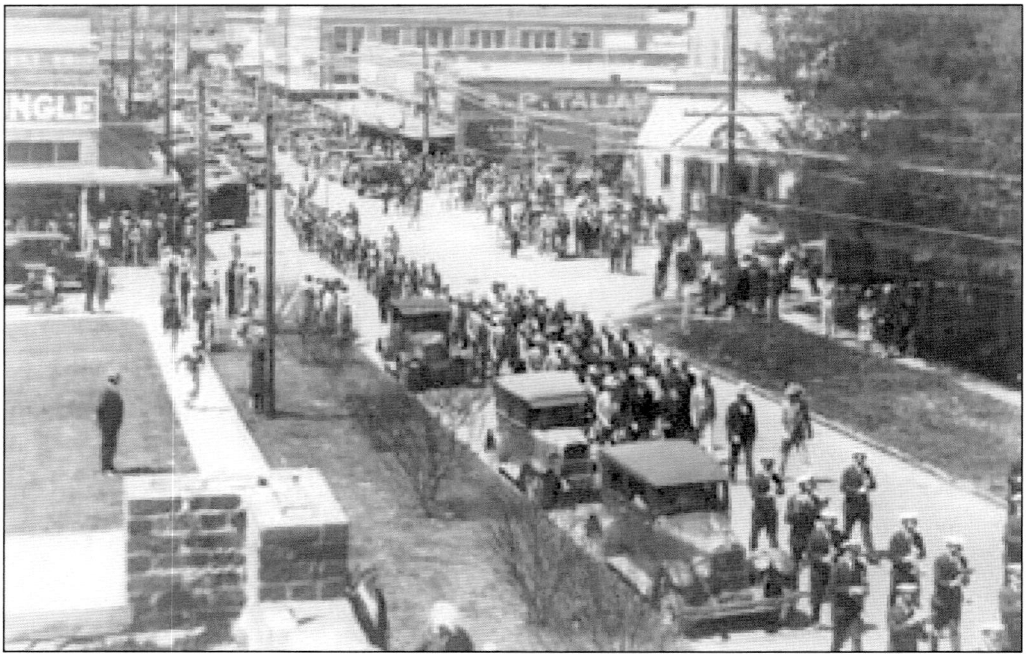

Here is another parade down Polk Street in Mansfield. This image gives the viewer an idea of what a prosperous downtown once existed in this southern town. When a parade passes by in Mansfield, all turn out to celebrate the event. (Courtesy of Louisiana State University in Shreveport, Noel Memorial Library, Archives and Special Collections.)

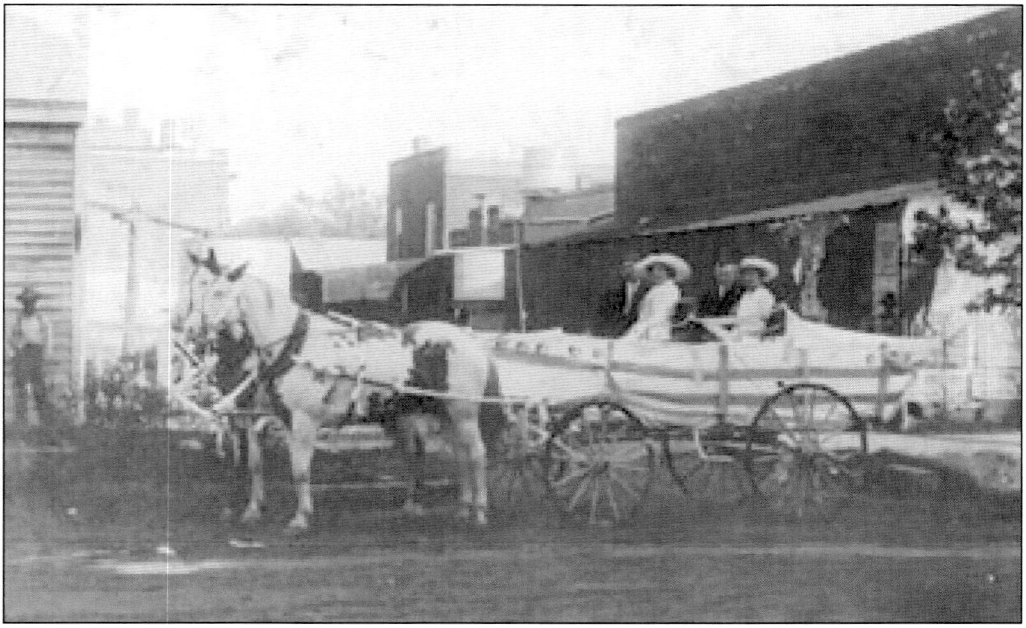

A wagon group in Mansfield is shown in this image. It is not known if the group was in a parade or dressed up for a special event, a visit to town from the countryside, or even church on Sunday, but from the appearance in the image they certainly drew a spectator or two. The riders are Mrs. J.A. Enloe, Jack Enloe, India Cook, Nelwyn Williams, and McHenry Nabors. (Photograph by E. E. George, courtesy of Raymond W. Powell.)

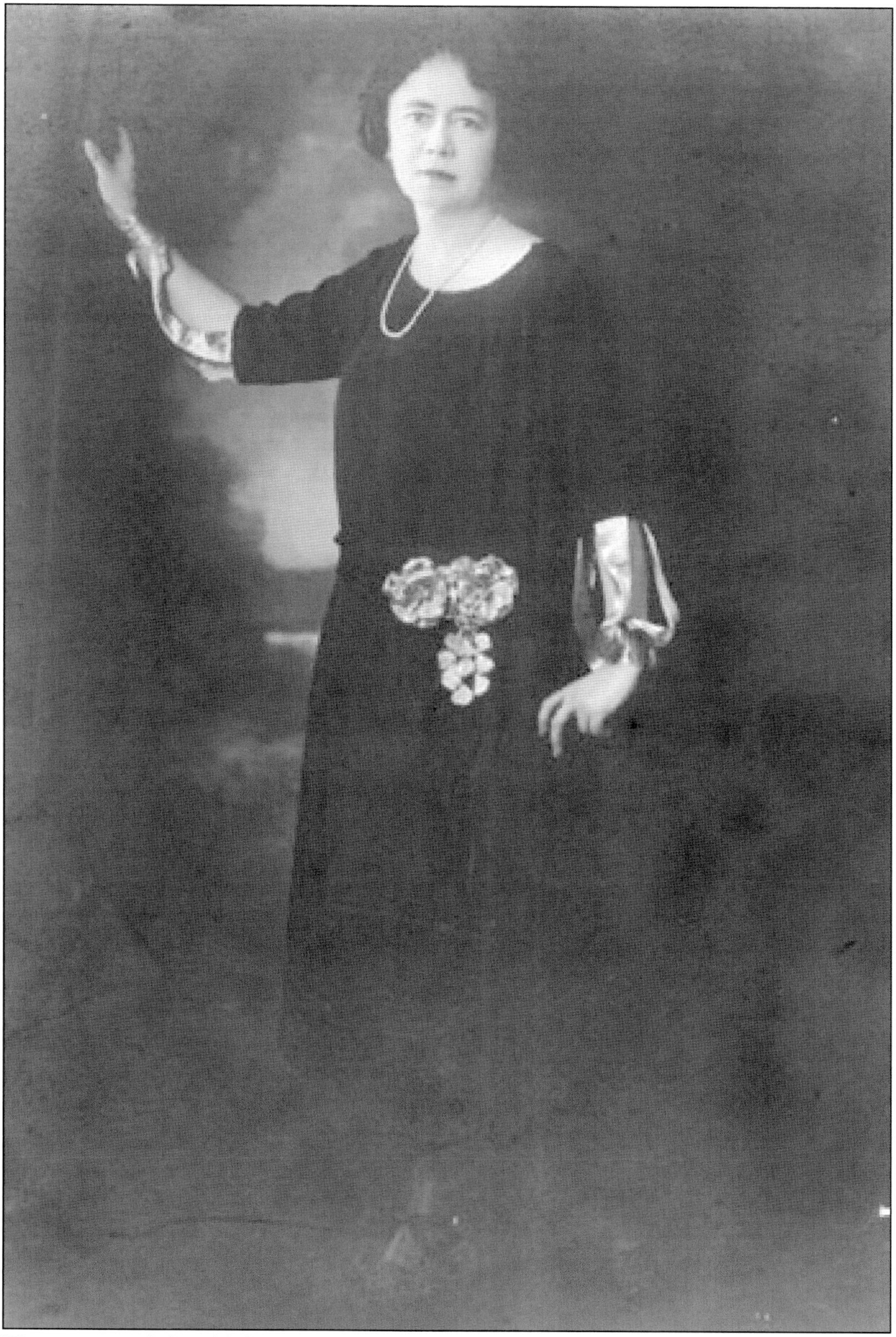

This attractive lady is likely a member of the Enloe family. (Courtesy of Raymond W. Powell.)

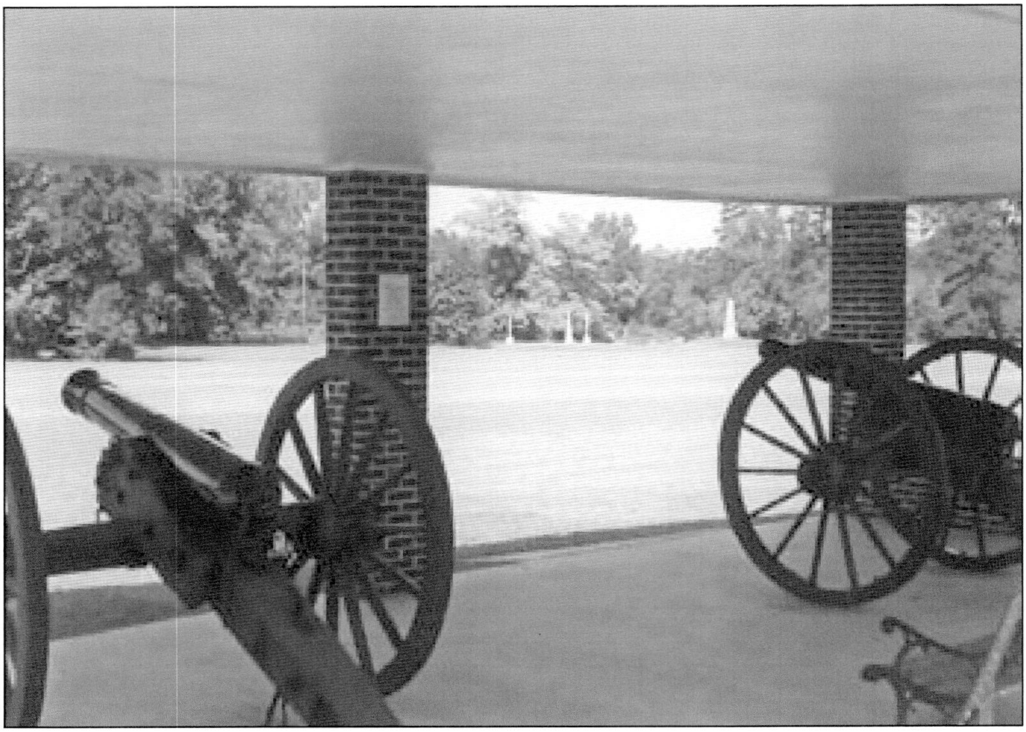

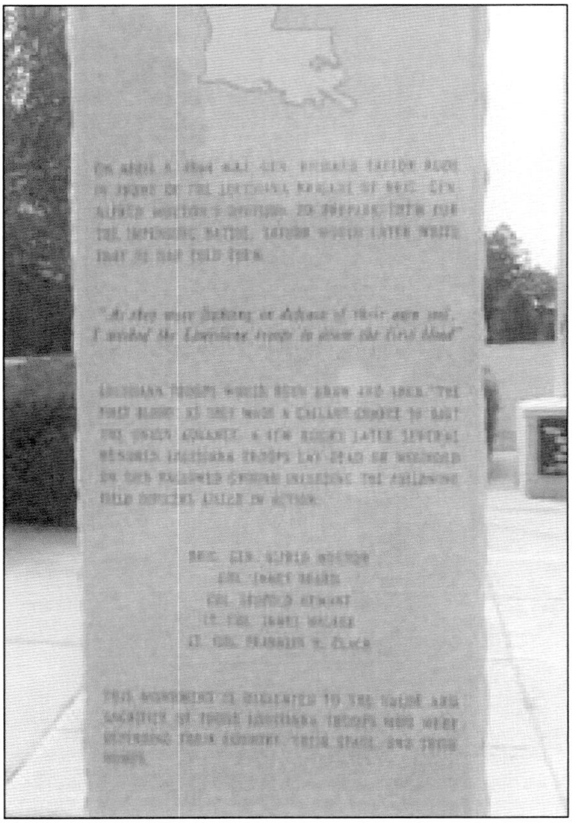

The Mansfield Battle Park plays a large role in the activities that occur in the area. Shown are the Val Verde cannon displayed at the park. (Photograph by George Meriwether Gilmer Jr.)

This illustration is of the Louisiana monument on the battlegrounds. It is dedicated to all Louisiana troops defending their homeland and in memory of Brig. Gen. Alfred Mouton, Col. James Beard, Col. Leopold Armant, Lt. Col. James Walker, and Lt. Col. Franklin Clack. (Photograph by George Meriwether Gilmer Jr.)

Six

Along Came the Railroads

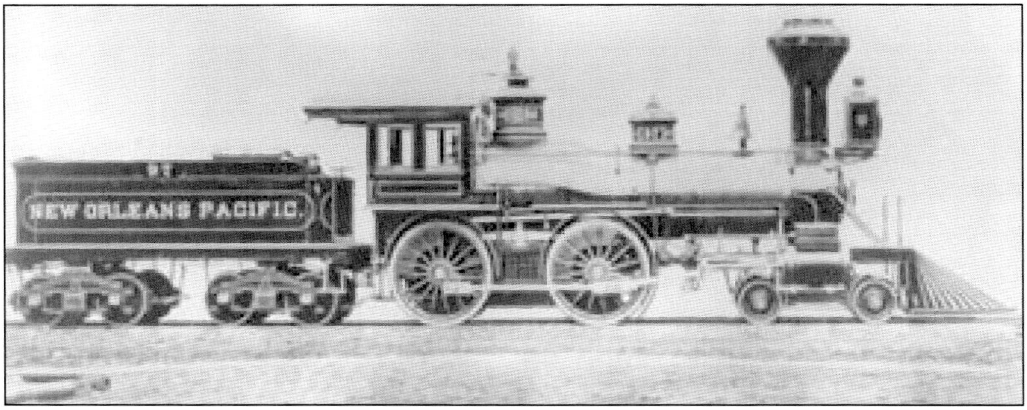

Rural outreaches of the southern frontier like DeSoto Parish long depended on crude wagon trails, small streams, and bayous to transport commodities like corn and cotton to markets abroad. North Louisiana farmers and planters, desperate for a more reliable means of transportation, vociferously clamored for railroads. Finally, the railroads came to DeSoto Parish, changing its entire settlement patterns. Pictured is an 1875 engine from the New Orleans Pacific. (Courtesy of Al Malone.)

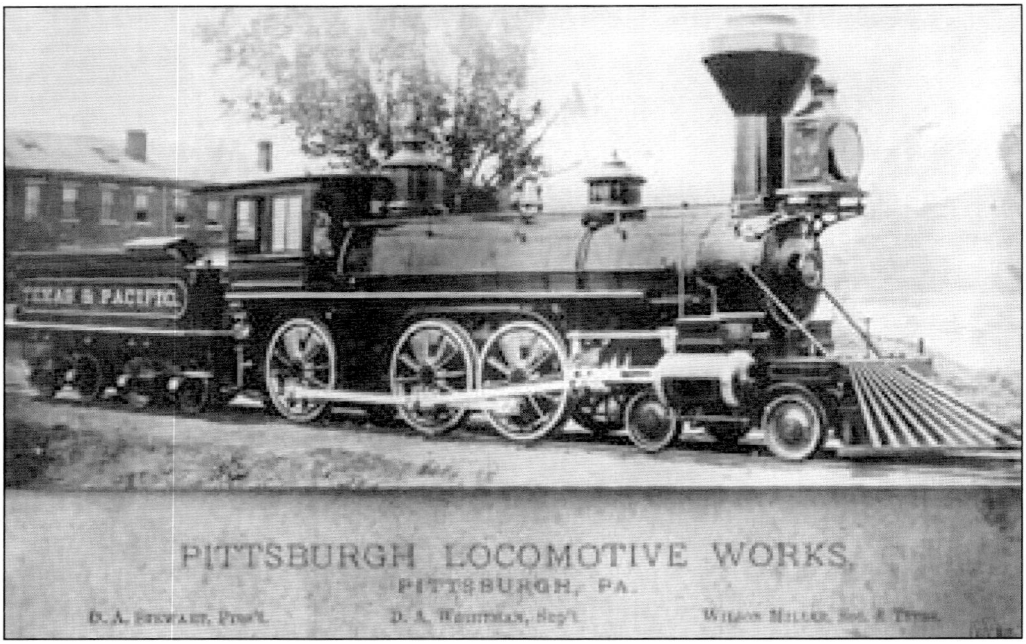

Shown is a Texas and Pacific Railway locomotive, Engine No.76, 4-6-0 type, D-2 class, Pittsburgh Locomotive Works in Pittsburgh, Pennsylvania. This is the type of locomotive (if not the exact one) that operated over the entire Texas and Pacific line and might have pulled the first train of cars from El Paso through South Mansfield and on to New Orleans. (Courtesy DeGolyer Library, Southern Methodist University.)

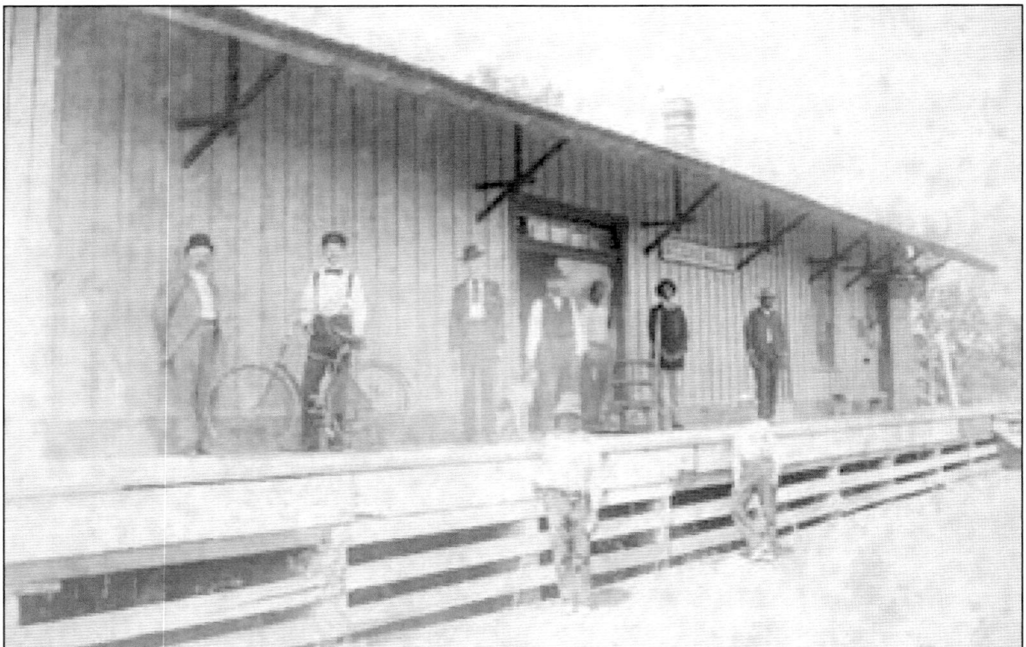

The Texas and Pacific Railway station at Stonewall is shown around 1890. The Stonewall station was constructed in 1881, and the town was named for Stonewall Jackson by the railroad. (Courtesy Curtis McCune.)

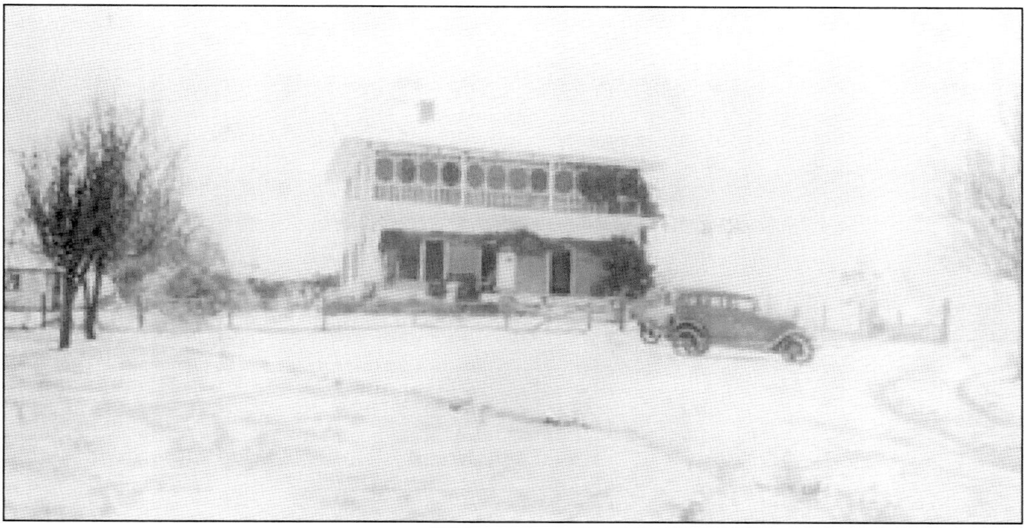

Pictured is the Gilmer home at Stonewall, and it is still a functioning farm. Mary Moseley and William Lewis Gilmer operated a dairy and creamery business and a general store named Rosehill Dairy. The Gilmers' various enterprises were located near the farm just west of the Texas and Pacific Railway (Courtesy of George Meriwether Gilmer Jr.)

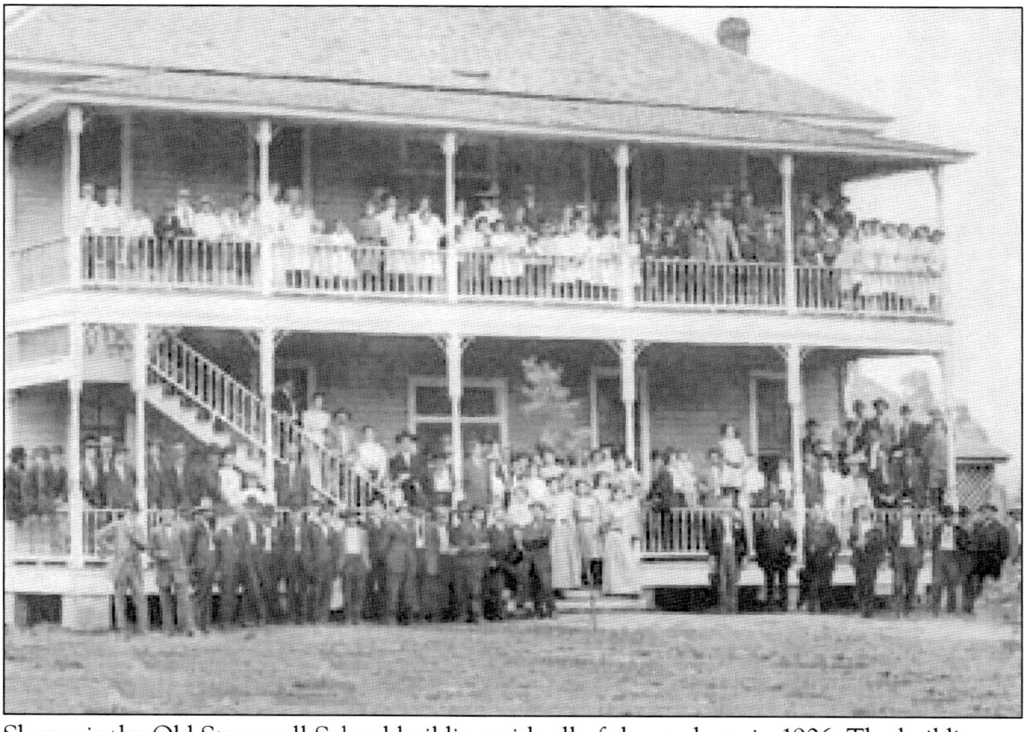

Shown is the Old Stonewall School building with all of the students in 1906. The building no longer stands. (Courtesy of Curtis McCune.)

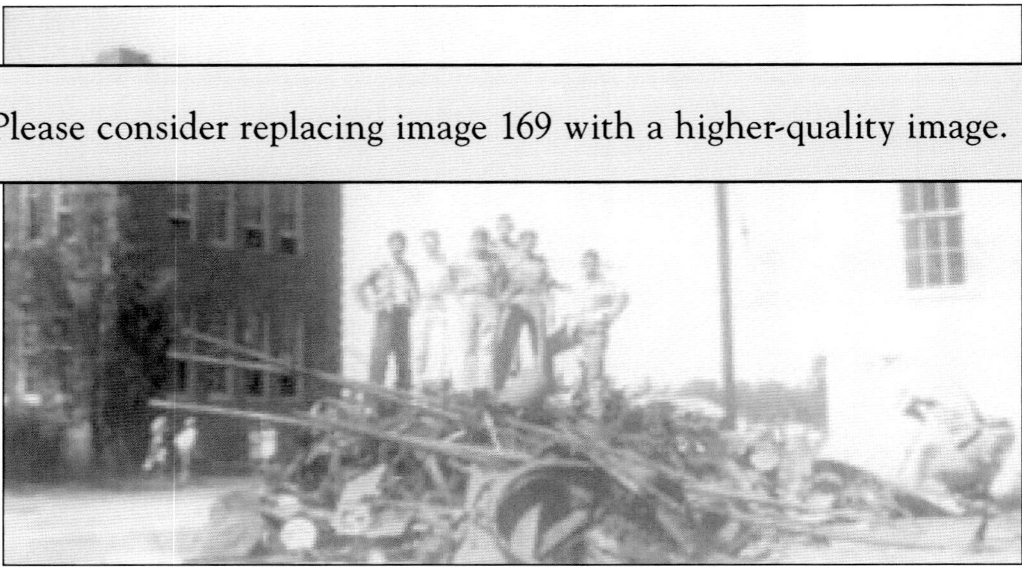

Pictured is Stonewall High School in 1943. This was during World War II, and the entire DeSoto Parish was scoured for scrap iron. For their part of the war effort, the students collected scrap iron, and they are proudly displaying it in front of their high school building. (Courtesy of George Meriwether Gilmer Jr.)

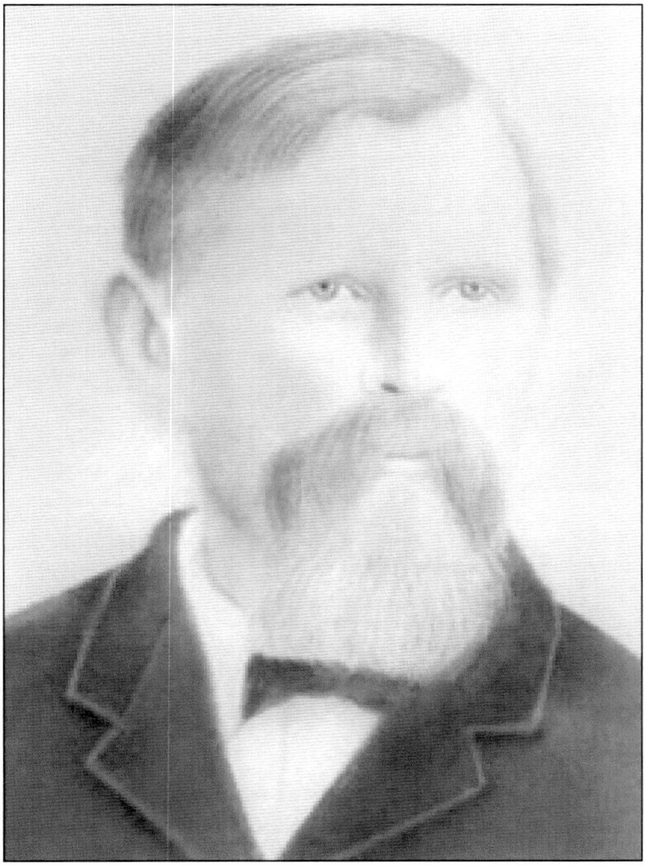

Shown is William Lewis Gilmer, husband of Mary Mosely Gilmer. He served on the DeSoto Parish School Board until his death September 22, 1915. He always worked diligently to improve education for the children of the community. It is said that he knew and called by name every child that attended Stonewall School. In 1924, students honored his memory by dedicating their yearbook to him. (Courtesy of George Meriwether Gilmer Jr.)

Mary Wortley Moseley married William Lewis Gilmer in the Keachie Methodist Church on January 2, 1896. She is shown with two of her children, George Meriwether Gilmer and Mary Wortley Gilmer. She served as Stonewall postmaster in 1914, continuing to hold that position for the next 12 years. (Courtesy of George Meriwether Gilmer Jr.)

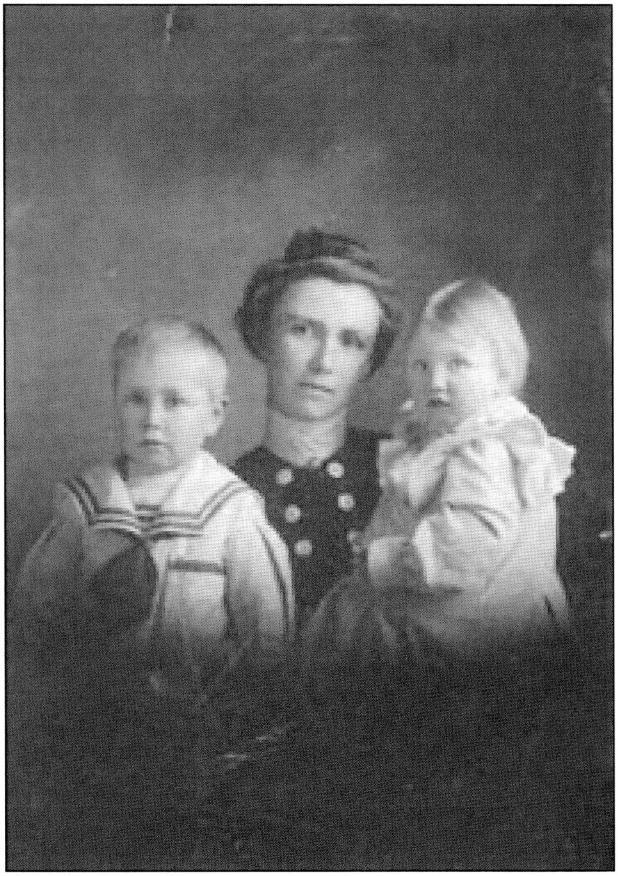

George Meriwether Gilmer is shown standing between two horses around 1910. (Courtesy of George Meriwether Gilmer Jr.)

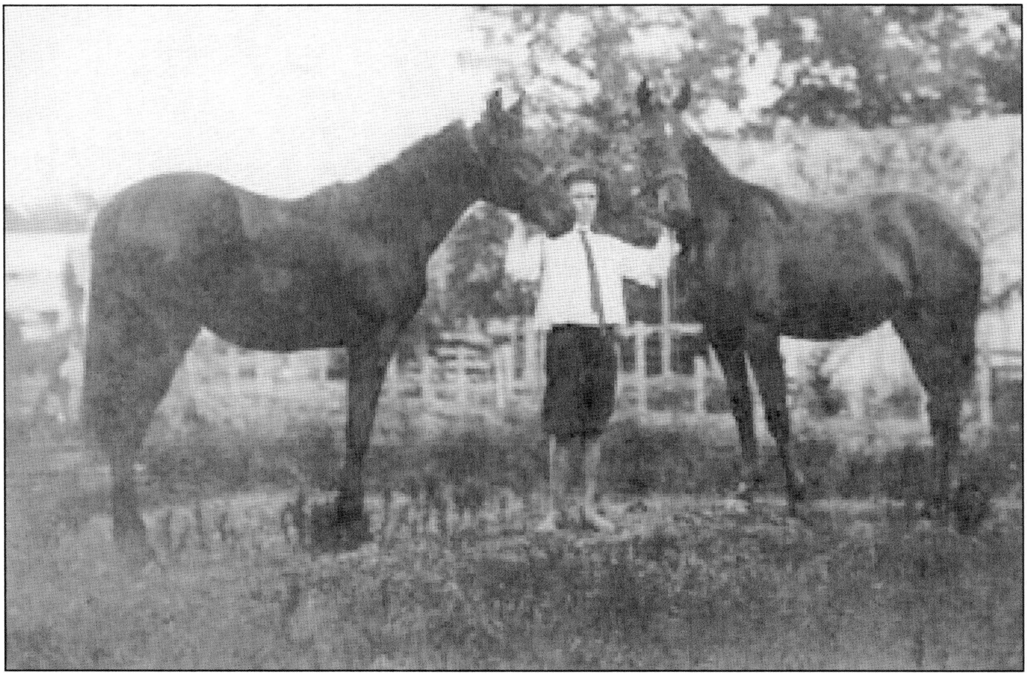

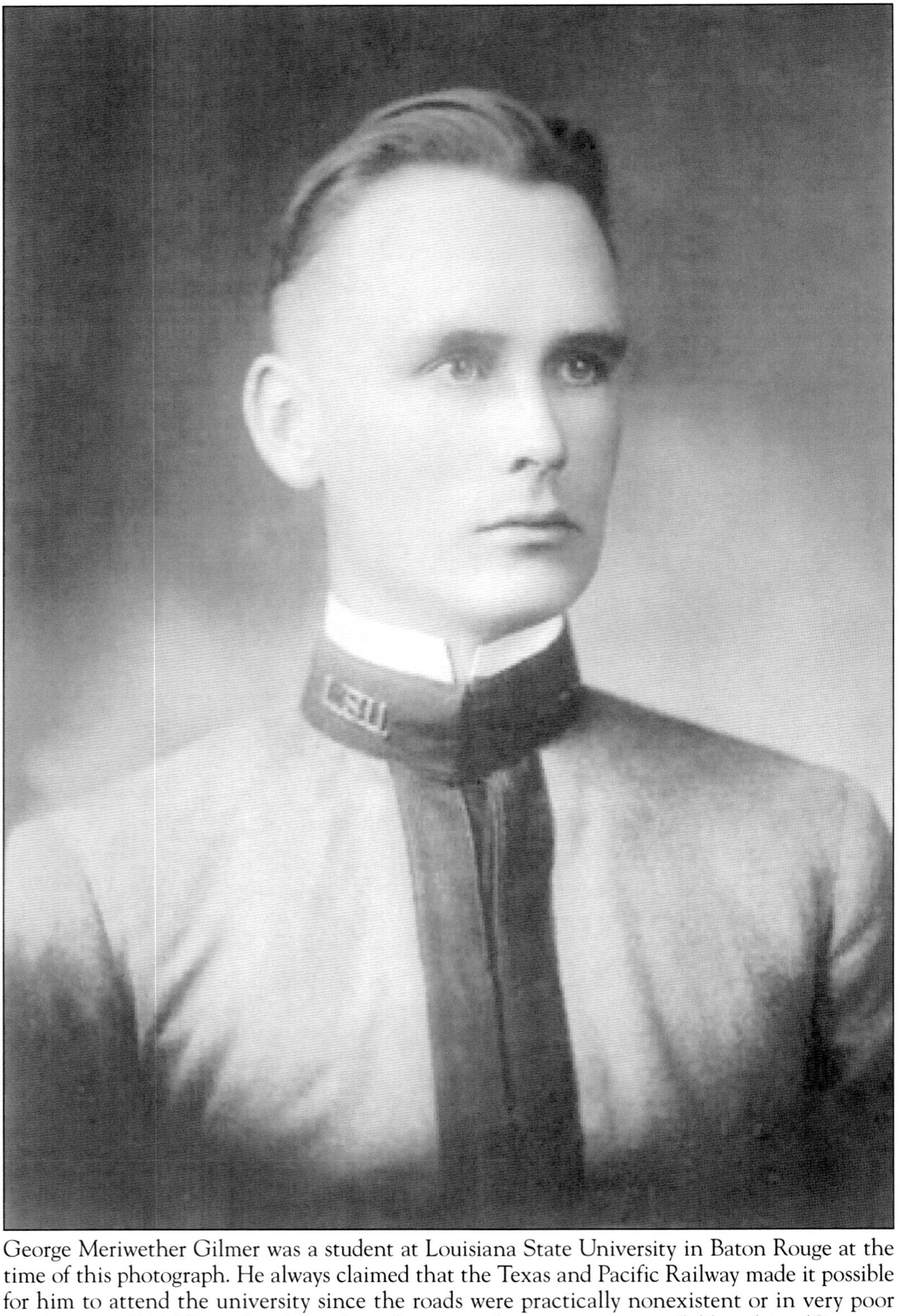

George Meriwether Gilmer was a student at Louisiana State University in Baton Rouge at the time of this photograph. He always claimed that the Texas and Pacific Railway made it possible for him to attend the university since the roads were practically nonexistent or in very poor condition in 1914. The railroad was the only means of transportation available to him. (Courtesy of George Meriwether Gilmer Jr.)

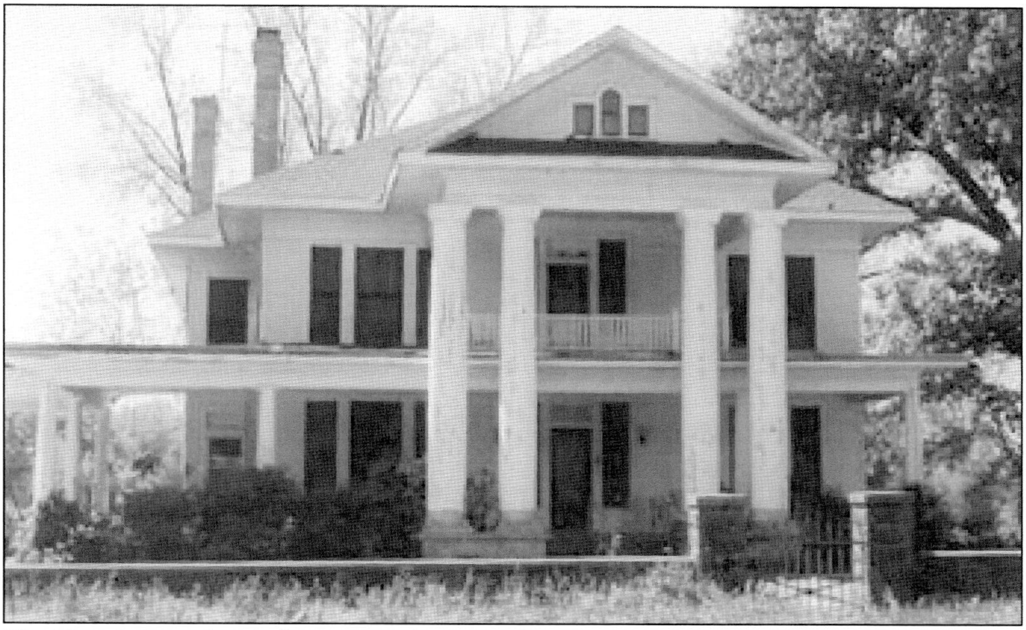

The New Orleans Pacific built its track on to Gloster, where this beautiful two-story home was constructed by Mason Dowling in the early 20th century. It has four huge columns rising from ground level, and a wide veranda expands across the front and continues around one side, where it turns into a porte-cochere (covered driveway). Chimneys frame either end of the mansion with fireplaces in the parlor, the dining room, and two of the upstairs bedrooms. A finely detailed wood staircase landing stands as a focal point in the front parlor directly across from the main doorway. (Photograph by Vicki Gourley.)

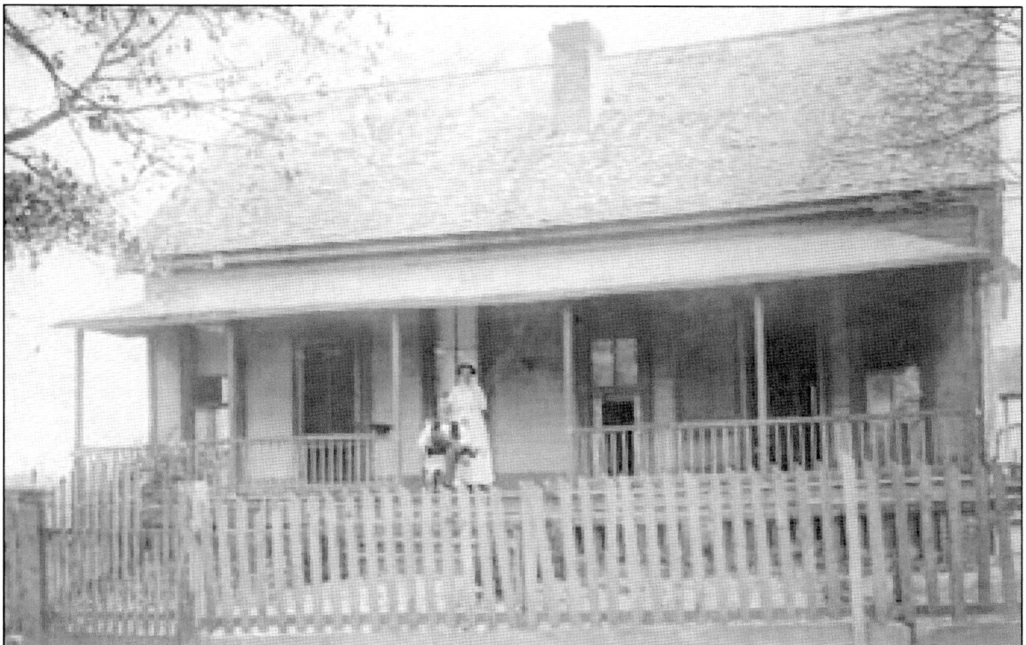

Robert Baldwin Burford and Blanche Rogers Burford are shown on their front porch around 1910. The home was in "downtown" Gloster in DeSoto Parish, Louisiana. (Courtesy of Libby Dady Alcorn.)

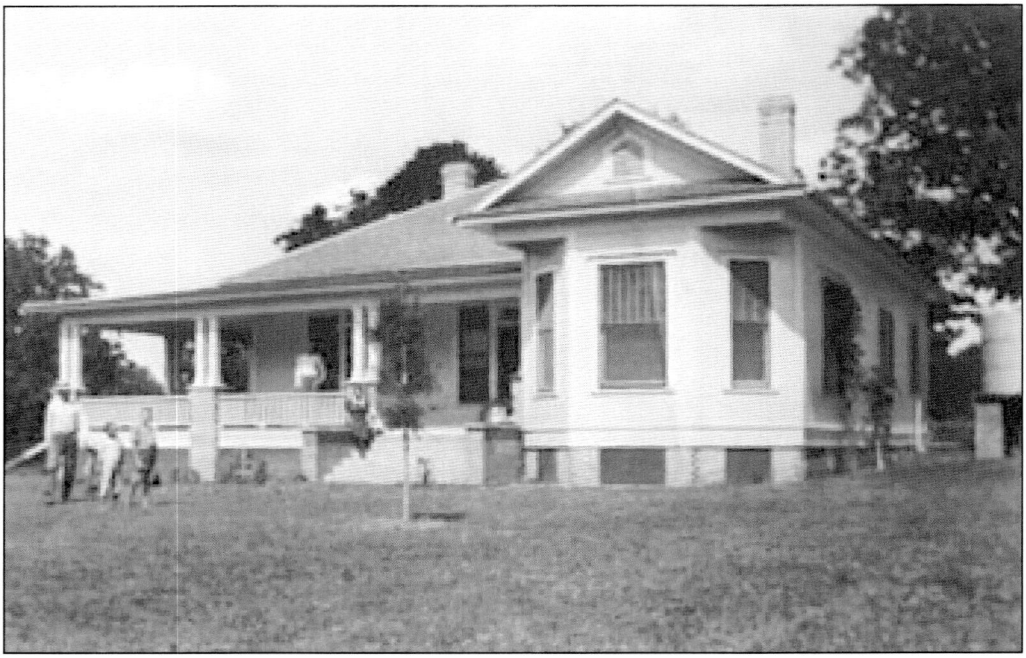

Shown is the home of John Green Burford and Minnie Hall Burford, who moved into it in 1922. Robert B. Burford (father of John Green Burford) is on the front porch, and John Green Burford is in the yard with two young boys (most likely his two sons, Charlie and Frank). The home still stands and is now owned by John Green Burford III. (Courtesy of Libby Dady Alcorn.)

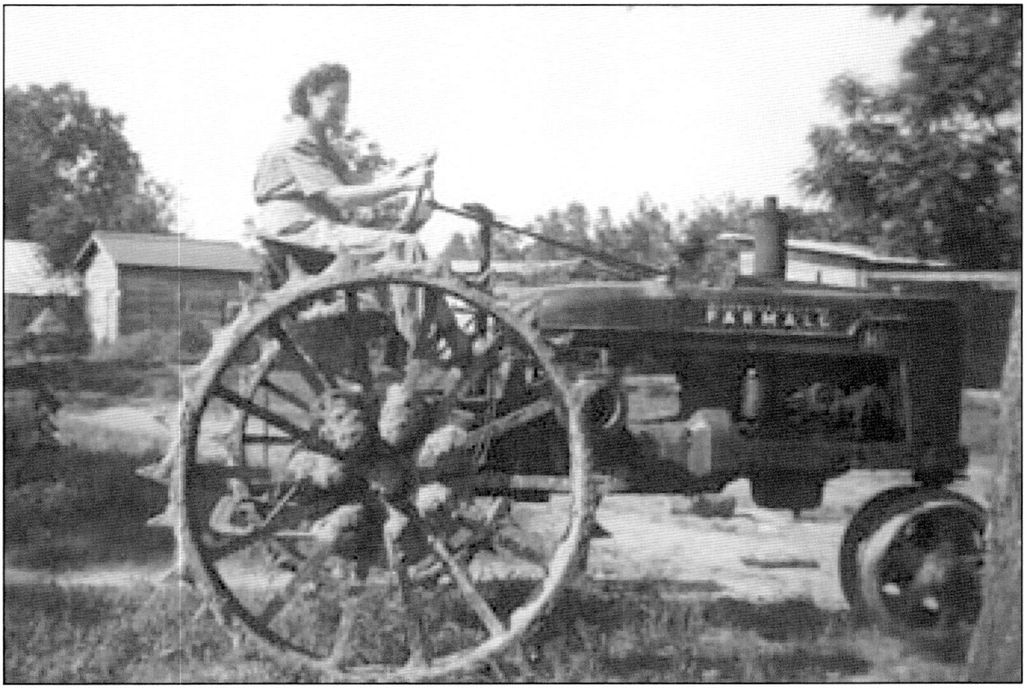

Mary Jackson Burford is shown on a tractor around 1940. She was married to Odell Hutchins about 1938, so depending on the actual date of this picture, she may have already been Hutchins. She is pictured on the farm of John Green Burford near the barn. (Courtesy of Libby Dady Alcorn.)

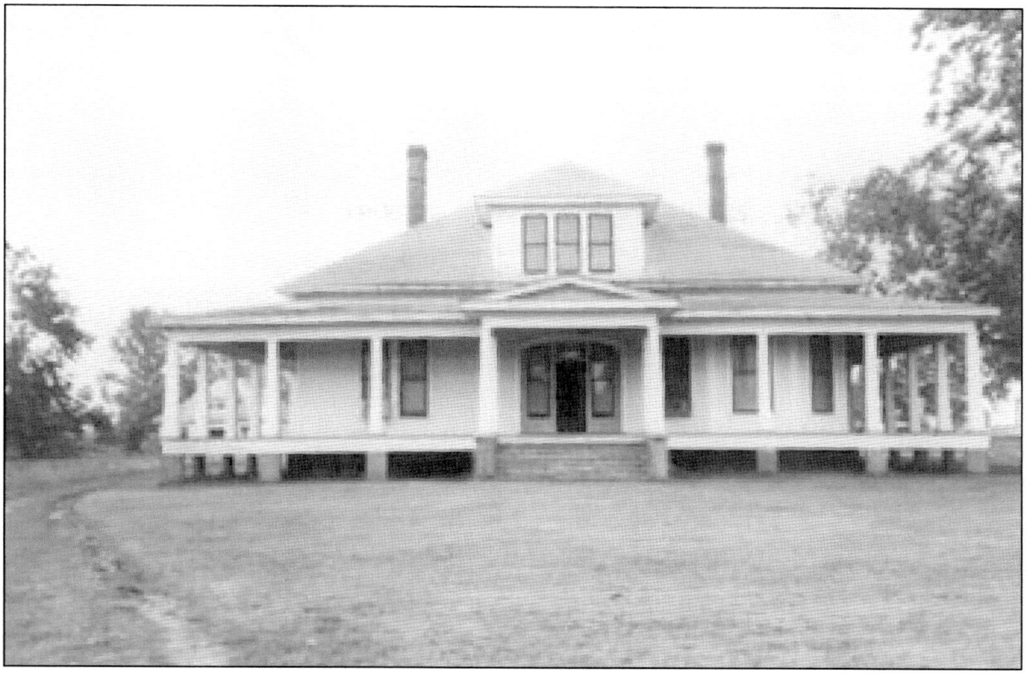

The John Long House was built about 1892 by Mr. and Mrs. John J. Long, parents of Mrs. Green Rives, Sr. The house was given to the Long's son when he got married. Built of the finest Lumber available at that time, the structure has ten rooms and four double fireplaces. The tiles making up two of the fireplaces were numbered in Sweden and imported to the plantation where they were used to build the fireplaces. (Courtesy of Raymond W. Powell.)

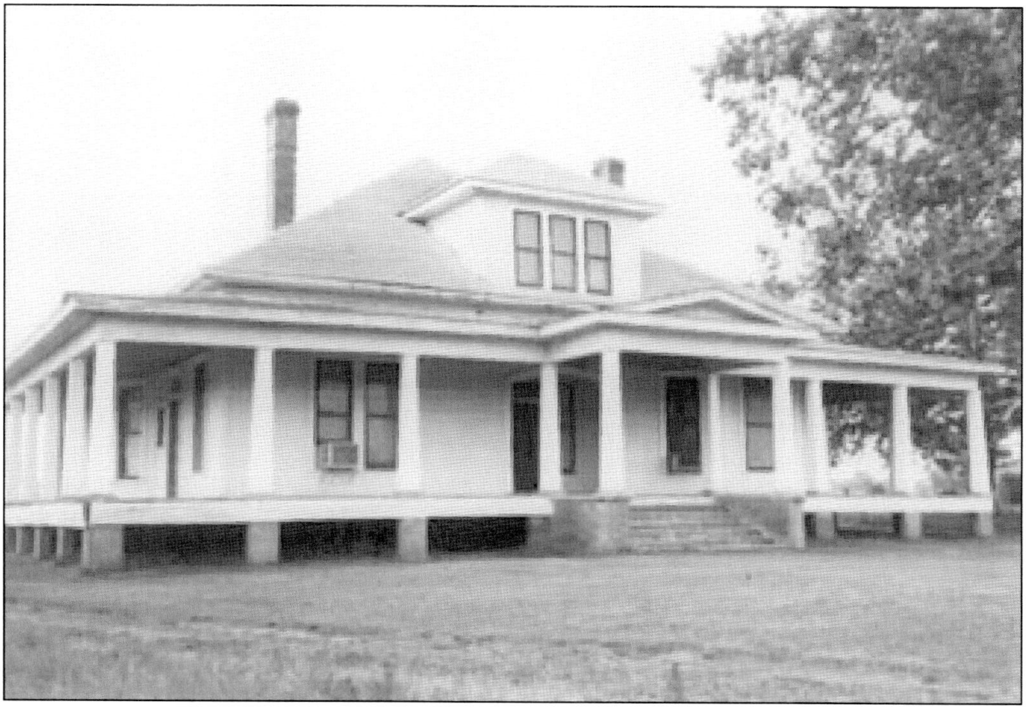

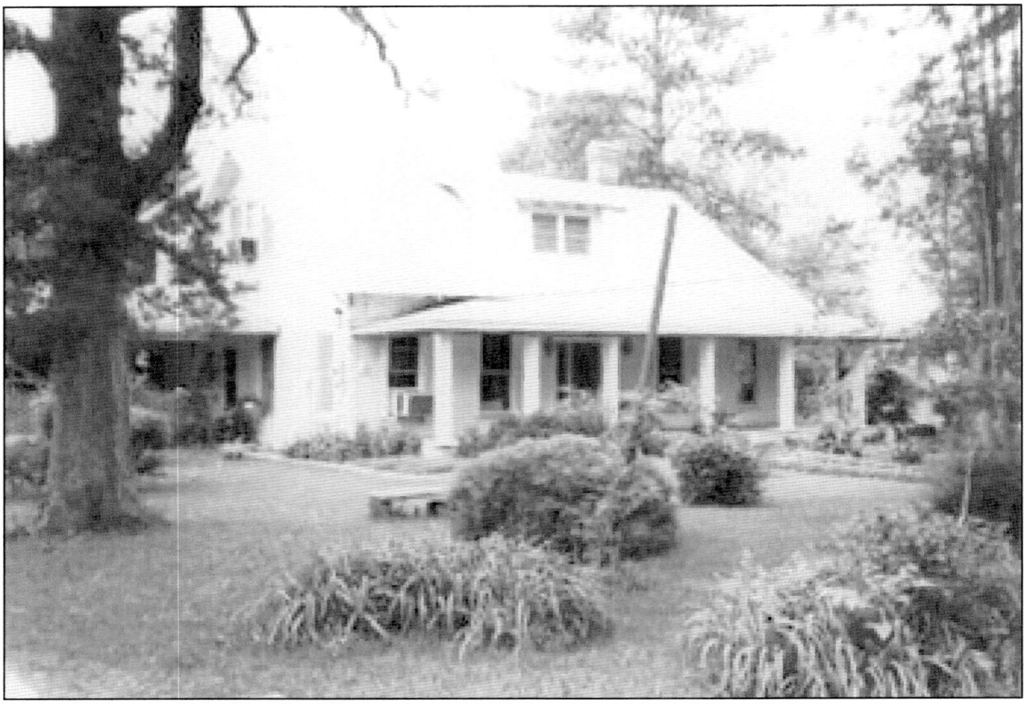

When the T.C. Hall home was built in 1887, it contained four rooms, an attic, and a kitchen. Later, a bathroom and plumbing were added. In 1956, the old kitchen was cut off and a new kitchen added on a concrete slab. Eventually, a carport was added and the front porch remodeled. The Halls have owned the home since 1975, when it was deeded by R.J. Riley to Mrs. Hall, who was his daughter. (Courtesy of Raymond W. Powell.)

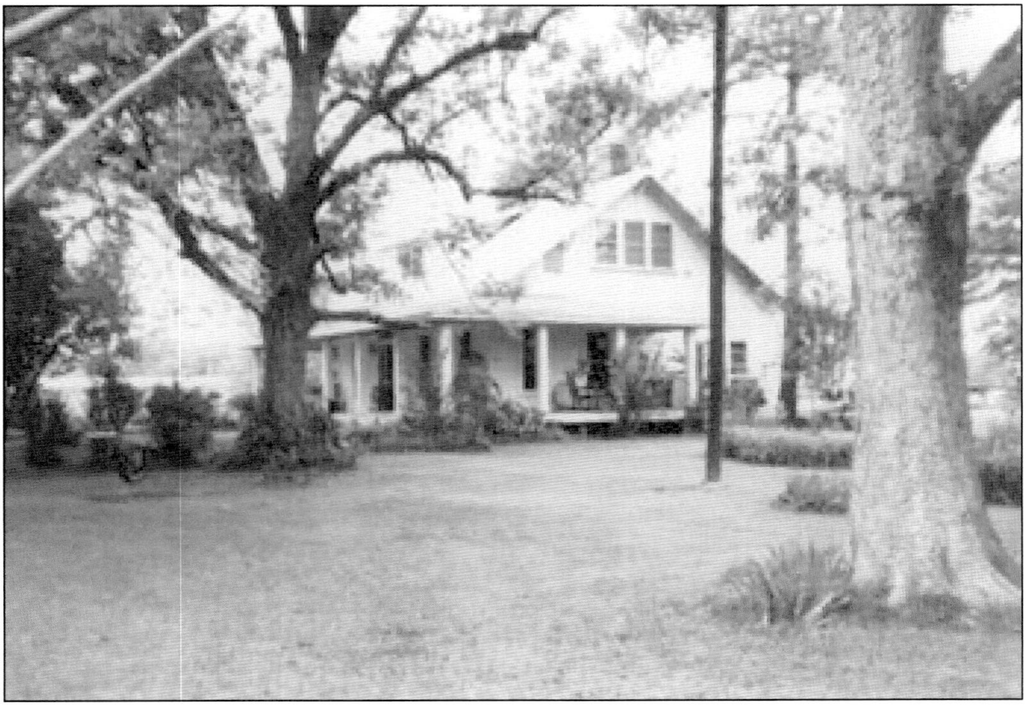

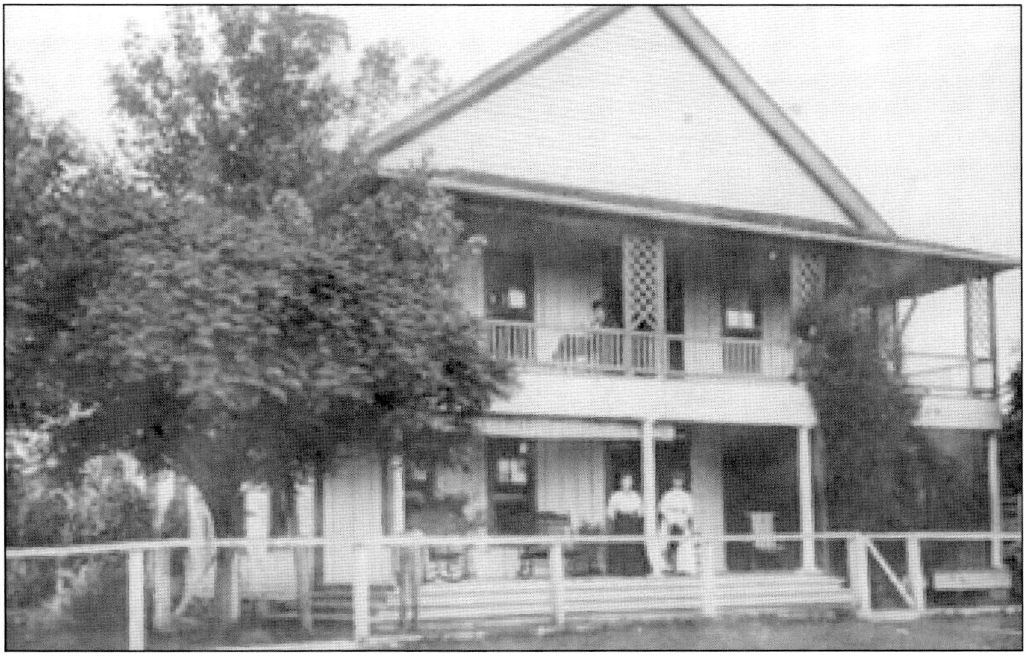

The New Orleans Pacific/Texas Pacific Railway laid out the village of Grand Cane. The Allen Hotel in Grand Cane was very near the railroad right-of-way and right behind the depot. It was built around 1890. (Courtesy of Edith Burgess Herring and the Grand Cane Historic Preservation Society.)

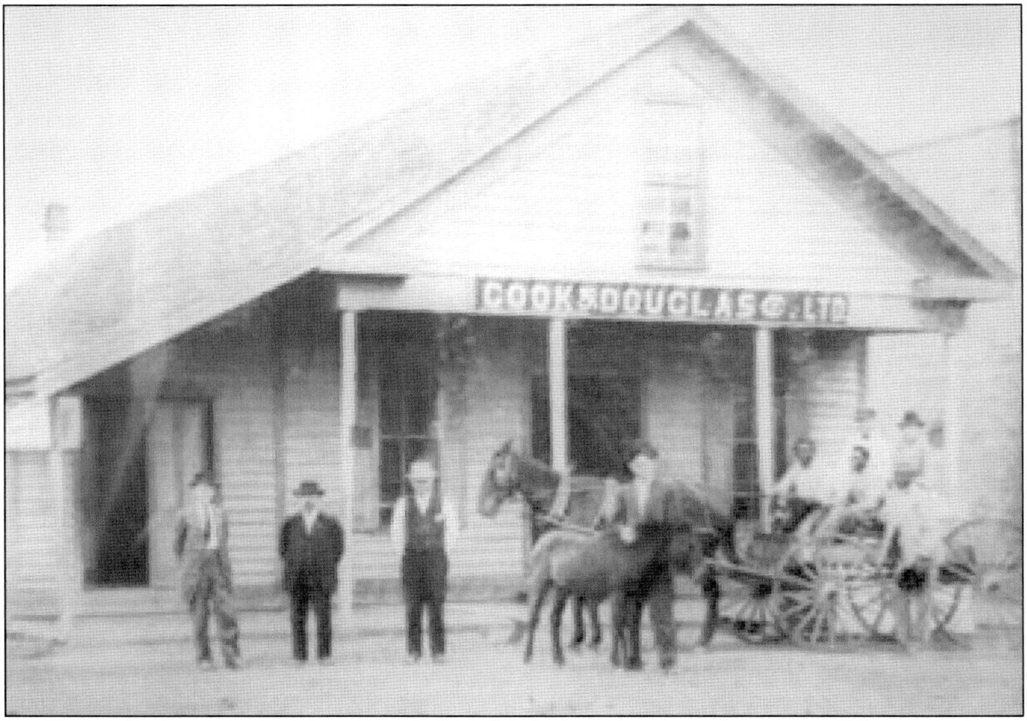

Shown is the inside of Rick's store in Grand Cane, Louisiana, around the late 1930s. Apparently, the store functioned as a café as well. In recent years, it was reopened as a restaurant. (Courtesy of Edith Burgess Herring.)

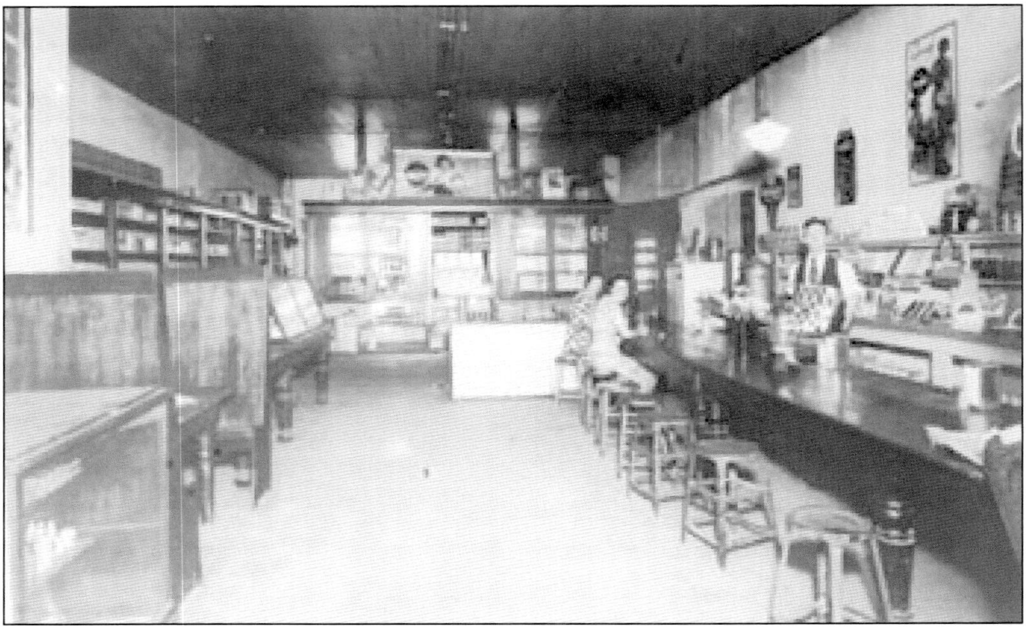

In 1903, Lodwrick Monroe Cook went into business with Charles A. Douglas, doing business as Cook & Douglas Co., Ltd. The firm bought a site consisting of Lots 7 & 8, Block 32 in the town of Grand Cane and built a store, which dealt in general merchandise and plantation supplies. The firm advertised that they paid the highest prices for cotton and cotton seed. (Courtesy of Edith Burgess Herring.)

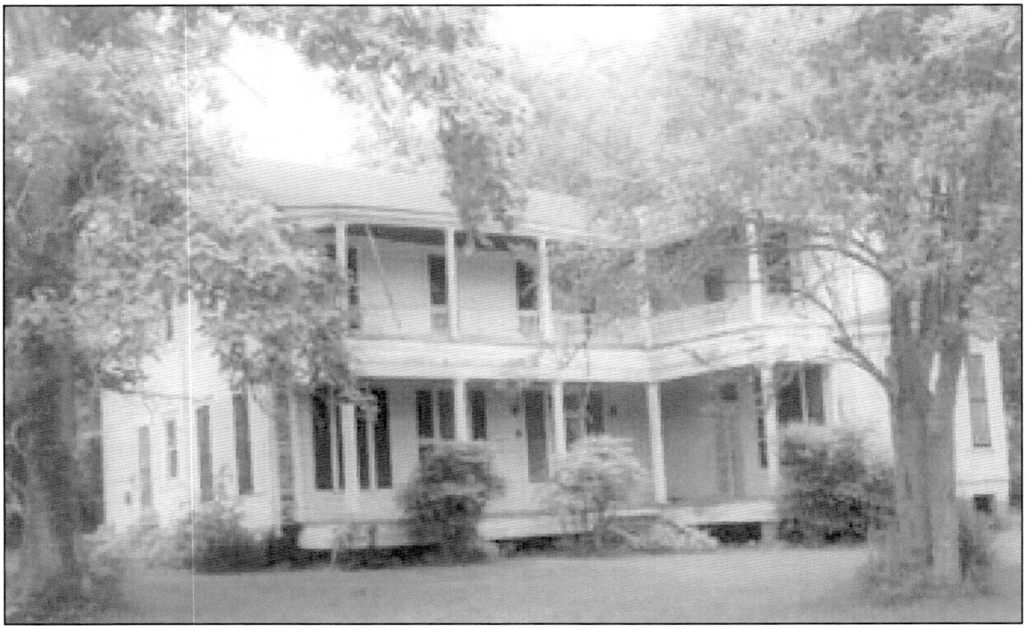

In 1835, Wright Drue Hobgood and his wife, Amanda, built the Cook Hill House on the site of an old Indian camp about two miles east of Screamerville. About 1890, the house was sold to Lodwrick Monroe Cook and his wife, Allie May Hood Cook. Under the supervision of Edith Herring, the house was moved nearer Grand Cane and is now a bed and breakfast. (Courtesy of Edith Burgess Herring.)

Children from farms and small towns found various ways of amusing themselves especially, around the barn and horses, cattle, hogs, and chickens. Pictured here is James Hill Cook of Grand Cane standing in a basket near a barn. Most people only needed a small amount of acreage to get by, and no home functioned without a dairy cow, chickens, and a small garden. Furthermore, neighbors and families shared with each another. (Courtesy of Edith Burgess Herring.)

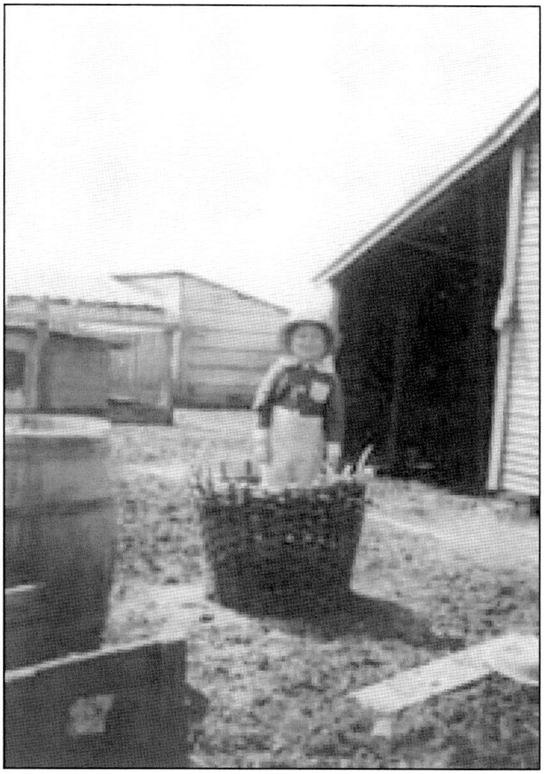

This photograph is of Providence Cumberland Presbyterian Church. Henry Storey, a resident of DeSoto Parish, donated the land in 1858 to the Providence Cumberland Presbyterian Church for a burying ground for the dead and apparently for the church building as well. (Photograph courtesy of Edith Burgess Herring and the Grand Cane Preservation Society.)

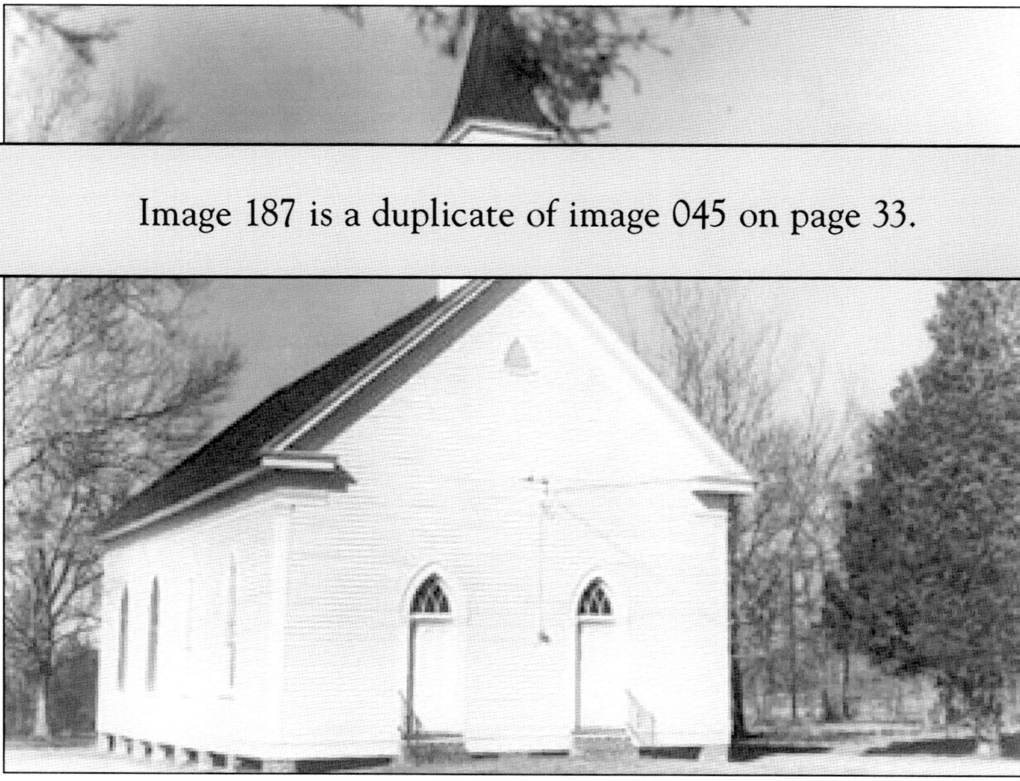

Image 187 is a duplicate of image 045 on page 33.

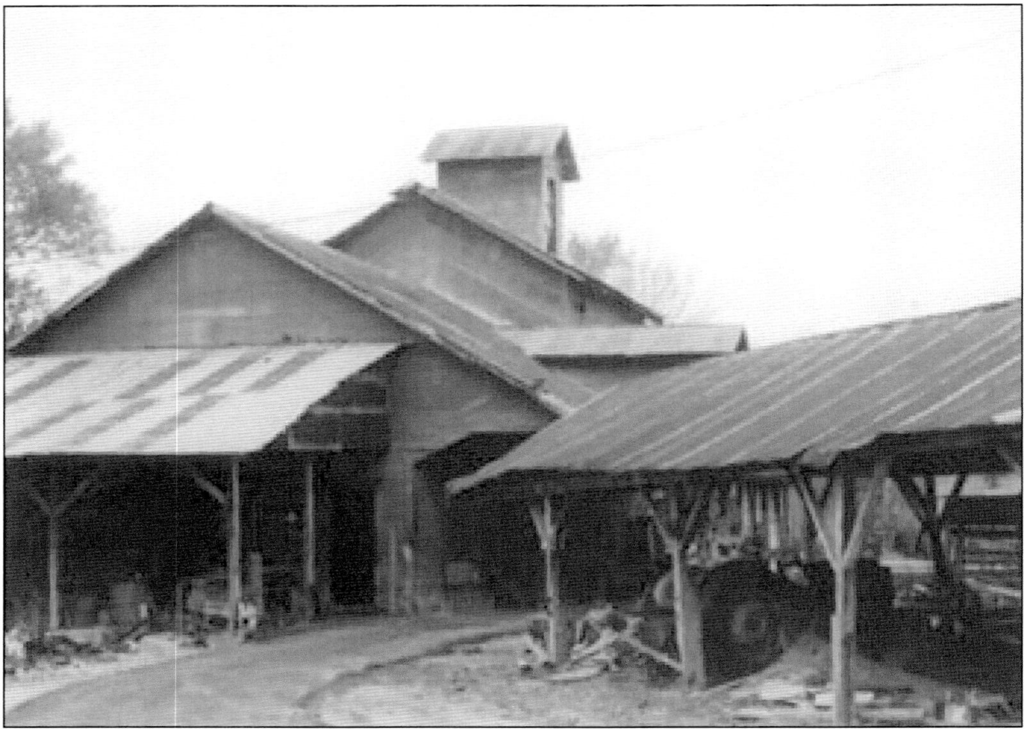

At one time, cotton was a large and important crop in the Grand Cane vicinity and other parts of northern DeSoto Parish. Shown is the cotton gin in Grand Cane, which appears to be in good condition although it is no longer in use. (Courtesy of Edith Burgess Herring.)

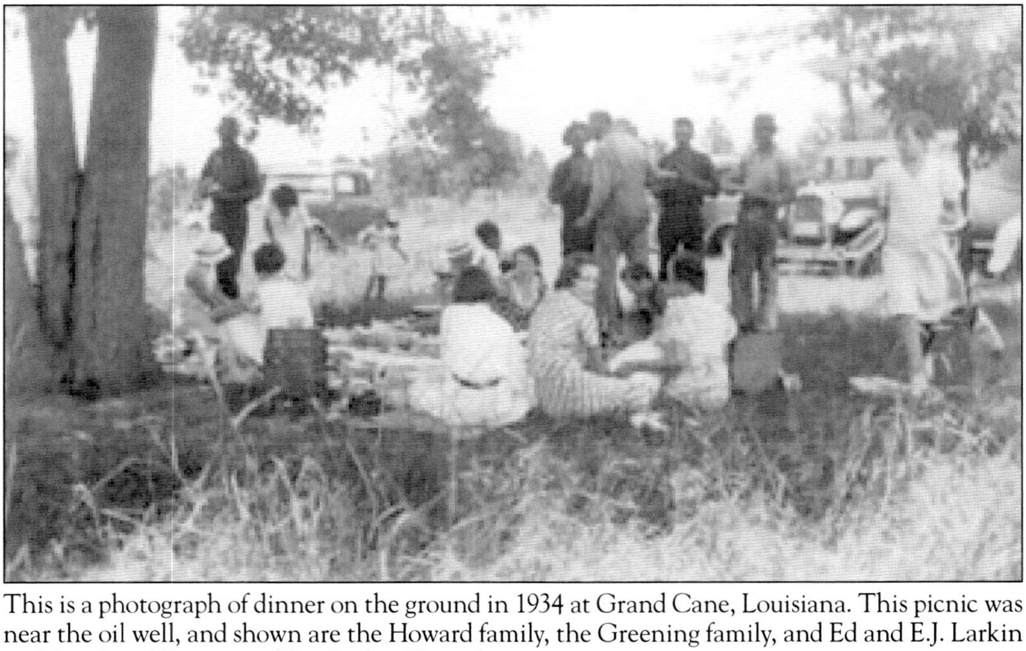

This is a photograph of dinner on the ground in 1934 at Grand Cane, Louisiana. This picnic was near the oil well, and shown are the Howard family, the Greening family, and Ed and E.J. Larkin and families. (Courtesy of Ina Larkin Young.)

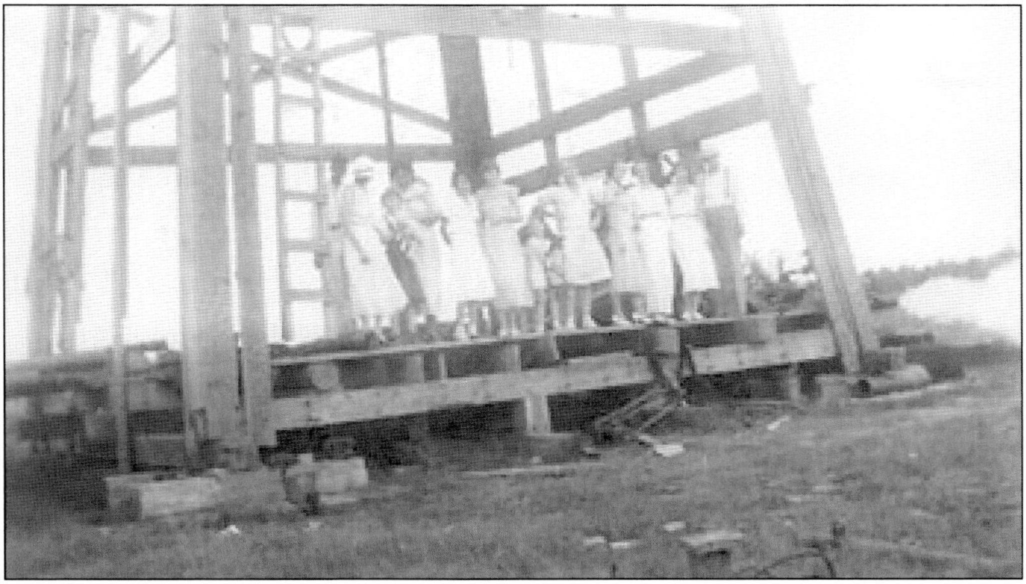

Pictured on an oil derrick near Grand Cane, Louisiana, around 1934 are the W.B. Larkin family (left) and the Greening family. (Courtesy of Ina Larkin Young.)

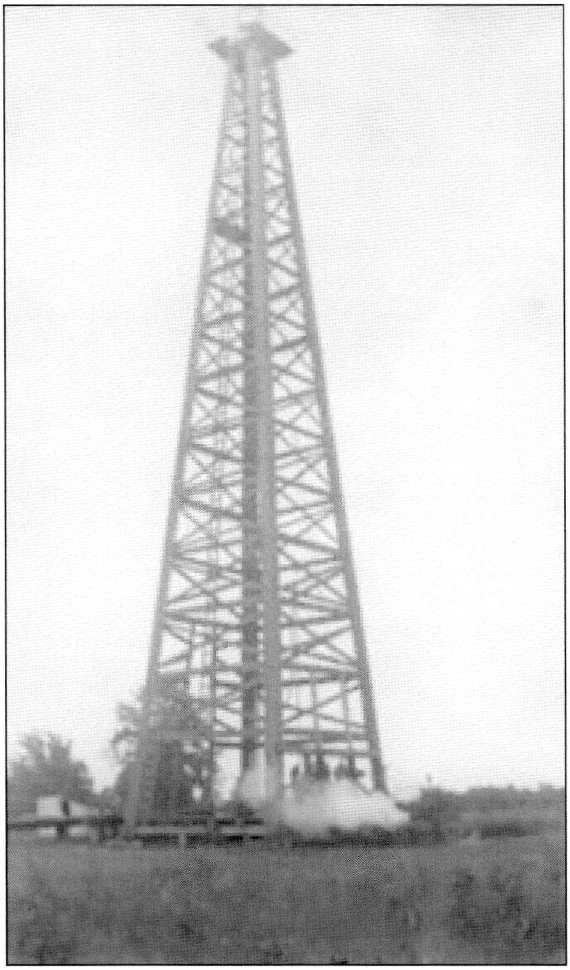

The oil derrick shown here was at Grand Cane around 1934. Apparently an oil derrick was a curiosity to those who lived in this small rural town, attractions being few and far between. (Courtesy of Ina Larkin Young.)

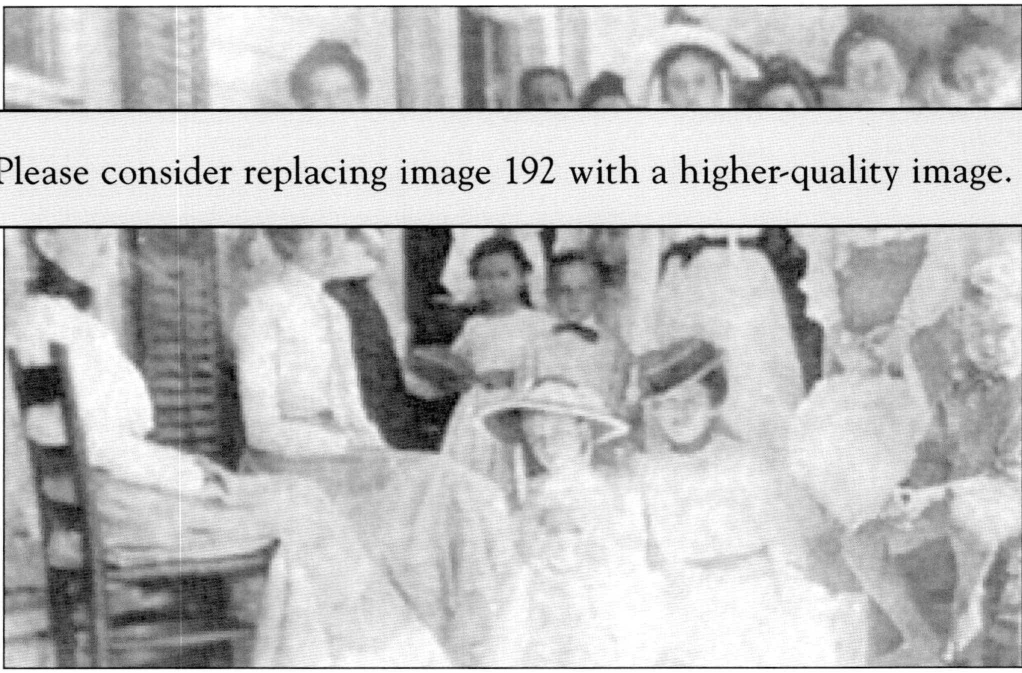

In the 1880s, Marmaduke Ricks opened a hotel known as Rick's Wells Hotel, famed for the healing waters from his mineral wells. He sent the water off for diagnosis and discovered the water had medicinal properties. The mineral properties were brought to notice of area medical practitioners, and they started prescribing the water for digestive problems, malarial disease, and other related ailments. (Courtesy of Liz Chrysler.)

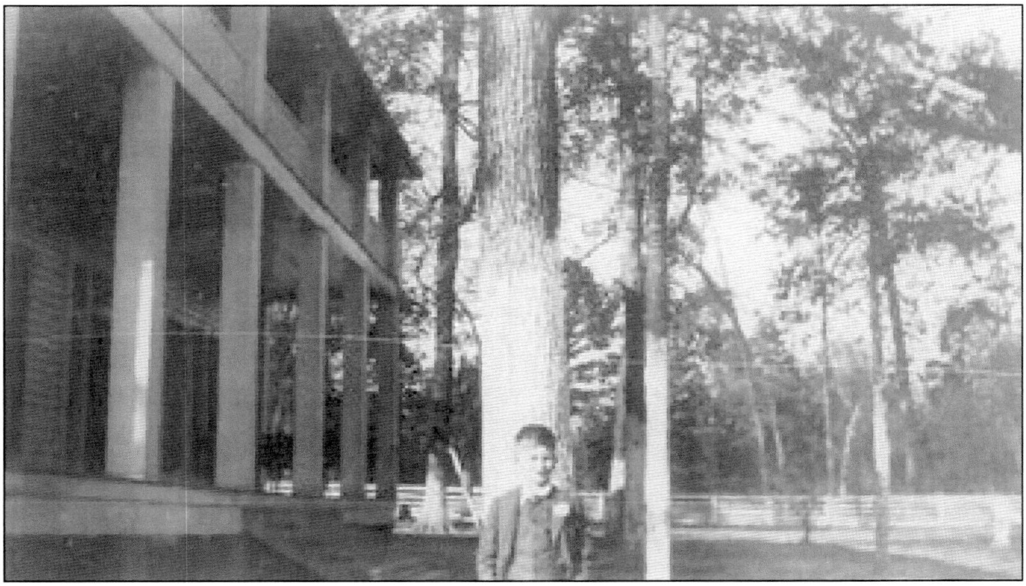

Pictured in front of Ricks Wells is 14-year-old Howard Griffith, son of Elizabeth Bailey and William Jasper Griffith. Those who are most familiar with the actual structure have concluded it was built sometime around 1866, but Ricks did not open the hotel until the railroad came. When his family home in South Mansfield burned in the early 1920s, W.J. Griffith purchased Ricks Wells for a home. (Photograph by Eureka Studios, courtesy of Louie Barnard Griffith.)

John Clifton Griffith Sr. served in World War I, worked for his father (William Jasper Griffith of South Mansfield) in the railroad cross tie business, and established Winston and Griffith Construction Company with offices in Shreveport and Dallas. He also went into the business of sodding the highways in Alabama, Mississippi, and the Dallas vicinity, using equipment for which he held several patents. John Clifton Griffith Sr. eventually retired to Grand Cane. Meanwhile, he fulfilled many civic responsibilities in the parish, such as the school board, the levee board, and the Grand Cane Methodist Church. (Courtesy of Carolyn Griffith Moffett.)

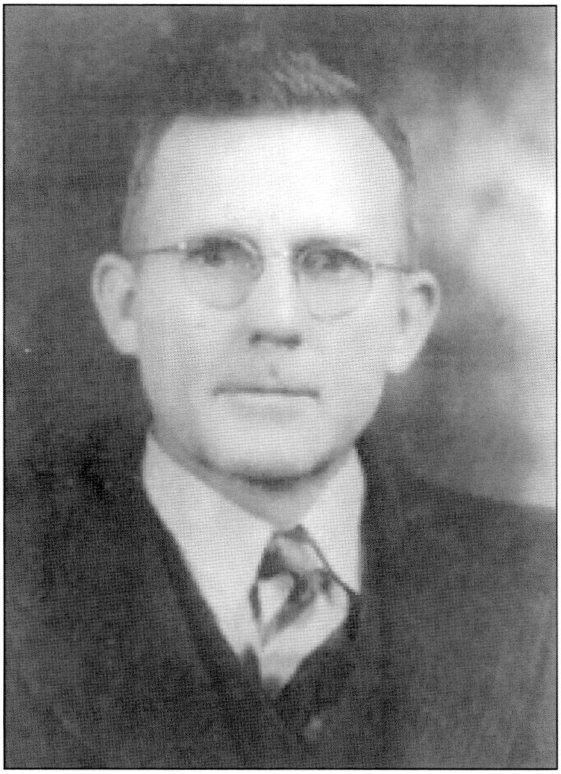

This photograph of the Ford House in Grand Cane shows a house designed by Sydney Platt. He ordered a plan from Sears Roebuck and varied the interior and exterior. Most exteriors were similar, but he refused to duplicate an interior. (Courtesy of Edith Burgess Herring.)

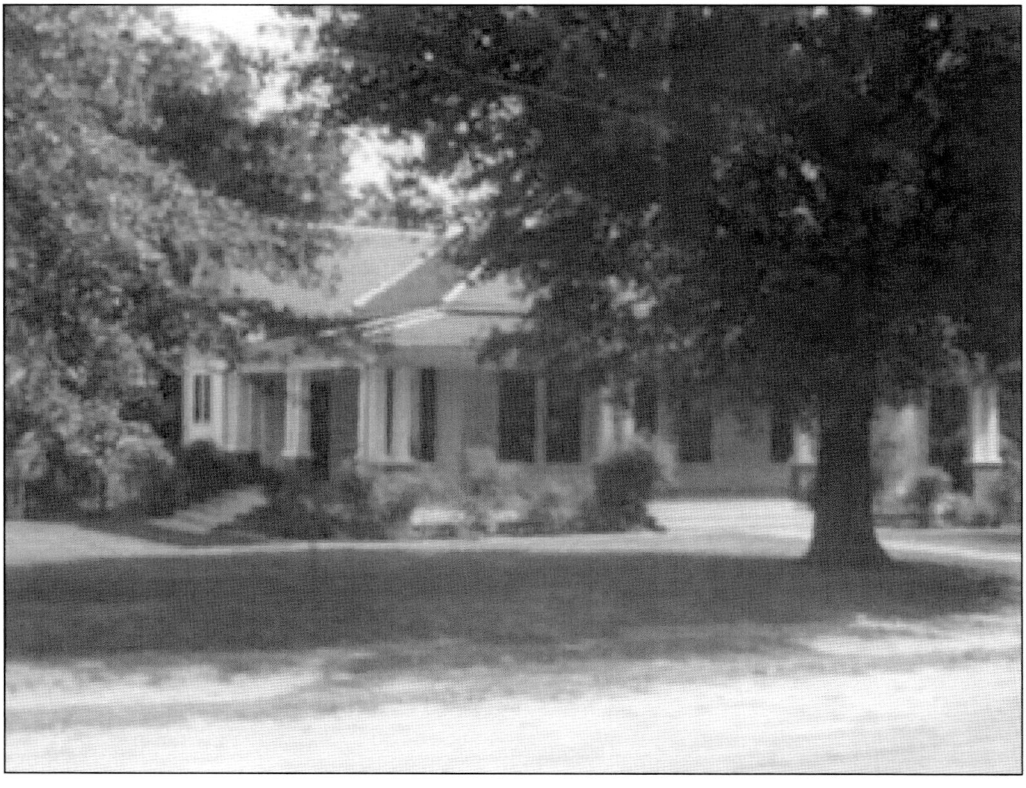

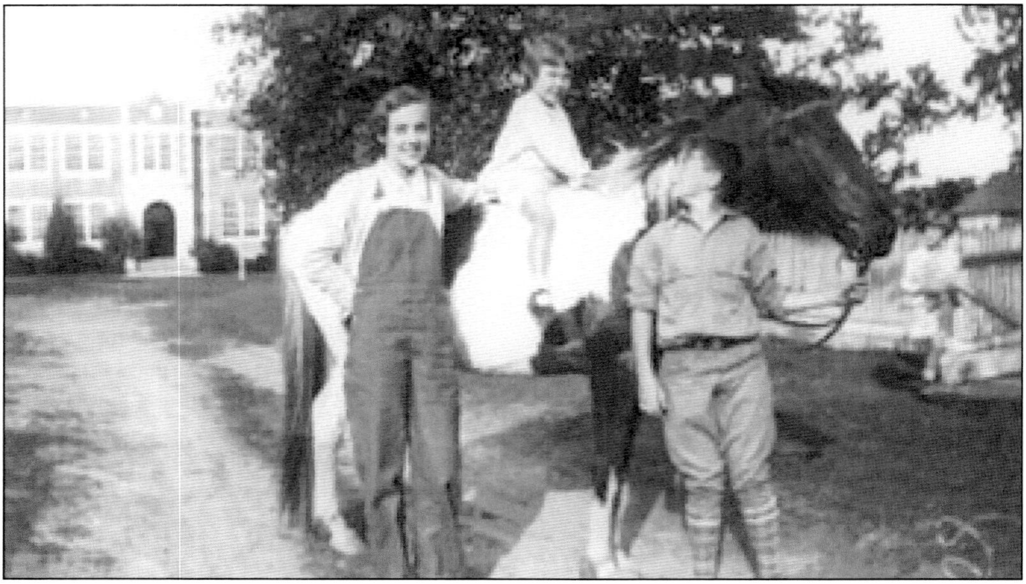

In the front of the house are the Ford children with horses. This photograph demonstrates the significance of horses to those who resided in Grand Cane and outside of cities in general. Grand Cane High School can be seen in the background. (Courtesy of Edith Burgess Herring.)

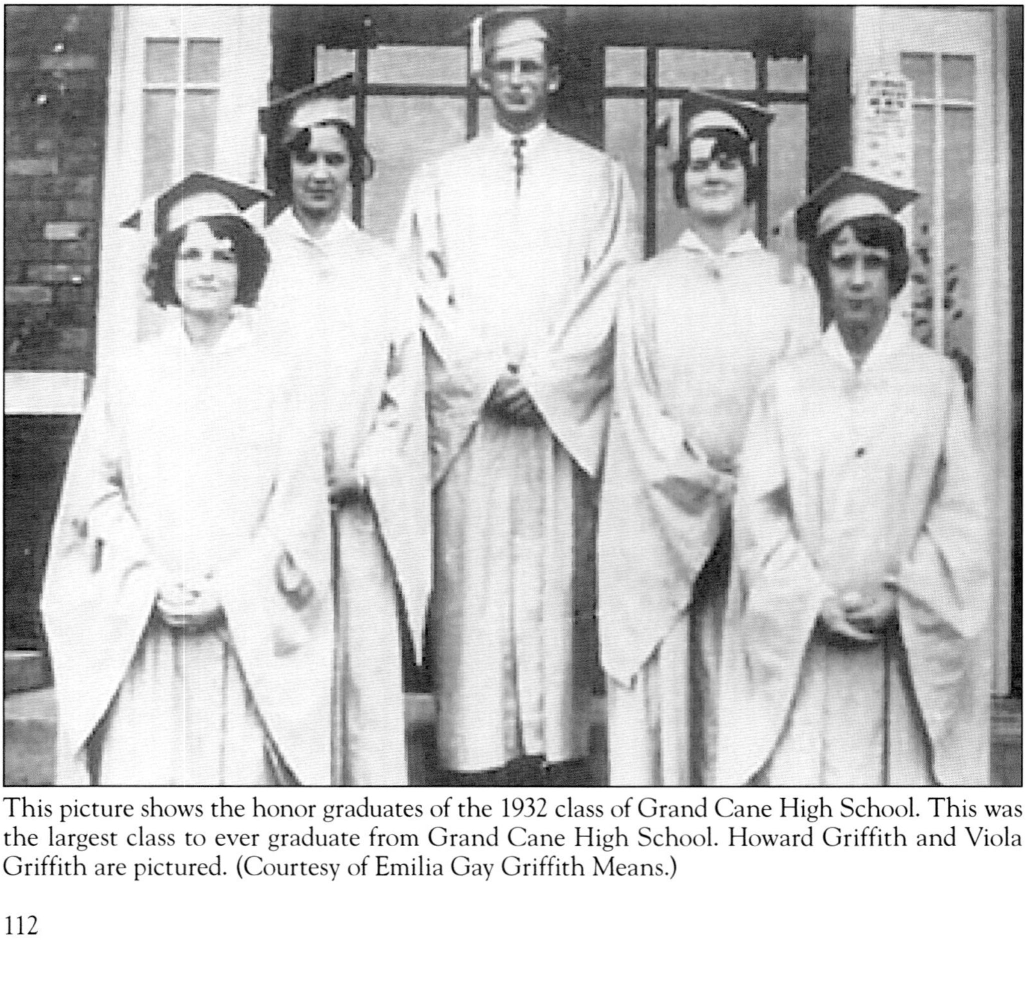

This picture shows the honor graduates of the 1932 class of Grand Cane High School. This was the largest class to ever graduate from Grand Cane High School. Howard Griffith and Viola Griffith are pictured. (Courtesy of Emilia Gay Griffith Means.)

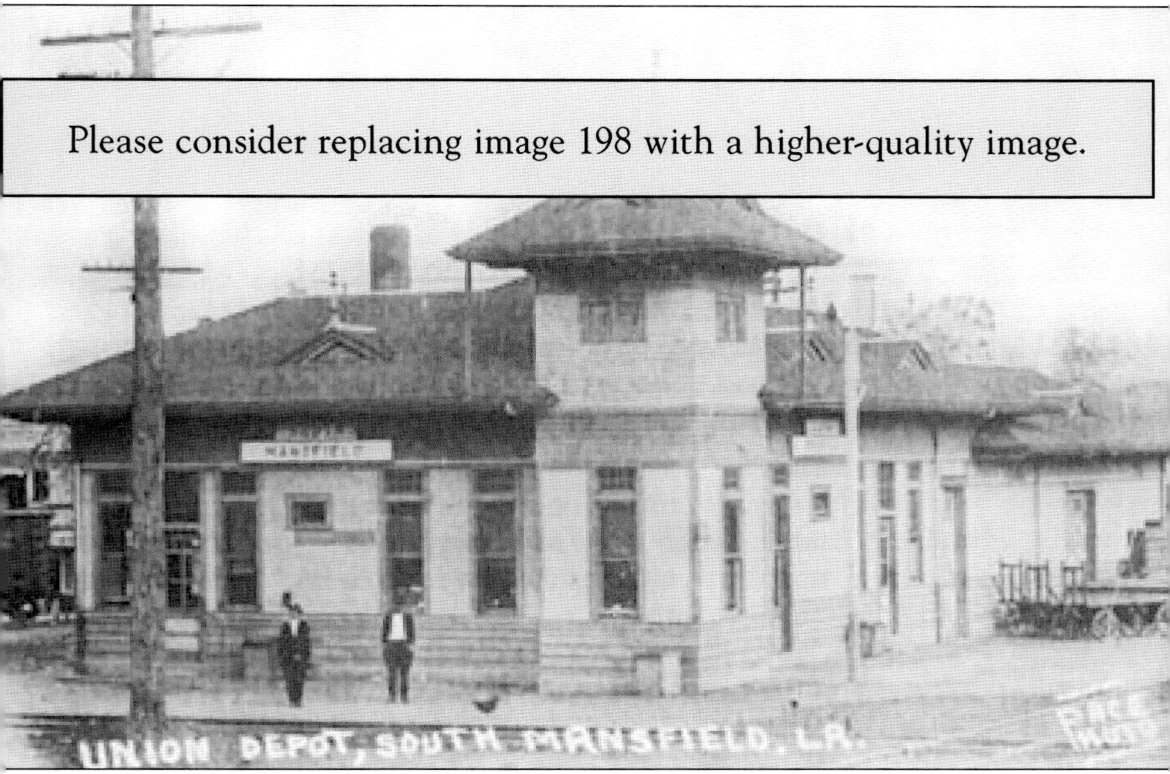

The New Orleans Pacific/Texas and Pacific bypassed the town of Mansfield. Therefore, the settlement of South Mansfield developed around the area where the track passed through. Mansfield developed the Mansfield Railway and Transportation Company, which exited to the junction at South Mansfield. Construction of the Kansas City Southern line followed in 1896 from Shreveport southward through the parish. With the two railroads came sawmills and the quick rise of the lumber industry. South Mansfield grew up with the lumber industry. It even prospered momentarily on the strength of its location as a rail crossroad. Shown is the railroad station, which was known as Union Station. There was also a post office, grocery store, five lumber mills, six hotels, a school, churches, Holloways Drug Store, Thackett's Ice Cream parlor, a year-round skating ring, ice and soft drink plants, an indoor theater, and the *South Mansfield Star* newspaper. (Courtesy of North Louisiana Historical Association and Scot Solice.)

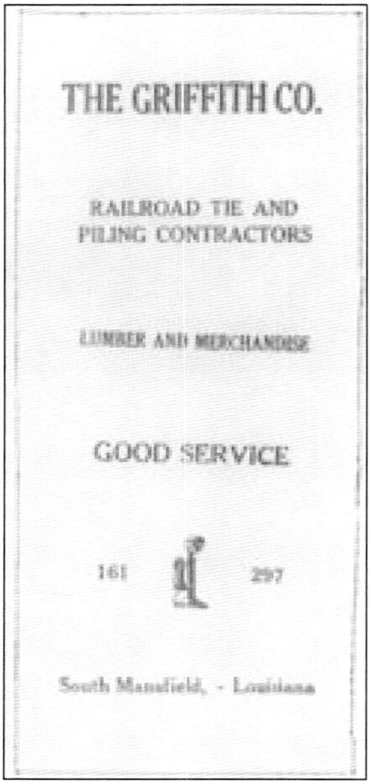

This advertisement for the W.J. Griffith Lumber and Tie Company at South Mansfield is from a 1922 *Mansfield Enterprise*. Most of the mills were located close to either the main line of the Texas and Pacific Railroad or the Kansas City Southern Railroad line that connected South Mansfield to the main city center of Mansfield. Next to the train depot was the Joshua Logan hotel which Joshua L. Logan, owner of the Logan Lumber Company, named for his son, the future New York playwright and director. (Courtesy of Nathaniel Means Collection.)

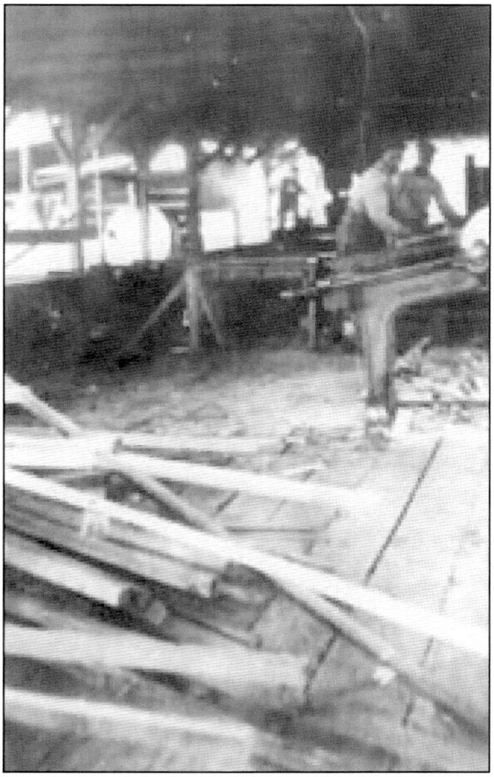

The illustration shows another location of the W. J. Griffith lumber mill at Clear Lake. With a population of 3,000 at one time, South Mansfield was home to the Frost Johnson Lumber Company, the Mansfield Hardwood Company and the Logan Lumber Company. The Sears Roebuck Company, famous for its catalogue that sold everything from needles to carriages, also operated a mill in South Mansfield. (Courtesy of W.J. Griffith family.)

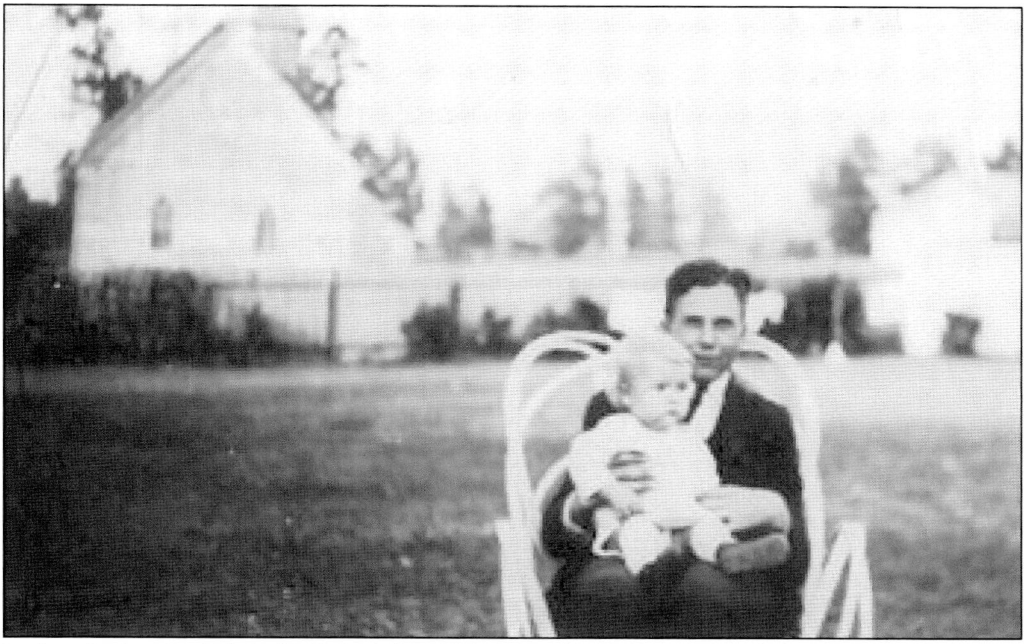

Luther Bailey Griffith holds baby John Clifton Griffith in 1921. It is believed that this was in the backyard of the Griffith home on Logan Avenue in South Mansfield. However, most who are familiar with the churches in Mansfield believe that this was taken on the then vacant land behind Christ Memorial Episcopal church. (Courtesy of Emilia Gay Griffith Means.)

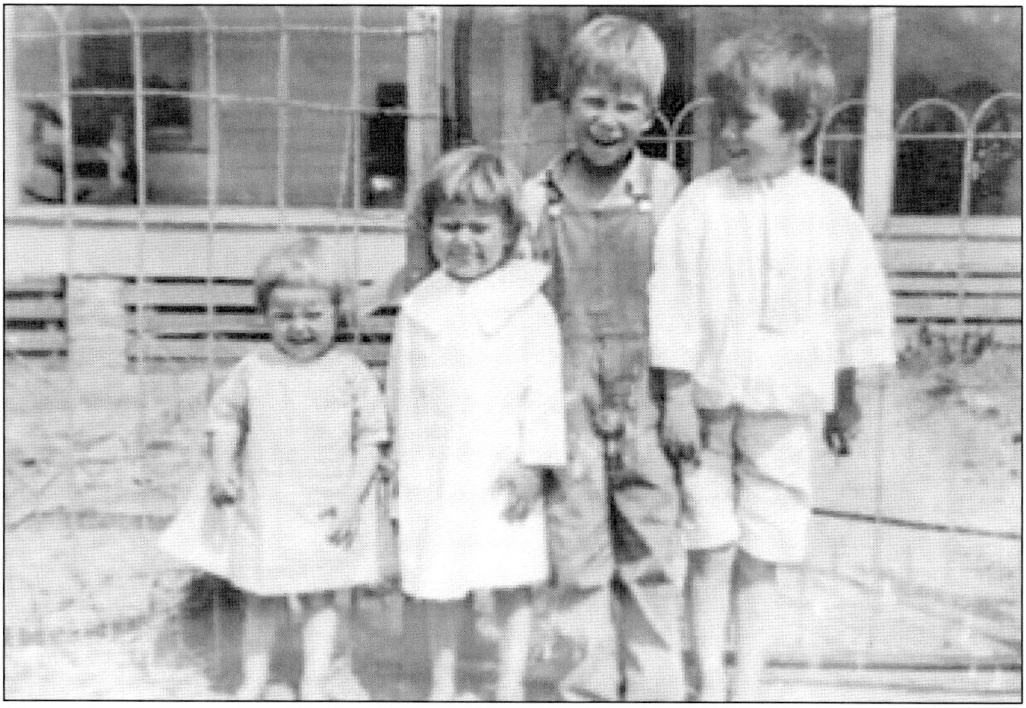

Shown from left to right are William Jasper and Elizabeth Bailey Griffith's children,Viola, Rebecca, Jay, and Fred. The children were photographed in front of the Griffith home on Logan Avenue in South Mansfield. (Courtesy of Emilia Gay Griffith Means.)

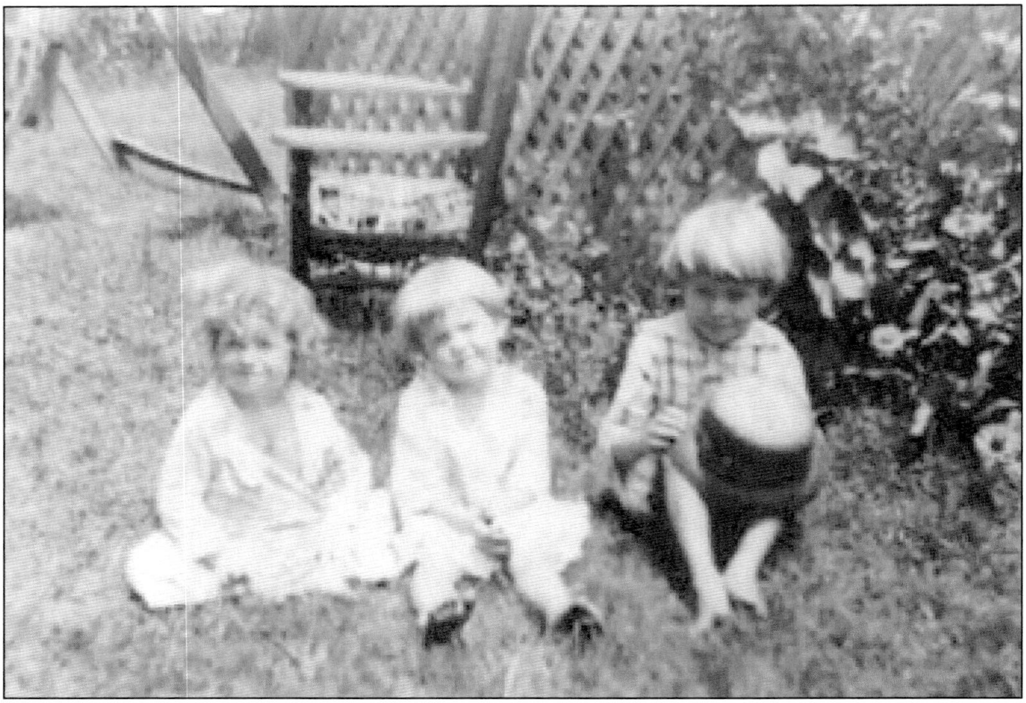

Here is another photograph of the Griffith children in the backyard of their South Mansfield home. They are, from left to right, Viola, Rebecca, and Howard. (Courtesy of Emilia Gay Griffith Means.)

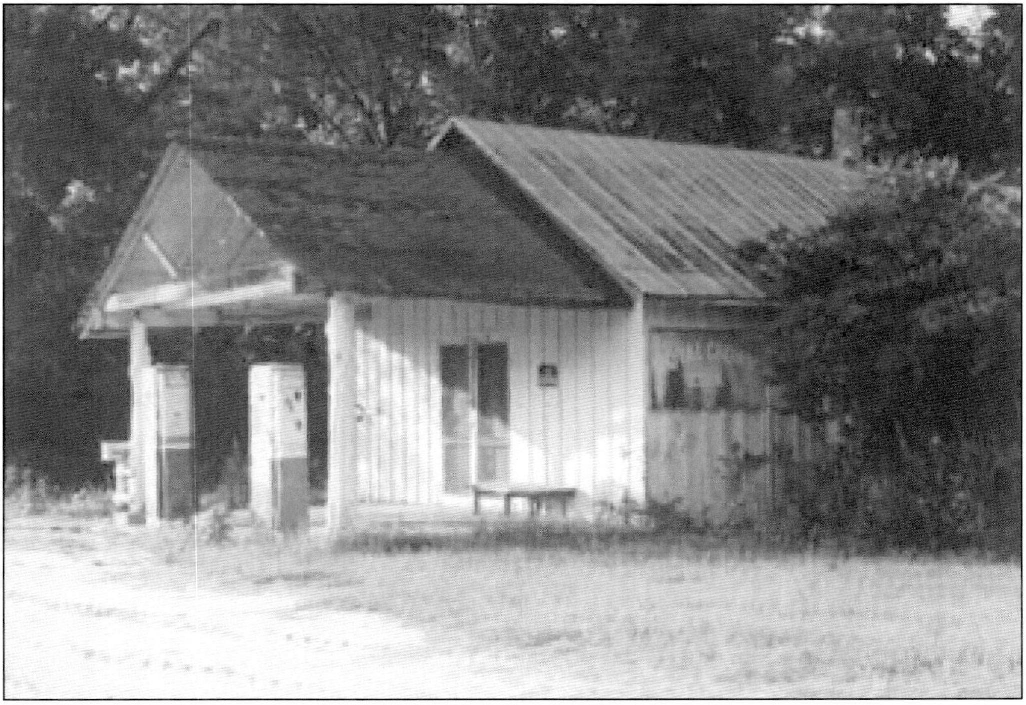

Another town on the New Orleans Pacific /Texas and Pacific line was Oxford. Shown here is a filling station which is one of the few structures remaining. (Photograph by W. Conway Link.)

Another gasoline station at Oxford is shown. The entire town, which once thrived with lumber mills, is abandoned. (Photograph by W. Conway Link.)

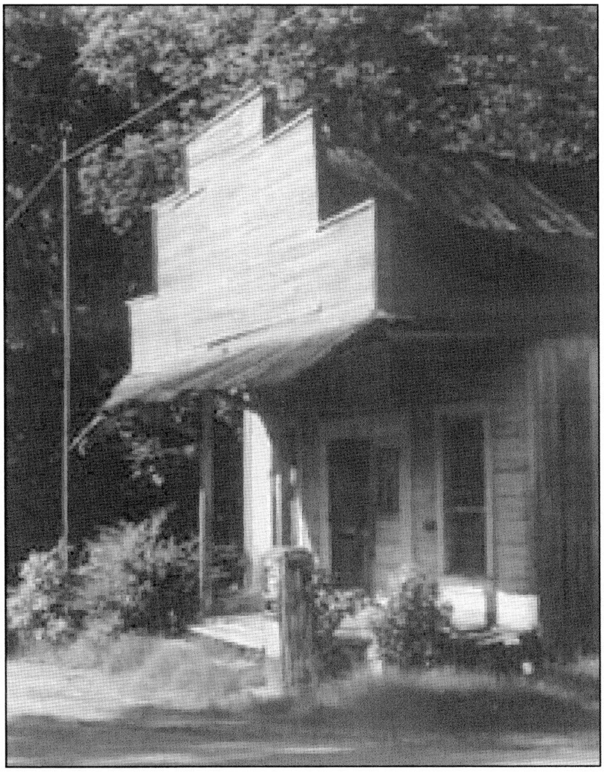

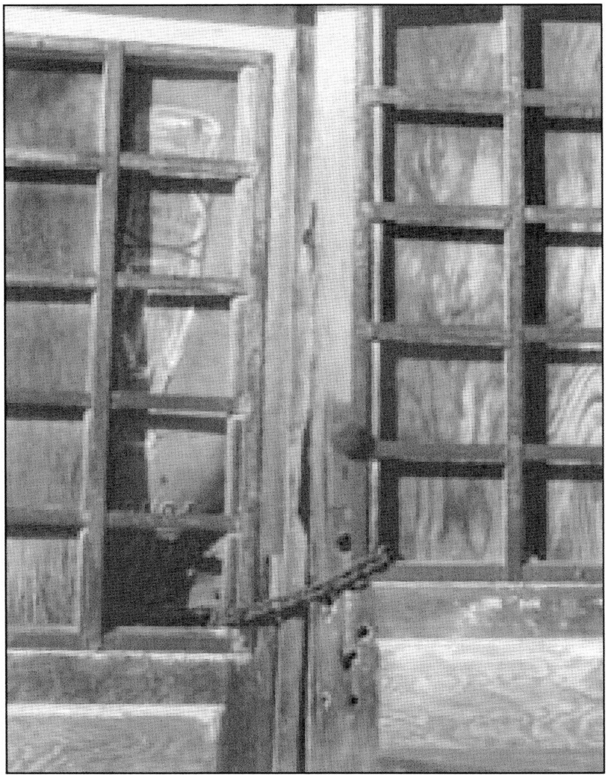

This image is of a boarded-up store at Oxford. These three buildings are all that remain. (Photograph by W. Conway Link.)

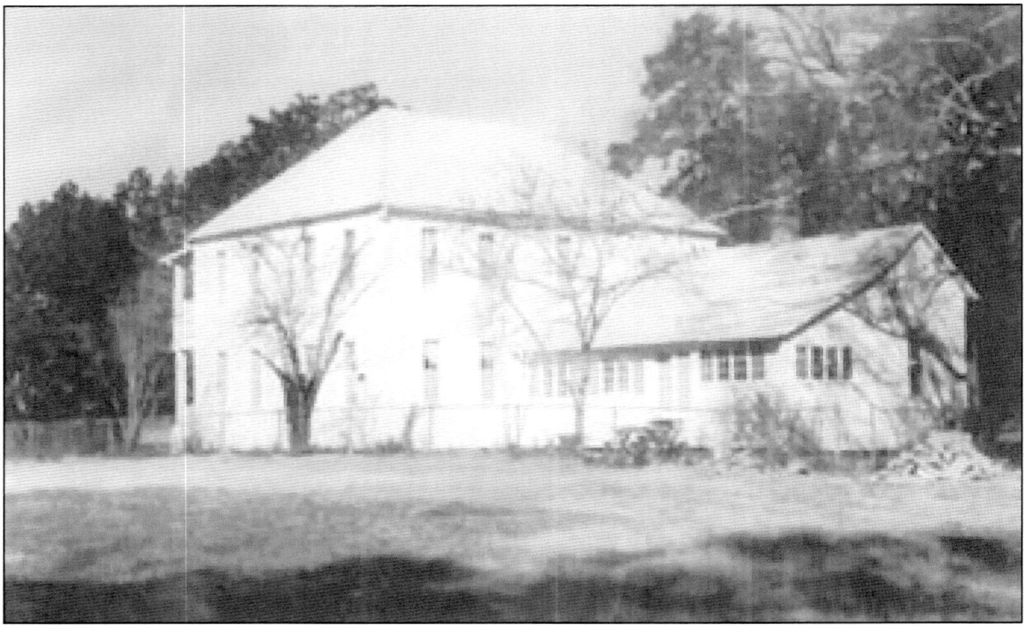

Benson was originally known as San Patice. The Sebastian house, one mile east of Benson on Highway 512, was constructed in the 1880s by Dan Sebastian. It has 13 rooms, 10 fireplaces, and 12-foot ceilings built of locally grown cypress and heart pine. The second story porch was blown away by a storm in the 1940s. The house was unoccupied from the 1950s through the 1970s and was severely vandalized while vacant. Patsy and Bernard Shadoin purchased the house in 1975 and over a 10-year period performed a complete restoration. They moved into the house full-time in 1986. They sold the property in 1992. Presently, the house is vacant and for sale. Benson, on the Texas & Pacific Railway line was once a thriving sawmill town. (Courtesy of Raymond W. Powell.)

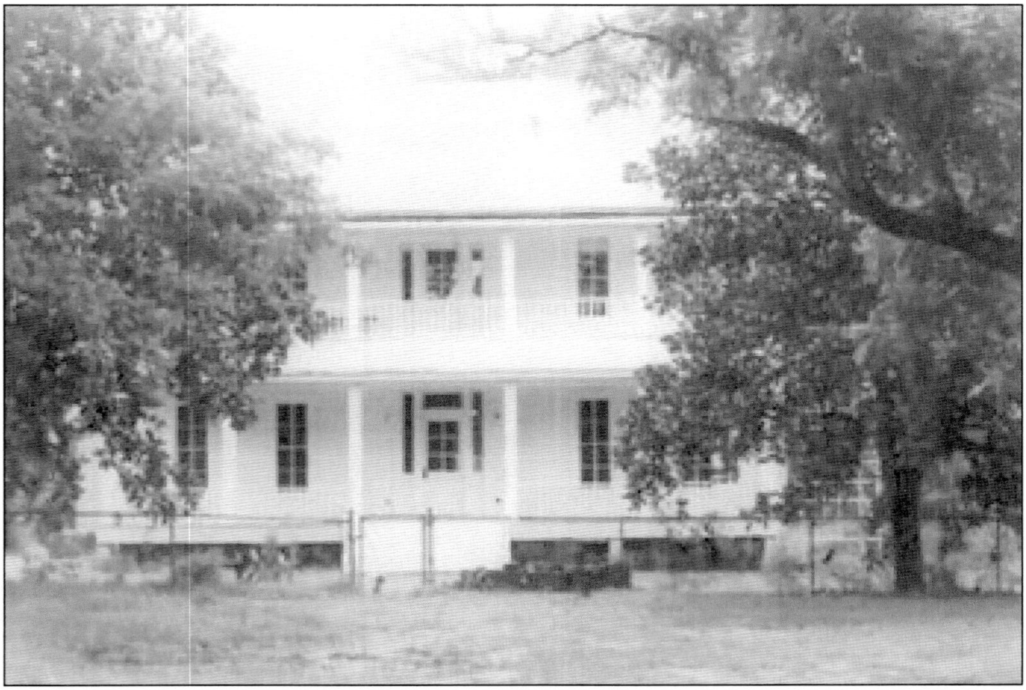

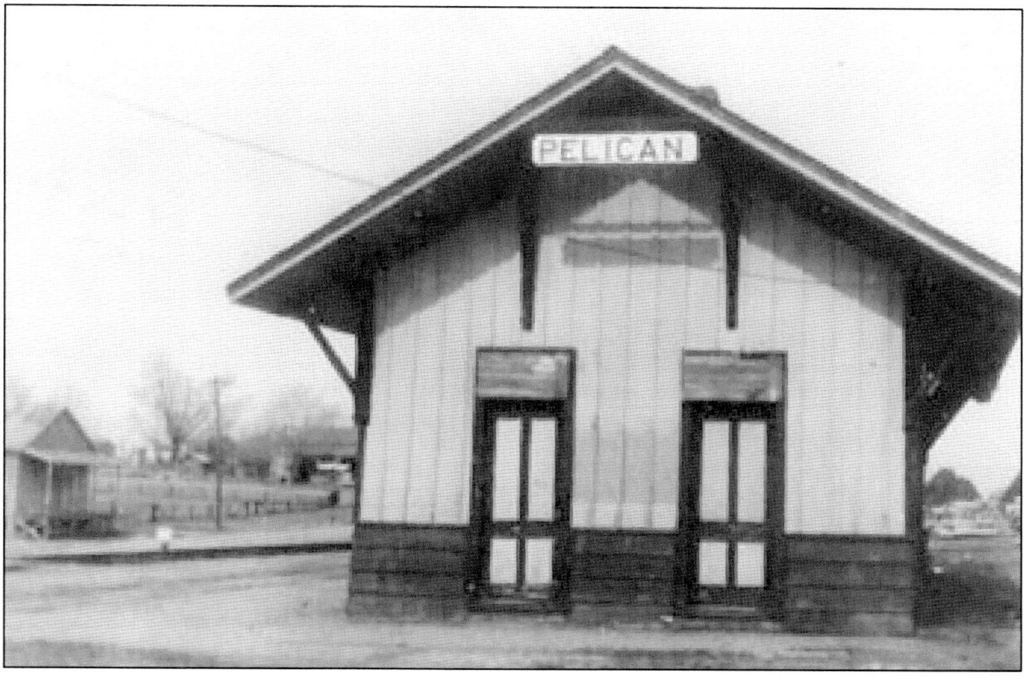

As the railroad activity decreased, there came a gradual improvement in roads and highways. Shown is the Pelican depot in later years. It was sold by the railroad and torn down before the railroad tracks were removed about 1960. (Courtesy of Kathleen Myers.)

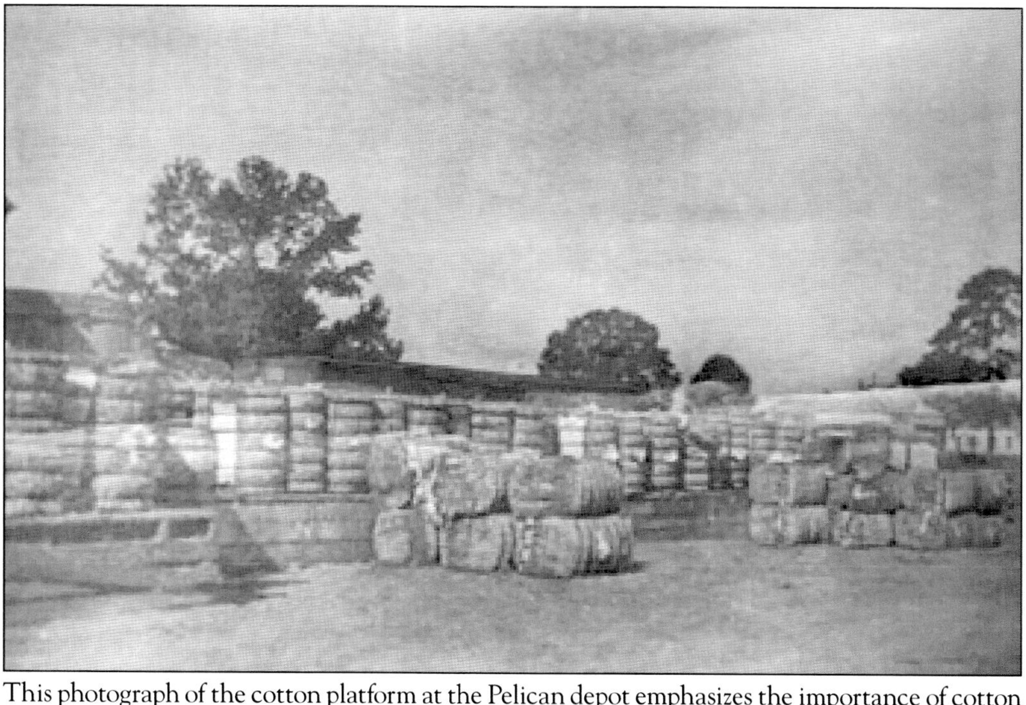

This photograph of the cotton platform at the Pelican depot emphasizes the importance of cotton to the area. Furthermore, it illustrates the role of the railroads and their importance in allowing cotton growers in the area to get their crops to the cotton buyers in Shreveport and New Orleans. (Courtesy of Kathleen Myers.)

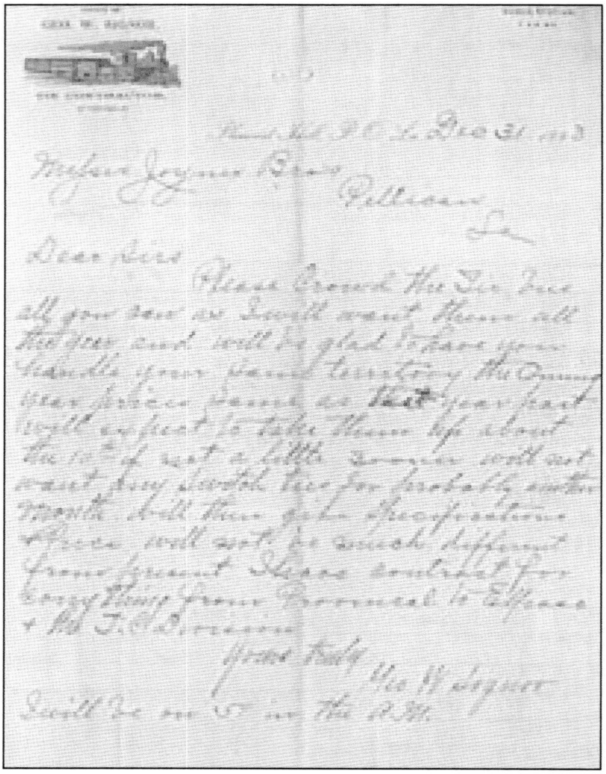

[illegible] Dec 31 [illegible]

Messrs Joyner Bros
Pelican
La

Dear Sirs
Please Crowd the Tie [illegible] all you can as I will want them all this year and will be glad to have you handle your [illegible] territory the coming year price same as last year [illegible] will expect to take them up about the 10th of next a little sooner will not want any Switch ties for probably another month till then [illegible] specifications Price will not be much different from present I have contract for everything from [illegible] to [illegible] + the T. & P. Division

Yours truly
Geo W Signor

I will be on 5 in the A.M.

Once the New Orleans Pacific Railroad/Texas and Pacific Railroad arrived in DeSoto Parish, there was much opportunity for those involved in the lumber and railroad cross tie business. One such person who recognized this opportunity was George W. Signor. (Courtesy of Emilia Gay Griffith Means.)

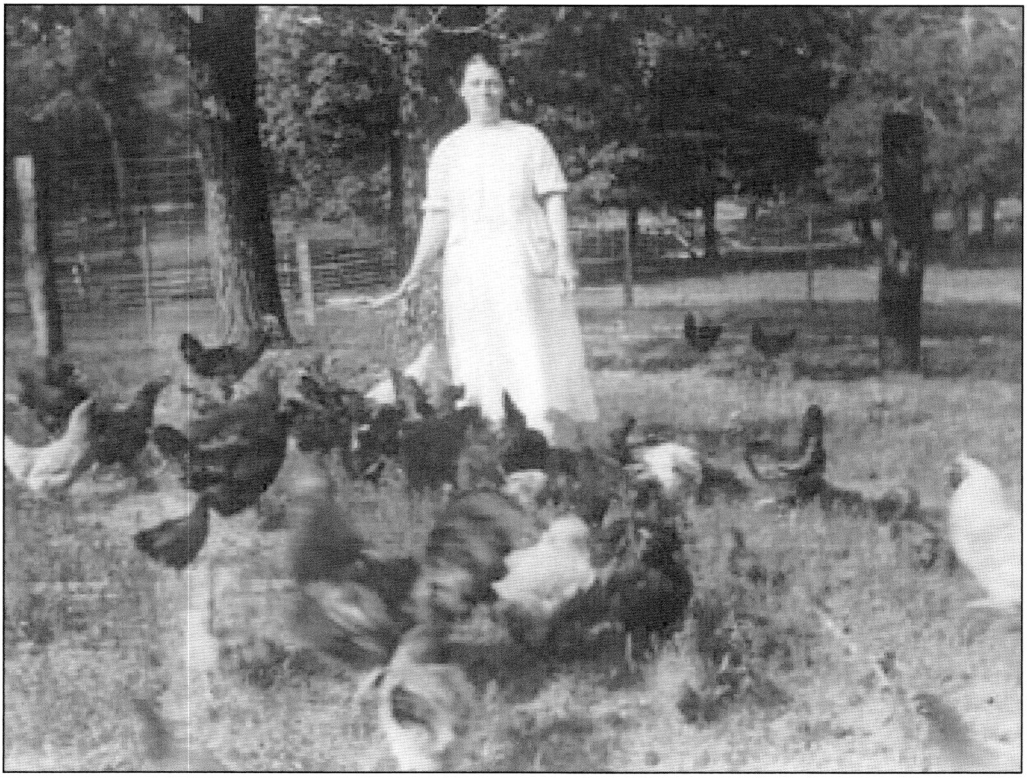

Photographed in her backyard with her chickens gathered around her is Ella Breazeale Robertson of Pelican, Louisiana. She was the grandmother of the late Haven Howell, the last of the Pelican wildcats. (Courtesy of Margaret Joyner.)

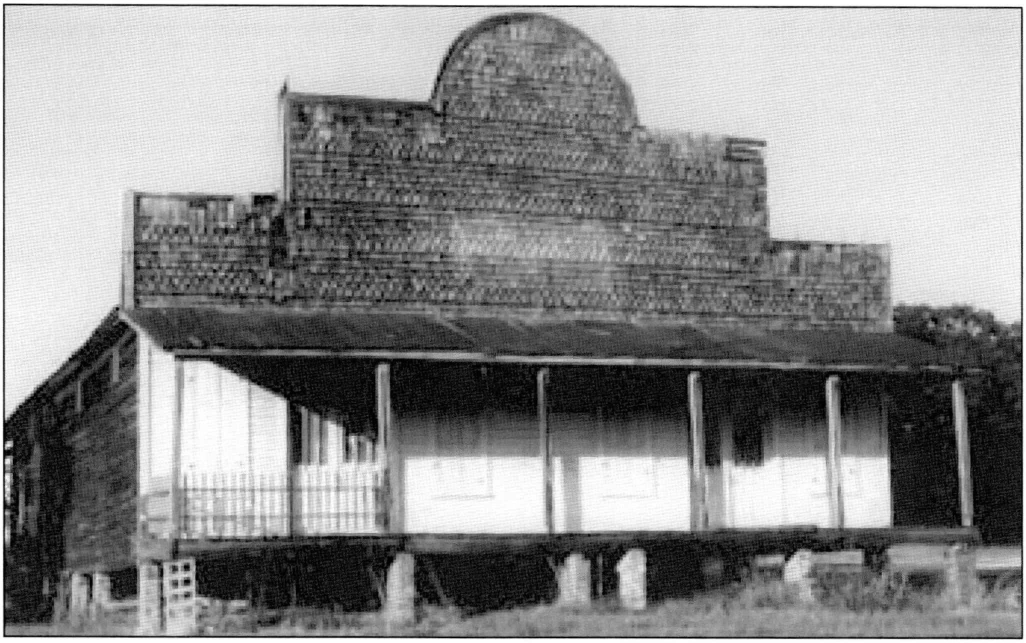

Joyners' Store, originally Jackson and Joyner, was built in 1889. The store was operated by Fred Breazeale and Henry Joyner in 1918, and by L.E Fincher and J.B. Gallaspy in 1934. It was the largest mercantile in operation. The imbricated or shaped shingles have been described as probably the finest example in northwest Louisiana and consist of alternating bands of straight edged, half octagon, and pointed shingles create the rugged texture that was popular in the late Victorian era. The building is no longer standing. (Photograph by W. Conway Link.)

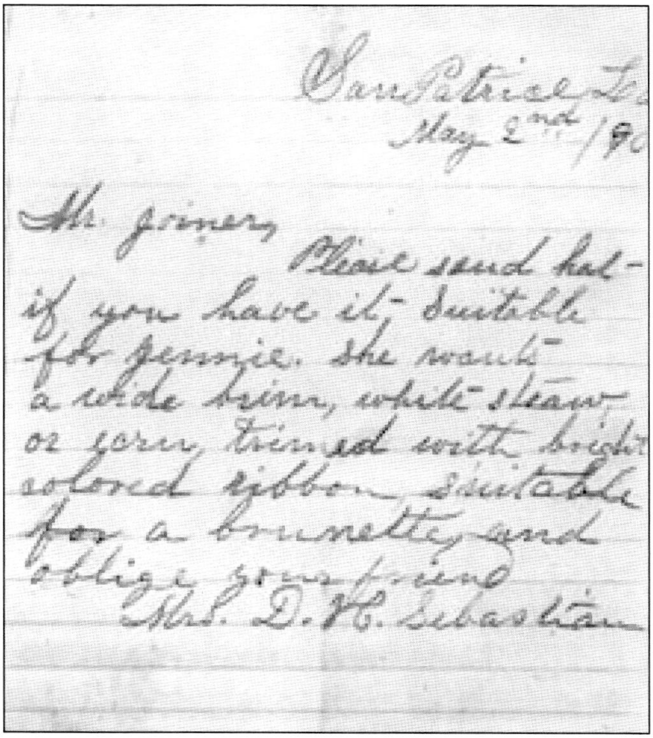

San Patrice
May 2nd /9

Mr. Joiner,
Please send hat -
if you have it - suitable
for Jennie. she wants
a wide brim, white straw
or corn trimmed with bright
colored ribbon suitable
for a brunette, and
oblige your friend
Mrs. D. H. Sebastian

Numerous notes flowed into the Joyner store. These were known as long paper tails because they were strung up on a long wire strand. Every conceivable type of paper found its way to the store in the form of an order. This one is from Mrs. D.H. Sebastian of San Patice, which later became known as Benson by the railroad. These notes poured in daily and usually were sent in by a servant. (Courtesy of Emilia Gay Griffith Means.)

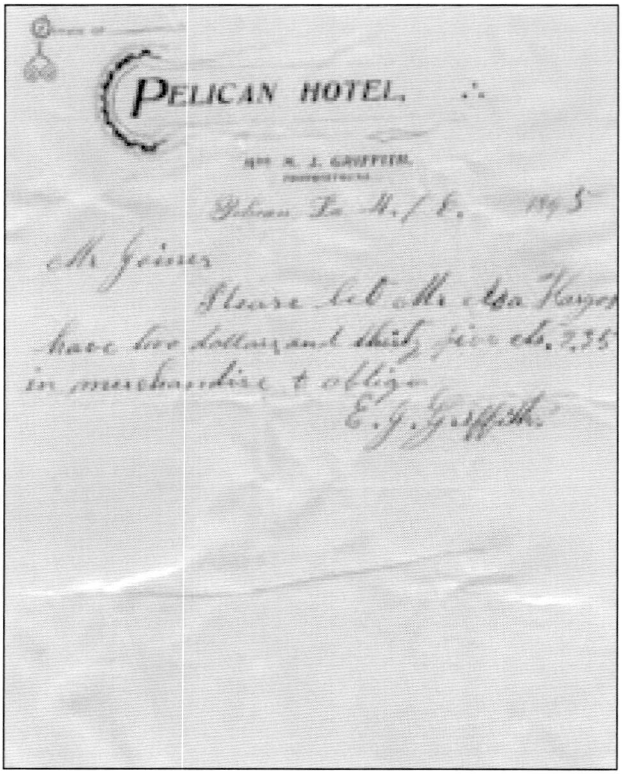
PELICAN HOTEL.

MRS. M. J. GRIFFITH,
PROPRIETRESS

Pelican La. 4/8. 1895

Mr. Geimer

Please let Mr. Asa Harper have two dollars and thirty five cts. 2.35 in merchandise & oblige

E. J. Griffith

Shown is another illustration of a long paper tail. This one is from Margaret J. Griffith, proprietress of the Pelican Hotel, and her husband, E.J. Griffith. Another one from E.J. Griffith asks "to let the girl Abi have a corset." More than likely this was for his wife or one of his daughters, as no decent woman in that day made an appearance without a corset. Mary Thomas Martin wrote, "Please send me a ham of meat by this girl if you have one." (Courtesy of Emilia Gay Griffith Means.)

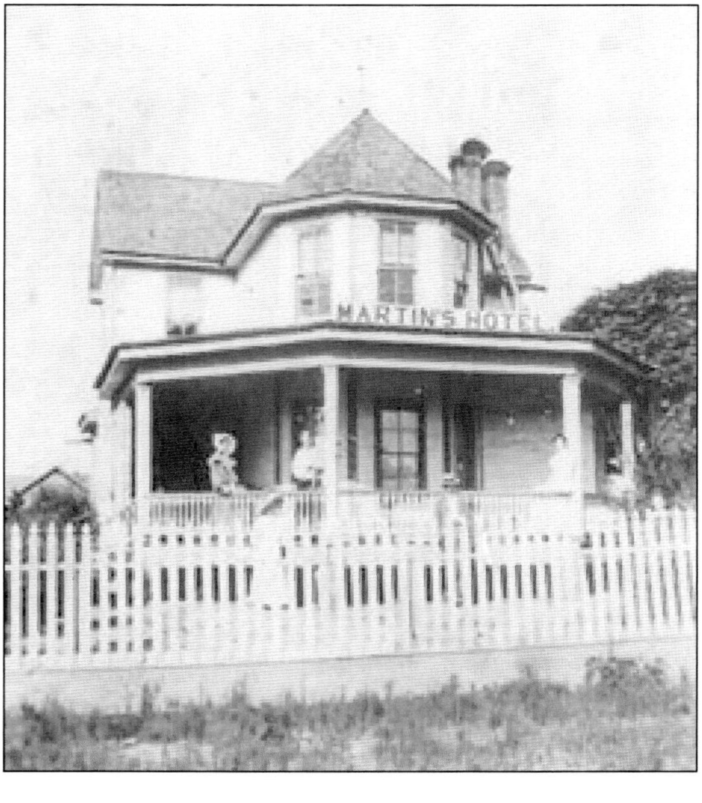

The Martin Hotel was one of two boardinghouses in Pelican. Drummers (salesmen) who came to visit the stores in town had a choice of boardinghouses, the other being the Pelican Hotel. G.W. Martin, husband of Mary Thomas Pace, operated the largest one, and in 1904 charged $2 per day. Boarders were also welcomed at several other homes in town. (Courtesy of Kathleen Myers.)

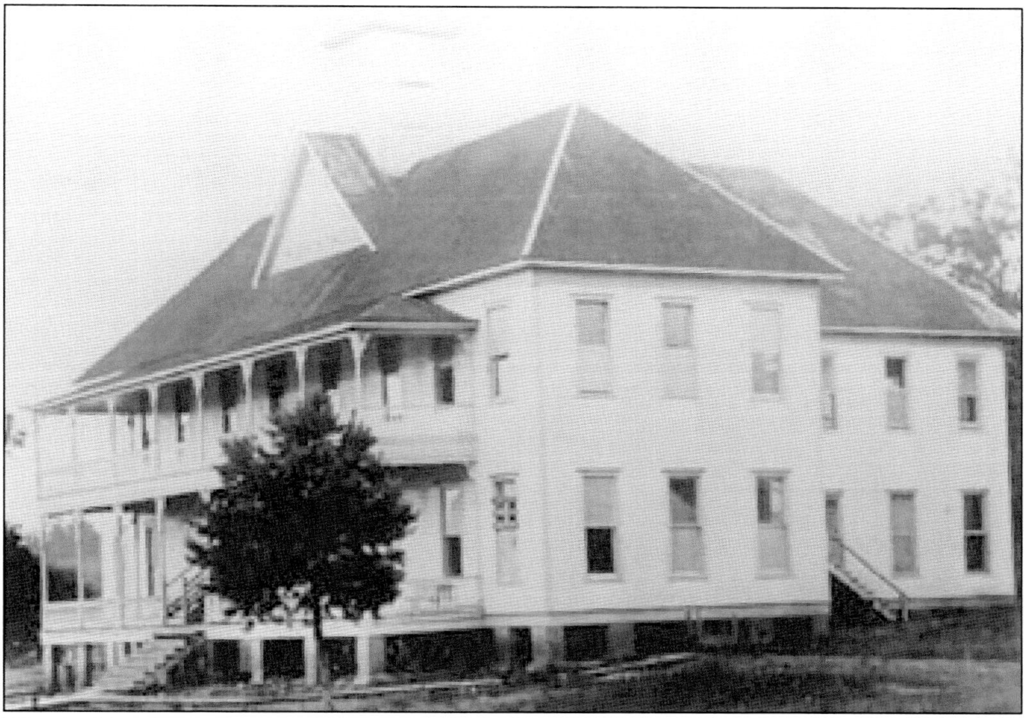

This building served from 1905 until 1919 as the school for the town of Pelican. Later it was owned by the Musgrove family and was therefore known as the Musgrove School. (Courtesy of Kathleen Myers.)

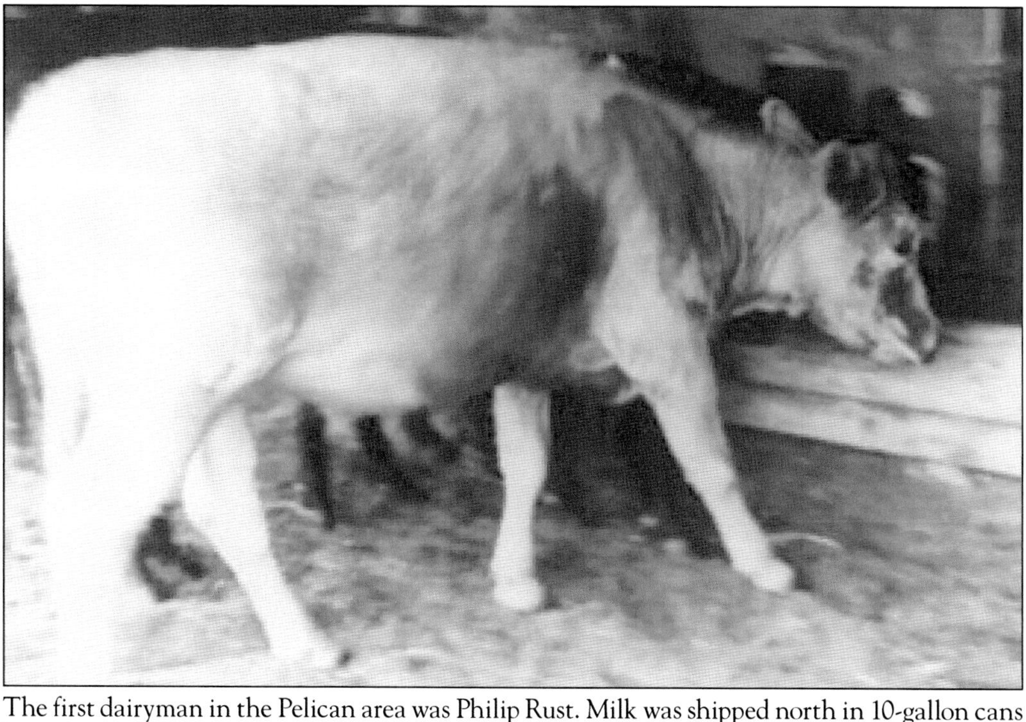

The first dairyman in the Pelican area was Philip Rust. Milk was shipped north in 10-gallon cans by train. However, many families had a milk cow. (Courtesy of Liz Chrysler.)

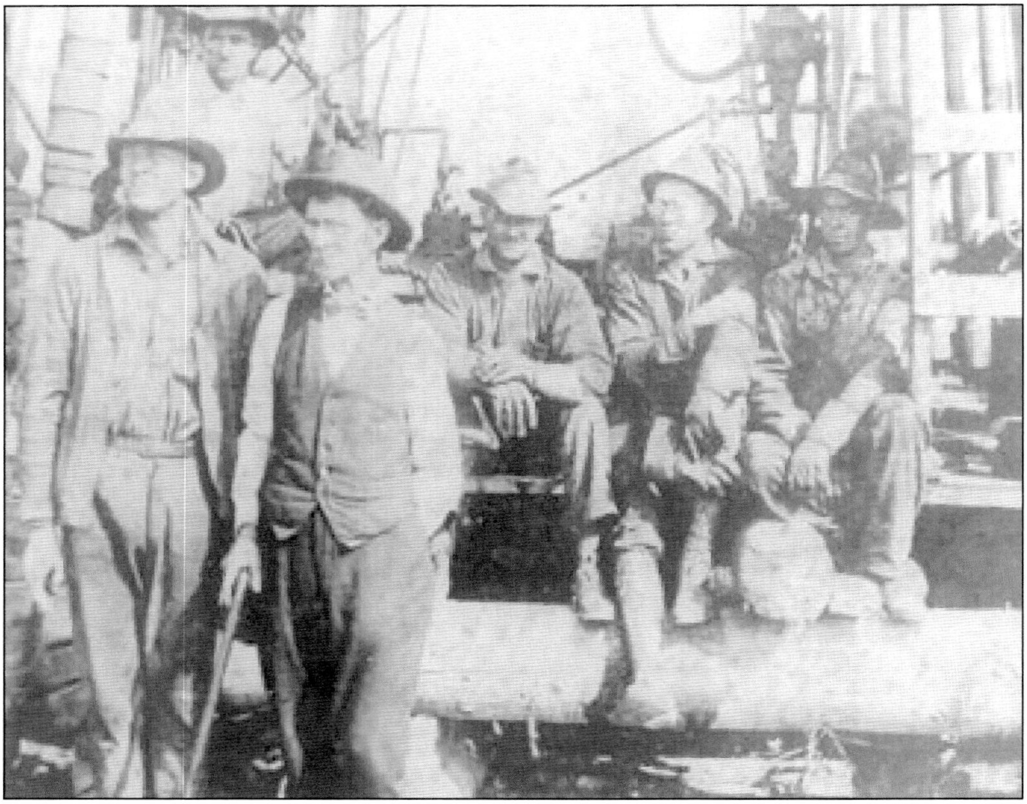

These oil workers were photographed at the site of the derrick near Pelican. The first oil well was drilled in Desoto Parish in 1913. (Courtesy of Emilia Gay Griffith Means.)

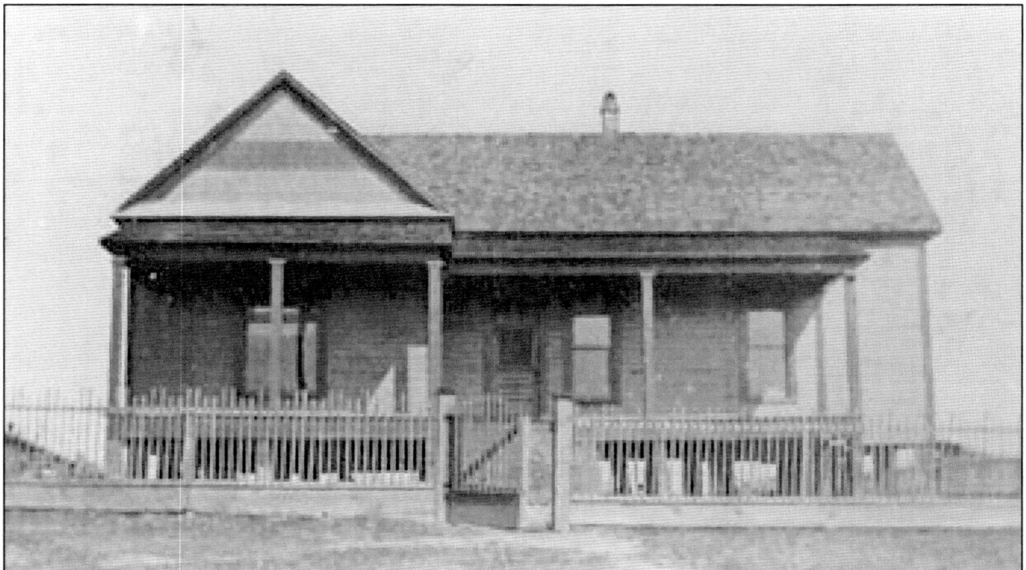

Pelican Methodist Episcopal Church South Parsonage served as one of three parsonages for the church. The original land was donated by A.F. Jackson. Today, this is homestead is known as the Buckley home. (Courtesy of Kathleen Myers.)

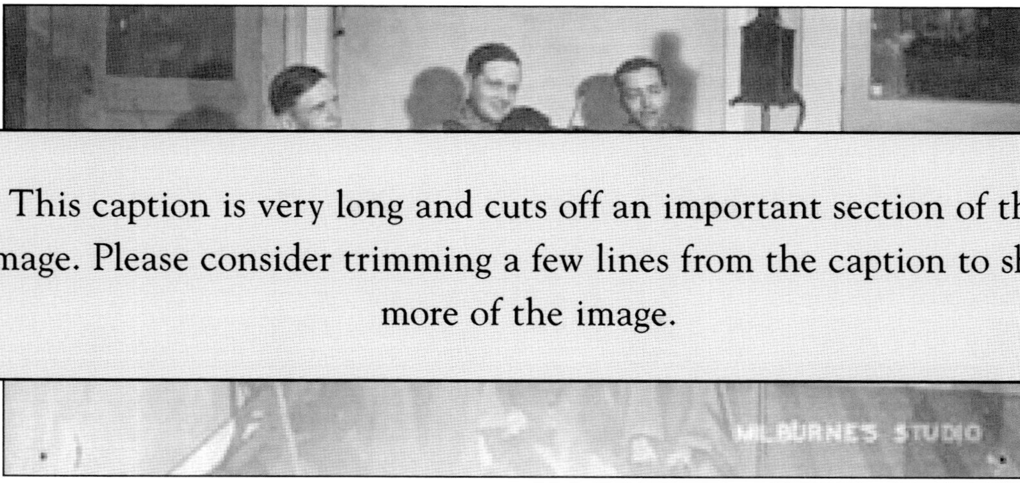

The Pelican Wildcats, DeSoto Parish musicians, played a central role in the evolution of live-music broadcasts in Shreveport. The rural populations of Northwest Louisiana, East Texas, and Southern Arkansas either suffered through the Great Depression or prospered in the oil boom of the times. Both situations provided an ideal audience for what is now country music. In 1928, Willie Ross Mayes (1899–1971) of Pelican organized a two-man country band with "Doc" Bass, also of Pelican. Doc sometimes failed to show up, so in 1929, Mayes pressed 17-year-old Kenneth Joseph Mayes into service with his guitar and harmonica. The Wildcats first played live on station KRMD under the guidance of "Paul, the radio man." When Paul moved to KWEA, a W.K. Henderson station, the Wildcats moved with him. Haven "Foots" Howell of Pelican, who died early this year, played with them. (Courtesy Louisiana State University in Shreveport, Noel Memorial Library, Archives and Special Collections.)

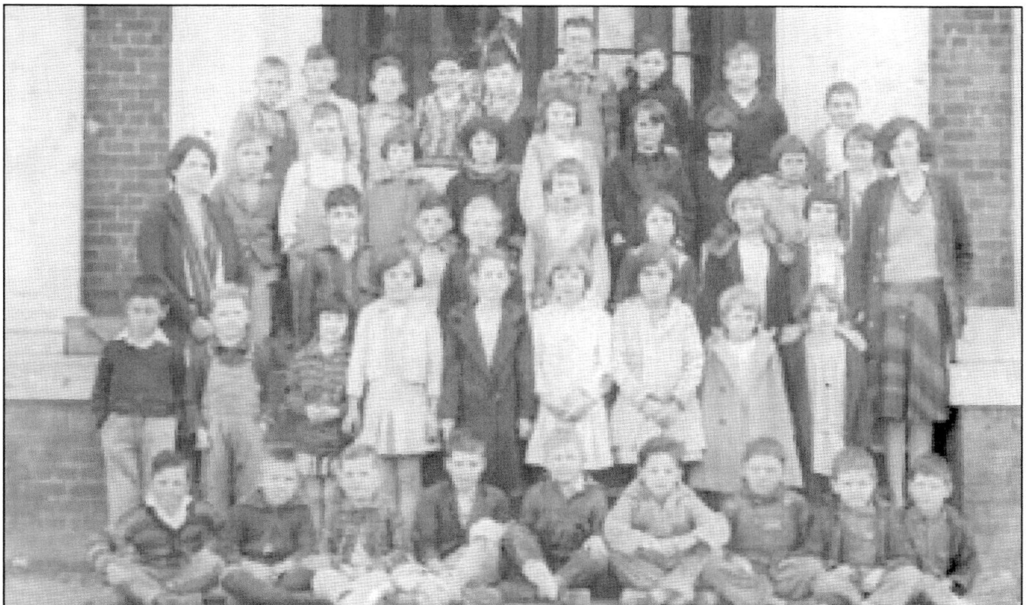

Shown are a group of children from Benson, Louisiana, in 1929–1930. The photograph was taken in front of Pelican School. (Courtesy of Louisiana State University in Shreveport, Noel Memorial Library, Archives and Special Collections.)

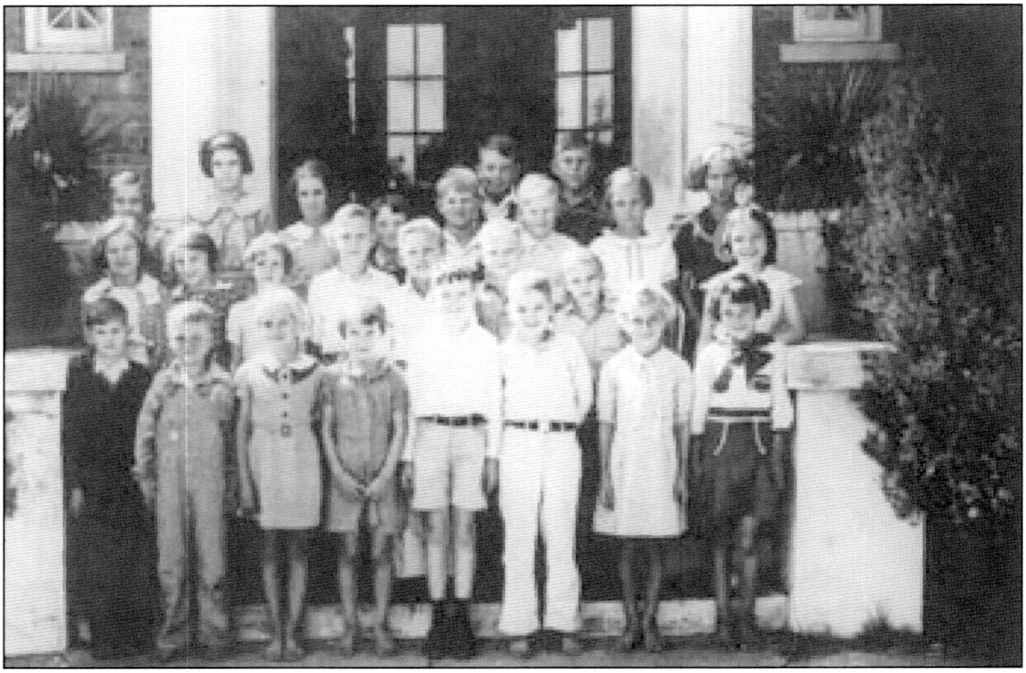

Pictured are a group of Pelican High School students in front of the school. Notice that some of the children were wearing shoes and others were not. Several among the group reported later that those shoes came off the minute they made it through the school door. (Courtesy of Margaret Joyner.)

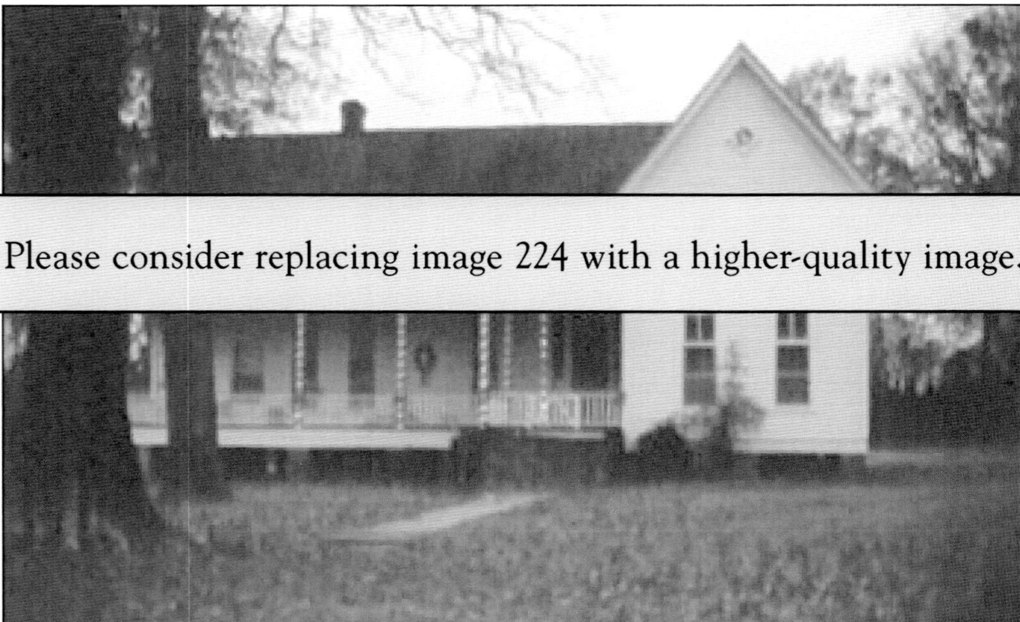

Shown is a Pelican home that was directly across from the Joyner Store. The photograph was taken at first dark during the Christmas season, and the occupants had decorated the exterior for the occasion. (Photograph by W. Conway Link.)

George W. Signor organized the Signor Burton Tie company with the purpose of manufacturing, buying, and selling railroad timbers, ties, and all such material used in the construction of railroad work. The board of directors was made up of George W. Signor, W.W. Burton, and Charles W. Billeiter. (Courtesy of Emilia Gay Griffith Means.)

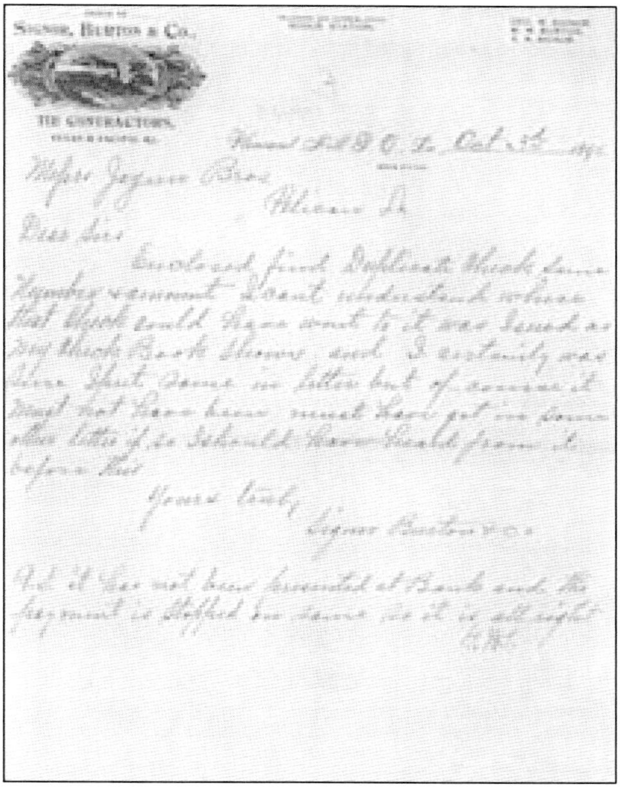

Signor, Burton & Co.

Tie Contractors

Messrs Joyner Bros
Pelican La

Dear Sirs

Enclosed find Duplicate Check same Number & amount. I cant understand where that check could have went to it was issued as my check Book shows and I certainly was sure I put same in letter but of course it must not have been must have got in some other letter if so I should have heard from it before this

Yours truly,
Signor Burton & Co.

P.S. it has not been presented at Bank and the payment is stopped on same so it is all right
G.W.

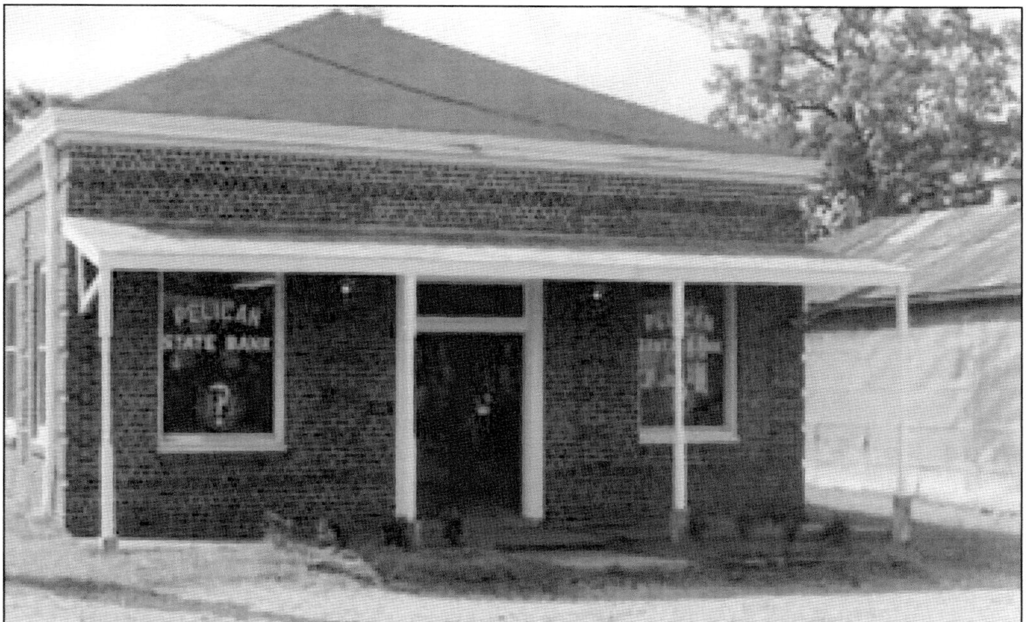

Pelican State Bank opened in 1911. The first board of directors consisted of E.L. Joyner, L.R. McGill, L.E. Fincher, J.B. Gallaspy, C.C. Payne, O.F. Moore, Charles McDonnell, S.T. Morrow, and W.S. Thigpen. The corporate seal was a pelican with a shield as a background encircled with the words "Pelican State Bank, Pelican, La." (Courtesy of Kathleen Gallaspy Myers.)